New Dimensions in
Body Psychotherapy

New Dimensions in Body Psychotherapy

edited by Nick Totton

Open University Press

Open University Press
McGraw-Hill Education
McGraw-Hill House
Shoppenhangers Road
Maidenhead
Berkshire
England
SL6 2QL

email: enquiries@openup.co.uk
world wide web: www.openup.co.uk

and Two Penn Plaza, New York, NY 10121-2289, USA

First published 2005

A catalogue record of this book is available from the British Library

ISBN-13 978 0335 21592 8 (pb)   978 0335 21593 5 (hb)
ISBN-10 0335 21592 0 (pb)   0335 21593 9 (hb)

Library of Congress Cataloging-in-Publication Data
CIP data applied for

Typeset by RefineCatch Limited, Bungay, Suffolk
Printed in Poland, EU by OZGraf. S.A.
www.polskabook.pl

Contents

Contributors

Jean-Claude Audergon (Lic. Phil. I, Dipl. Process Work; www.cfor.info, www.processwork-audergon.com) teaches process work internationally. Originally Swiss, he is a co-founder of the Process Work Organization in Zurich, Switzerland, and in Portland USA, as well as the School of Process Work in the UK – the Research Society of Process Oriented Psychology UK (www.rspopuk.com). He is interested in the creative process found within body experience and body symptoms, and the interplay between personal development and community-building. Jean-Claude works in various countries with issues of cultural and ethnic diversity, minority issues, youth violence and conflict resolution. He emigrated to Los Angeles in the early 1990s to focus his studies on Process Work interventions in violence. He is involved in the field of mental health, offering training seminars for working with acute and chronic mental health issues within psychiatric hospitals, and facilitating community forums on mental health for patients, staff and community members. Jean-Claude originated the 'Arts Atelier' and works with actors, improvisers, puppeteers, opera singers, directors, writers and other artists in the 'Atelier' in London, as well as consulting privately. Jean-Claude teaches and consults in organizations in the UK and internationally, has a private practice and trains and supervises students in London.

Katya Bloom is a movement psychotherapist in private practice in London. She recently completed her Ph.D. under the auspices of the Tavistock Clinic, to be published in 2006 by Karnac Books, entitled *The Embodied Self: Movement and Psychoanalysis*. Her passionate interest in the interrelationships between psyche and body has also been explored through teaching in wide-ranging settings on both sides of the Atlantic, including the past 15 years at the Royal Academy of Dramatic Art. She has co-written *Moves: A Sourcebook of Ideas for Body Awareness and Creative Movement* (Routledge 1998), and is the author of two stage plays.

Roz Carroll is a trainer at the Chiron Centre for Body Psychotherapy and at the Minster Centre in London. She is a body psychotherapist, supervisor and author, specializing in neuroscience, psychotherapy and health. She has given talks on these themes in a wide range of contexts, including hospitals, universities and training organizations. Her seminar series 'Emotion and Embodiment' was described by Allan Schore as 'a great synthesis of theory, as well as practical application of the advances in neuropsychoanalysis. Truly creative.' Articles, lectures and details of current courses are available at www.thinkbody.co.uk.

Emilie Conrad, founder and director of Continuum (www.Continuum-Movement.com), is a visionary whose work continues to inspire an international audience of therapists and movement educators. Born and raised in New York City, she studied ballet and Afro-Haitian dance. As a result of her groundbreaking work with Dr Valerie Hunt at UCLA, she developed a radical new technique for neuromuscular innovation and spinal injury rehabilitation. Emilie is an international teacher and guest speaker at various universities, healing arts centres and movement therapy institutions.

Ruella Frank Ph.D. has been teaching in the field of movement re-education for more than 25 years and has been practising Gestalt psychotherapy since 1982. She is director of the Center for Somatic Studies (www.somaticstudies. com/), on the training faculty of the New York Institute for Gestalt Therapy and the Gestalt Associates for Psychotherapy, New York City, and teaches throughout the USA and Europe. Ruella wrote *Body of Awareness: A Somatic and Developmental Approach to Psychotherapy* (Gestalt Press/Analytic Press 2001), now available in four languages.

Linda Hartley is a UKCP registered psychotherapist, practitioner and teacher of Body-Mind Centering®. A senior registered dance movement therapist, she has an MA in somatic psychology. She has taught internationally for many years in the fields of bodywork, dance and somatic movement therapy, and has worked as a therapist since 1982. Currently she practises at the Cambridge Body Psychotherapy Centre where she is a staff member. As founding director of the Integrative Bodywork & Movement Therapy Institute, she has run training programmes in England and Germany since 1990. Linda is the author of *Wisdom of the Body Moving* (North Atlantic Books 1995), *Servants of the Sacred Dream* (Elmdon Books 2001) and *Somatic Psychology: Body, Mind and Meaning* (Whurr 2004).

Gottfried Heuer is a training analyst and training supervisor with the Association of Jungian Analysts. He works in private practice in West London, and teaches and lectures. He started his therapeutic career 30 years ago as a neo-Reichian bodypsychotherapist. In this capacity he worked individually as well as with experiential and training groups in many European countries, the Americas and Australia. He also engaged with graphic arts and photography, and exhibited and published internationally. He writes and publishes widely on the early links between radical politics and analysis. The co-founder and chair of the International Otto Gross Society (http://www.ottogross.org/), he has co-edited the proceedings of four International Otto Gross Congresses he co-organized in Berlin, Zurich, Munich and Graz.

Peter A. Levine Ph.D. holds doctorates in medical biophysics from the University of California-Berkeley, and psychology from International University. With over 35 years of research in the psychology and physiology of trauma, he has developed 'Somatic Experiencing' and teaches his work throughout the world. He has contributed to a variety of scientific and medical publications and is a member of the Institute of World Affairs Task Force of Psychologists for Social Responsibility. He serves on the World Presidential Initiative on Ethnopolitical Warfare, which developed a training and postgraduate curriculum for dealing with large-scale disasters and ethnopolitical conflict. Peter is the author of the best-selling book *Waking the Tiger: Healing Trauma* (North Atlantic Books 1997), available in 13 languages as well as three audio learning series for Sounds True: *Healing Trauma: Restoring the Wisdom of the Body*; *It Won't Hurt Forever: Guiding Your Child Through Trauma* and *Healing Sexual Trauma: Transforming the Sacred Wound*. He heads The Foundation for Human Enrichment (www.traumahealing.com).

Yorai Sella is a clinical psychologist and an integrative psychotherapist based in Israel. Having originally trained as a Zen-Shiatsu and acupuncture therapist, his focus in clinical practice, writing and teaching has been the integration of oriental and western psychodynamic approaches to the issue of body-mind-spirit. He is the founder and co-director of the 'Maga' School for Zen-Shiatsu therapy and of the 'Dmut' Institute for East-West Psychotherapy. He teaches body-oriented psychotherapy and lectures on psychodynamic and phenomenological psychopathology at Tel-Aviv University. His clinical work centres on issues of boundaries, containment and holding, in therapy with people who have experienced trauma and with clients suffering from somatic symptoms. He is currently coordinating a research study on the effectiveness of Shiatsu therapy with victims of terrorist attacks suffering from post-traumatic stress disorder.

Michael Soth is an integrative body psychotherapist, trainer and supervisor, living in Oxford, UK. He is training director at the Chiron Centre for Body Psychotherapy in London and over the last 20 years has been teaching on a variety of counselling and psychotherapy training courses. In his practice and teaching he brings together a range of psychotherapeutic approaches, including analytic and humanistic perspectives. Although he calls himself 'integrative', he is equally interested in integration and dis-integration. His work is informed by the image of the wounded healer, in that he thinks of the therapeutic process as a relationship between two people who are both wounded and whole. Other areas of work include organizational consultancy, group facilitation, conflict resolution, work with men, plus a project applying body psychotherapy to illness, chronic symptoms and psychosomatic disease. Some of his writing and published articles are available at www.soth.co.uk. You can contact him via the website.

Nick Totton is a psychotherapist and trainer in private practice based in Calderdale, West Yorkshire, UK. Originally trained in post-Reichian therapy, over the last 20 years (originally in collaboration with Em Edmondson) he has developed the form of work which he now practises and teaches, Embodied-Relational Therapy. He is the author of several books, including *The Water in the Glass: Body and Mind in Psychoanalysis; Psychotherapy and Politics* (Rebus 1998); *Body Psychotherapy: An Introduction* (Open University Press 2003) and *Press When Illuminated: New and Selected Poems* (Salt 2004). He edits the journal *Psychotherapy and Politics International* and has an extensive website at www.erthworks.co.uk.

David Tune has been a practising body psychotherapist for over 25 years. He trained in New York and London and now works within an integrative perspective. He is also a trainer and senior lecturer in counselling, currently conducting research for a Ph.D. into the use of touch in counselling and therapy. Other areas of interest include the politics and ethics of therapy, and communication between physical selves in the therapeutic relationship. David's previous work has included psychiatric nursing and social work. He now works in Essex and York, UK, and lives with his partner and daughter in North Essex.

Introduction

The body is our general medium for having a world.

(Merleau-Ponty 1962: 146)

O let me teach you how to knit again
This scattered corn into one mutual sheaf,
These broken limbs again into one body.

(Shakespeare, *Titus Andronicus*, V. iii)

This book has two main purposes and two main audiences. Firstly, I want to celebrate and demonstrate the arrival of body psychotherapy as a unique and respected modality within the community of psychotherapies. Secondly, I would like to share some of the important contributions which body psychotherapy, as it goes through an extraordinary renaissance of energy and creativity, is currently making to that community. The two audiences, therefore, are on the one hand everyone interested in exploring the 'turn to the body' in psychotherapy; and on the other hand, body psychotherapists themselves, who will be heartened and inspired by these new perspectives.

New readers start here

This section is primarily for those not yet well acquainted with body psychotherapy and its history (for a much fuller account, see Totton 2003). Those who already know something about body psychotherapy may be familiar with much of what I have to say, and might even want to skip on to the next section – although it is often surprisingly useful to read a new account of what one thinks one knows already!

Our subject is the ensemble of approaches which, on appropriate occasions, *work psychotherapeutically through the body*, understanding that 'mind' does not function over and against 'body', but that the two are complementary, and ultimately only facets of the same whole. Body psychotherapy recognizes that there is no human mind without a body, and no living human body without a mind; and therefore, that in approaching a mind we are also approaching a body, just as in approaching a body we are also approaching a mind. Hence body psychotherapists, as well as having their own special skills and techniques, employ the full range of tools available to verbal therapists. Body psychotherapy is *verbal psychotherapy plus*, not minus; it would be fair, if provocative, to call it 'holistic psychotherapy'.

Body psychotherapy has always been around, although not always under that name. Psychoanalysis as it emerged from and through Freud's adventurous career was always a bodily theory – indeed, often a bodily practice. Freud massaged his early patients, 'pinched', 'kneaded' and 'stroked' them (Freud 1895: 54, 137–8), pressed their foreheads (Freud 1895: 110) and chests (Masson 1985: 120), lay for hours on the floor with them (Ferenczi 1988: 33) and paid minute attention to their ailments, aches and pains, tics and fidgets, smells, secretions, toilet behaviour, energy cycles, states of sexual arousal or otherwise. Psychoanalysis was from the start a theory of how the body and its impulses are represented in the mind, and of how 'mind' and 'body' can come to be experienced as conflicting and competing forces (Totton 1998); its method of interpretation mapped the body onto the world, discovering an abundance of bodily imagery in every dream, image and activity – 'a subterranean passage between mind and body underlies all analogy' (Sharpe 1940: 202).

Although Freud himself became increasingly taken up with the mental aspect of human experience, the bodily emphasis of his theory was developed in the 1920s and 1930s by his distinguished colleague Sandor Ferenczi, who worked with states of extreme trauma where 'if a trauma strikes the soul, or the body, unprepared . . . its effect is destructive for body and mind, that is, it disrupts through fragmentation' (1988: 69). Ferenczi was in turn influential on Wilhelm Reich, the founder of body psychotherapy as a clinical discipline, who in the 1930s and 1940s carried Freud's approach to embodiment beyond the perceived boundaries of psychoanalysis (from which he was promptly expelled – see Heuer, this volume).

Reich was the first to work systematically with the bodily aspect of experience, focusing in particular on the breath, and encouraging his analysands to relax and allow their breath to happen spontaneously. With Reich's support, and his feedback on how he saw them interrupting and controlling their breath, analysands gradually released the blocks against free breathing which functioned to suppress emotion. Their bodies began to offer movements, tremblings, twitchings, jerks, spasms, gestures, grimaces, sensations of hot and cold, itching and prickling, pain and pleasure, streaming energy, gestures, sounds, visions – opening up a whole world of feeling, memory and meaning which Reich explored verbally as well as physically (for an extended account, see Totton 1998: 107–12).

Reich developed a methodology which used pressure and manipulation to release the tension held in his patients' tight muscles, the 'armouring' which we develop in order to repress and deny unbearable emotion. This 'muscular armouring' is the bodily aspect of 'character armouring', the corresponding, functionally identical psychological repression: 'every muscular rigidity contains the history and meaning of its origin . . . the spasm of the musculature is the somatic side of the process of repression' (Reich [1945] 1972: 300, 302).

Although Reich was originally an analyst, and remained so in many of his basic attitudes, his expulsion from psychoanalytic institutions meant that his work became best known in the context of the 'growth movement', the flourishing of humanistic psychology in the 1960s and 1970s. Along with other body-focused therapies like Gestalt (whose founder, Fritz Perls, was analysed by Reich), Reichian therapy was swept up into the countercultural project of 'liberating the body'. Much, though by no means all, of the body psychotherapy practised during this period now seems crude, simplistic and often insufficiently boundaried – assuming that physical and emotional pressure leading to emotional catharsis was not just necessary, but also sufficient, to heal neurosis. Sometimes it left people in bits.

At the same time, much of this work was powerfully transformative, even if unintegrated, and many fine therapists continued to work and develop their ideas. The extremes of the period perhaps help to explain why body psychotherapy fell out of mainstream acceptance – indeed, fell almost out of view, identified with what in the 1980s and 1990s was seen as the radical fringe of psychotherapy. However, the central reason for its fall from credibility was undoubtedly the drag created by our culture's drastic inhibition concerning embodiment, its tendency to fear and despise the body and all its works. (This is not incompatible with the present cult of the objectified body – see below.)

In that sense, society is right to be wary of body therapy. Beyond its belief that increased body awareness is a way into alleviating physical and psychological problems, body psychotherapy is one element in a cultural coalition which keeps alive a vision of a possible future where human beings are no longer alienated from either their own embodiment or the rest of the natural world. It holds that surrender to our own embodied experience will tend to dissolve the dualisms on which oppression rests – between male and female, black and white, civilization and nature: that the false dualism of mind/body is the keystone on which the structure depends (Totton 2003: 47–52, 143–6). Not all body therapists identify with this vision, but it is still a potent force.

So far I have briefly described what seems to me the central element in body psychotherapy, the Reichian and post-Reichian tradition. But there are other important and autonomous forms of body-centred therapy, which are now starting to link up with each other and with the post-Reichian world. The most important of these (for a full survey see Totton 2003) are

Dance Movement Therapy and Process-Oriented Psychology, both of which are represented in this volume.

The new wave

The renaissance of body psychotherapy which we are now experiencing has several roots:

- the 'turn to the body' in western culture and intellectual theory;
- a parallel but somewhat later 'turn to the body' in psychotherapy and counselling;
- the striking confirmations from contemporary neuroscience;
- the coming to maturity of a generation of body psychotherapists trained in the 1970s and early 1980s;
- the confluence of a number of streams of embodiment-focused work previously compartmented away from each other.

Turning to the body

From the 1980s onwards, bodies have become a subject of intense interest within and between several intellectual fields including sociology, anthropology, psychology, cultural studies, philosophy and politics (Frank 1990; Csordas 1994; Hancock *et al.* 2000). In many ways this echoes, and no doubt in part responds to, an increasing focus on the body in western culture itself – what is known as 'lifestyle culture', with its emphasis on appearance, fitness and sexual desirability (Jagger 2000). The negative aspects of this narcissistic positioning of the body as an object of consumption are easy to identify, but more positive readings are possible, for example Turner's (1994: 28) insistence that

> This new 'life politics' . . . of personal identity has focused so largely on issues of bodiliness because, I suggest, the appropriation of bodiliness in all its aspects . . . is the fundamental matrix, the material infrastructure, so to speak, of the production of personhood and social identity. What is at stake in the struggle for the control of the body, in short, is control of the social relations of personal production.

Emily Martin argues that these cultural shifts represent 'the end of one kind of body and the beginning of another kind of body' (1992: 121), and from a Jungian perspective, McNeely suggests that they constitute an unconscious programme of radical restitution: 'The objective psyche . . . has come to recognize the beauty and value of the individual body, resulting in a wave of narcissism whose purpose may be essentially creative . . . From this point of view, self-preoccupation reflects the collective need to reunite body and soul' (1987: 107).

The intellectual exploration of embodiment may have originated in the hope that the body would constitute some sort of bedrock reality in the shifting sands of postmodernism. What has emerged, however, is not a simplification but a tremendous increase in complexity. Intellectual attention to the body has revealed it as – to use the appropriate academic discourse for a moment – a socially constructed object, a site for the inscription of multiple narratives:

> If behind the turn to the body lay the implicit hope that it would be the stable center in a world of decentered meanings, it has only led to the discovery that the essential character of embodiment is existential indeterminacy ... embodiment is reducible neither to representations of the body, to the body as objectification of power, to the body as a physical entity or biological organism, nor to the body as an inalienable center of individual consciousness.
>
> (Csordas 1994: xi)

Body psychotherapy is just beginning to engage with this complexity.

Therapy rediscovers the body

Alongside and partly in response to this intellectual and cultural turn, many psychotherapists and counsellors are also developing a new interest in embodiment. Significant new books on the topic are multiplying (Aron and Anderson 1998; Staunton 2002; Aposhyan 2003; Shaw 2003; Solomon and Siegel 2003; Totton 2003; Hartley 2004; Macnaughton 2004; White 2004 and many others). Journals are producing special issues or features on the body in psychotherapy (e.g. *AHP Perspective*, June–July 2004; *British Journal of Psychotherapy*, 19(4); *Gestalt Review*, 4(4); *Person-Centred Practice*, 10(2); *The Psychologist*, 15(4); *Psychotherapy in Australia*, 8(2); *Self and Society*, 26(2) and (4)), and a new international journal, *Body, Movement and Dance in Psychotherapy* is launching in 2006 (www.tandf.co.uk/journals/titles/17432979.asp). Increasing numbers of professional conferences are being focused on the embodiment theme – for example, the Freud Museum in London, 2000, on 'The Therapist's Body'; The Bowlby Memorial Conference, March 2003, on 'Touch: Attachment and the Body'; the UK Council for Psychotherapy, October 2004, on 'The Body in Psychotherapy'; and in March 2005, the Association for Cognitive-Analytic Therapy on 'Body, Brain and Beyond: Neuroscience, Embodiment and Transpersonal Experience in Psychotherapy'. In April 2005 the Association of Chiron Psychotherapists considered 'Embodied Relationships in Psychotherapy' and Counsellors and Psychotherapists in Primary Care, in May

2005, looked at 'Mind, Body and Emotion' – one conference a month in the UK alone! In parallel, many body psychotherapists report increasing demand for their services in workshops, talks, articles and individual therapy and supervision.

As I have suggested, this new fascination probably partly reflects the cultural shift described above. I suspect that there are also more complex dynamics at work within the therapy and counselling subculture. One could emphasize either an increasing maturity in the therapy world leading to less defensiveness and more adventurousness; or, conversely, a groundswell of rebellion against the restrictive paradigms of orthodox training programmes. Perhaps the bottom line is that therapy is reintegrating the body into its vision simply because *the body needs to be there*: without it, the picture just doesn't make sense.

Neuroscience

Another factor, though, is the tidal wave of new data and theory emerging from the field of neuroscience: directly relevant to psychotherapy, and almost uncanny in its support for the precise positions which body psychotherapy has always taken – for example, that 'we need our body to think with' (Totton 2003: 30; for neuroscientific support see Pert 1986; Damasio 1994); that emotions are embodied, and crucial to therapeutic change (Schore 1994; Panksepp 1998; Damasio 2000); that the autonomic nervous system is a key to therapeutic efficacy (Schore 1994); that the details of infant development are embedded in permanent aspects of body-mind (Schore 2001a, 2001b); that trauma is crucially important to this embedding (Perry *et al.* 1995; Perry and Pollard 1998; Schore 2001b); and even that the degree of affection and freedom given to infants in a given society is reflected in its degree of violence and authoritarianism (Prescott 1975, 1996). Roz Carroll's chapter expands on several of these issues.

A new generation

Many body psychotherapists trained towards the end of the 'growth movement' era have now come to maturity, and several are represented here. Surviving in an often hostile climate has, it seems, strengthened and deepened their commitment to working through the body, while at the same time they display an openness to the wider realm of psychotherapy, a drive to take body psychotherapy out of the ghetto without sacrificing any of its unique value. Many of this new generation have four things in common: an openness to and interest in psychoanalytic thinking; an equal interest in neuroscience; a relational approach to psychotherapy; and an integrative impulse.

Pychoanalysis

As explained above, body psychotherapy originates in Wilhelm Reich's development of what he saw as key positions of psychoanalysis, even while the analytic movement was abandoning them. In recent years psychoanalysis has been in a revisionary mood, undertaking a return to and reappraisal of its original discoveries. Important to this has been the rehabilitation of Sandor Ferenczi, a giant of early psychoanalysis, deeply concerned with issues of embodiment. It seems unlikely that psychoanalysis will go so far as to rehabilitate Reich, but the new generation of body psychotherapists have, conversely, 'rehabilitated psychoanalysis', rediscovering the analytic foundations of Reich's work obscured by his honorary membership of the humanistic psychotherapy movement (Totton 1998). This has meant giving serious attention to analytic concepts like transference and countertransference (Soth, this volume), projection (Bloom, Sella, Soth, this volume), and fantasy (Bloom, Sella, this volume) – bringing such concepts into dialogue with body psychotherapy, and working out what adjustments might be required on both sides.

Neuroscience

Another aspect of the revisionary tendency in contemporary psychoanalysis has been a widespread interest in the findings of contemporary neuroscience; a new field of 'neuro-psychoanalysis' has emerged (Kaplan-Solms and Solms 2001; Solms and Turnbull 2002). Partly following this trend, body psychotherapists have also turned their attention to neuroscience – and, as already indicated, have found powerful support for the intuitions and discoveries of early body psychotherapy. In particular, the new wave of body therapists have drawn on neuroscience for a highly developed theory of trauma (Levine, this volume; Rothschild 2000).

Relational

The new generation tend to be strongly *relational* in their approach to psychotherapy. The expression 'embodied relationship' or some variation on it seems to have been independently generated by a number of different writers (e.g. Soth, Totton, Tune, this volume; cf. Barlow and Coverdale 2004); it certainly summarizes the current *Zeitgeist* of body psychotherapy – perhaps even of psychotherapy in general, well summarized thus:

> We have used the term 'embodiment' to refer loosely to the totality of body-mind communication processes that allow the individual to know her or himself simultaneously as a separate entity and as a functioning part of relationships in her or his family and community. For us, 'embodiment' describes a set of processes, not a state.
>
> (Carswell and Magraw 2001)

Again, there is strong support for this approach from neuroscience, which has drawn mainly on attachment theory for its psychotherapy input (Carroll, this volume).

However, classical attachment theory perhaps does not in itself provide a sufficiently rich and broad model for body psychotherapy; there may be more to discover from engaging with the new integrative movement of 'relational psychoanalysis' (Aron and Anderson 1998). My personal view is that body psychotherapy cannot do without some equivalent of analytic drive theory, and a good starting point would be Reich's prescient and synthesizing remark that 'There is but one desire which issues from the biopsychic unity of the person, namely the desire to discharge inner tensions ... Hence, the *first* impulse of *every* creature must be the desire to establish contact with the outer world' (Reich [1945] 1972: 271, original emphases).

Integrative

As well as being instinctively relational, the new generation is instinctively *integrative*. Their strong interest in psychoanalysis does not mean that the values of humanistic psychotherapy have been abandoned. Good ideas and practices are gathered in from whatever source. However, this doesn't mean magpie eclecticism: there is a striking commitment to theoretical coherence.

Meeting streams

As well as integrating different styles of therapy in general, the new wave of body psychotherapy is dismantling the bulkheads which have long divided its own space. Communication and cross-fertilization is taking off between the different schools of body psychotherapy itself. There are still gulfs between Reichian and post-Reichian therapy, dance movement therapy, process approaches, primal therapies and so on: as one so often sees, the smaller the pond the bigger the quarrels (the Reichian field in particular is often reminiscent of Trotskyist splinter groups).

But bridges are beginning to span the gulfs, and parties of explorers are venturing across them. In fact, certain practitioners – some of them represented in this volume – no longer identify exclusively with any one of the traditional groupings. The work is underway of developing a shared language which can connect up the different traditions (see especially Bloom, this volume). And from these multiple cross-fertilizations, a vigorous hybrid growth ensues.

This book

What follows showcases some of the most exciting and innovative work going on in the field of body psychotherapy. It is by no means exhaustive – a single volume could not possibly be; there are several other figures who could have substituted equally well for those writing here (e.g. Babette Rothshchild, Pat Ogden, Courtenay Young, Will Davis, David Boadella, Christine Caldwell, William Cornell), but I believe that the most important strands of innovative work are represented.

The book consists of two parts, 'New dimensions of theory' and 'New dimensions of practice'. Such a division can never be absolute – theory constantly informs practice and vice versa – but the first section focuses on work which is generally independent of any particular orientation, and useful to all, while the second section samples the huge range of specific styles and methods currently available – also hopefully useful to all, but each working within its own paradigm.

Part 1 begins with Roz Carroll's account of some of the contribution contemporary neuroscience makes to body psychotherapy. Out of the wealth of material, Carroll has focused on a theme historically and immediately important for body psychotherapists, the autonomic nervous system. Peter Levine's chapter then takes up other neuroscience material, along with ethology, in a compelling and already highly influential model of trauma treatment.

In a groundbreaking (and heavily abridged) chapter, Michael Soth addresses the currently much discussed concept of embodied countertransference, staking out territory for a specifically body-psychotherapeutic interpretation of the concept. Katya Bloom integrates concepts from dance movement therapy, infant observation and elsewhere into a fascinating new synthesis, and David Tune offers a contemporary reading of the perennial question: is touch permissible in therapy, and if so when and how? (I am sadly aware that some psychotherapist readers will rigidly distinguish between chapters which favour the use of touch – unacceptable – and those which do not – acceptable.)

Part 2 opens with chapters on the application of traditional psychotherapy paradigms to the field of body psychotherapy: Yorai Sella on a Freudian approach, and Gottfried Heuer on a Jungian one. Ruella Frank's chapter works as a bridge – her approach grows out of the Gestalt paradigm, and is also strongly movement orientated, linking it with the next two chapters: Linda Hartley's account of two movement systems, Body-Mind Centering® and Authentic Movement, followed by Emilie Conrad's description of her own Continuum Movement approach. The book ends with two process-focused therapies. Jean-Claude Audergon describes the bodywork aspect of Process Work, an enormously creative and influential school; and finally, my own chapter on Embodied-Relational Therapy integrates process-focused methods with the more state-oriented approach of Reich and his heirs.

Papers are written in a great variety of styles, from the scholarly to the personal, the abstract to the concrete, helping to illustrate the full range of the field. This collection is, I believe, an exemplary showcase for what body psychotherapy has to offer. Including authors from the UK, the USA, Israel, Germany and Switzerland, it portrays an international discipline which has come of age, and is still growing and learning: both a unique and autonomous therapeutic approach, and a valuable contributor to new syntheses and discoveries in psychotherapy as a whole.

PART 1
New Dimensions of Theory

1 Neuroscience and the 'law of the self'

The autonomic nervous system updated, re-mapped and in relationship

Roz Carroll

Reich came to identify Freud's id with the autonomic nervous system [which is] a highly organized and wonderfully co-ordinated physiological system and not a 'seething chaos' as Freud described the id. The appearance of functional rather than structural chaos may appear in the ANS [autonomic nervous system] in pathological conditions.

(Smith 1989: 118)

Interdisciplinary dialogue

After giving a paper at the 2004 United Kingdom Council of Psychotherapists (UKCP) conference 'About a Body' I was asked by a delegate, 'Why do you need to turn to neuroscience for confirmation about what you are doing?' I answered that it wasn't confirmation I was seeking, but engagement with the *different perspective* offered by neuroscience. The body psychotherapists Reich, Perls, Boadella, Keleman and Boyesen turned to physiology, embryology, morphology, systems theory – science in the mainstream and at the edge – to stimulate their thinking. Indeed many psychotherapists, starting with Freud, have engaged with scientific research in a creative way, just as others have turned to mythology, anthropology, alchemy and the arts. Scientific knowledge is not privileged: it is as provisional, political and approximate as psychotherapeutic knowledge. But, at this point in history, it is providing a wealth of exciting data-rich and paradigm-shifting hypotheses about human functioning (Carroll 2003).

Neuroscience means 'the study of the nervous system' but it has become an umbrella term for a group of disciplines, including cognitive and experimental psychology, infant observation, psychiatry, physiology, philosophy, neurobiology, neurochemistry and genetics.[1] Schore, Panksepp, Trevarthen,

Damasio and others are forging creative bridges between neuroscience and various traditions of psychoanalysis, psychology and social theory (Carroll 2002a). They present genuinely new models based on a considerable amount of assimilation and contextualization of theory and raw data, drawing on multiple sources, including hundreds of research papers. Their formulations are interlinked, differing in some details but agreeing on some key ideas: that there is an intrinsic relationship between bodily structure and psychological function; that the brain requires a body to think through and with; and that regulation of affect is the central organizing principle of human development and motivation.

At the cutting edge, neuroscience is making strides towards linking self-object states with specific subsystems in the brain and the body. Panksepp has looked at intrinsic potentials of the nervous system and identified specific brain circuits, neurochemicals and motoric patterns relating to seven core affects (1998). Trevarthen has developed the concept of intersubjectivity with an emphasis on coordinated, reciprocal rhythmic patterns of movement, vocalization and gesture (Trevarthen and Aitken 2001). Schore proposes that the sense of self emerges from early synchronized energy exchanges between mother and baby which evolve into more complex differentiated interactions (1994, 2003a, 2003b, 2003c). In great detail he shows how the perception, representation and regulation of bodily and emotional states lies at the heart of human relations. Together these models provide the basis for a 'new anatomy' of body-mind-brain, as a system of systems, with each dimension (autonomic, motoric, peptidergic) mapped more coherently in a relational and developmental context (Carroll 2004).

The autonomic nervous system (ANS) is a core structure involved in the management of basic body states – that is, the metabolism of energy, the regulation of affect, and the survival and health of the organism. There has been a spectacular increase in interest in the ANS linked with the emergence of the newly-designated area of 'affective neuroscience' (Damasio 1994; Schore 1994; Panksepp 1998). One of the critical discoveries is that the ANS is not simply autonomous but regulated through interaction with others, and that these interactions are laid down as internalizations at every level of the microstructure of brain and body (Schore 1994).

An increasing number of therapists are turning to neuroscience to refine and develop the theory and practice of psychotherapy, especially in the realm of trauma, attachment and psychopathology (De Zulueta 1993; Schore 2003b; Gerhardt 2004). Body psychotherapists have an advantage here in having grown up with a psychotherapeutic model which is grounded in an understanding of the ANS.[2] Body psychotherapists are trained to observe, attune to and work explicitly with autonomic states in their clients and in themselves (Totton 2003).

In this chapter I will focus on the ANS – this highly organized and wonderfully coordinated physiological system – outlining important developments from neuroscience. It will be a journey into the labyrinth of the complex structures of body-brain, now more fully mapped and elaborated. My emphasis will be not proving the accuracy of models through an accumulation of facts (I invite you to go to my sources, and the sources of those sources, for the detail) but rather running and playing with the concepts, metaphors and possibilities presented mainly in the work of Allan Schore.

The ANS regulates emotional-physiological cycles

> The physiological operations that we call mind are derived from the structural and functional ensemble [of endocrine, immune, autonomic etc. components] rather than from the brain alone.
>
> (Damasio 1994: xix)

The central nervous system (CNS) consists of the brain and spinal cord and extends throughout the body via the peripheral nervous system. This is subdivided into the somatic nervous system and the ANS. The word 'autonomic' is derived from the Greek *auto* (self) and *nomos* (law), hence my favourite translation of this as 'the law of the self', although the usual term is 'self-regulating'. In evolutionary terms the ANS is older than the CNS and its anatomical circuitry is broadly dispersed, creating a general response, quite unlike the highly specific pathways and response of the CNS. The somatic nervous system controls musculoskeletal movement and operates within a feedback loop which continually sends and receives motor and sensory information between the brain and the body.

The ANS has two branches which regulate the viscera, sense organs, glands, muscles and blood vessels. In standard physiology the two parts of the ANS have been perceived as functioning reciprocally: the sympathetic governing arousal, the fight or flight reaction, and the parasympathetic involving relaxation, recuperation and digestion (see Table 1.1). The sympathetic nervous system is activated by any stimulus over an individual's threshold, which generates an immediate anticipatory state through the release of adrenaline. This causes the heart to beat more quickly and strongly, increases blood supply to the muscles, raises blood pressure, dilates the bronchii and increases the breathing rate, raises the blood sugar level for increased energy, speeds up mental activity, increases tension in the muscles, dilates pupils and increases sweating.

The parasympathetic nervous system comes into operation after the stimulus has been responded to and action taken. It has the opposite effect to sympathetic activity, allowing the body to wind down and rebalance. The activation of the parasympathetic nervous system encourages relaxation of muscles, slowing the heart rate and lowering the blood pressure. It assists the

Table 1.1 The autonomic nervous system

	Sympathetic	*Parasympathetic*
Summary	Arousal, action, outer focus fight/flight Speeding up	Inhibition, inner focus, rest, digestion, repair Slowing down
Standard physiology	Faster breathing (in breath) increases heart rate, increases blood pressure Blood goes to muscles, increases muscle tension, releases glucose for energy Pupils dilate Pale skin, cold sweating Digestion inhibited	Slower breathing (out breath) Decreases heart rate Decreases blood pressure Blood to organs and skin Relaxes muscles Enhances immune function Pupils contract/flushing, flushed skin, warm blushing Increased digestive secretions
Neurobiological associations	Dopamine, CRF (corticotrophin releasing factor), adrenaline, endorphins	Cortisol, serotonin, noradrenaline, oxytocin
Development of connection to orbitofrontal cortex	Ventral tegmental limbic circuit from 10–12 months	Lateral tegmental limbic circuit from 14–16 months
Schore's correlations with object relations	Amplifying object: 'time moves forward'	Inhibiting object: 'time stands still'
Body psychotherapy	Feelings that go 'up' – anger, fear, excitement, joy, desire	Feelings that go 'down' – shame, sadness, contentment, reflection
Resources Defences	purpose/goal/focus agency, projection – push away	assimilation, presence, introjection – take in
Response to stress	Active coping Fight-flight to remove source of stress	Passive coping Immobility and withdrawal to reduce effects of stress

breathing to return to its normal rate, digestive juices to flow, bladder and bowels to function, and supports rest, sleep and immune functions.

Since Reich, body psychotherapists have recognized the function of the ANS as a barometer of emotional intensity and internal conflict. Sympathetic activation has been seen as an indicator of an impulse or a feeling being stirred (*sym pathos* means 'with feeling'). It is often experienced as a wave of feeling coming *up* – anger, fear, excitement, desire, hatred – which, if expressed, involves movement out, or towards, or in the case of fear, away from, an object. Sympathetic physiology increases energy and readies the body for action – so it is also about the need to do, express and act. Conversely the parasympathetic action is a concomitant of coming *down* – disappointment, grief, shame, guilt, despair; and contentment, peacefulness and satisfaction – feelings which involve a decrease in tension, withdrawal of energy inward and tend more towards introspection.[3]

The two parts of the ANS together form a self-regulating cycle, but more complex layers of emotional regulation overlay this basic homeostatic template (Carroll 2000). Body psychotherapy has mapped prototypical cycles in terms of contact quality, changes in blood flow, muscle tension and movement. This model also considers how the cycle is interrupted defensively through habitual patterns and as a result of developmental vicissitudes (Boyesen *et al.* 1980).

Tracking of these cycles and their intrapsychic and interpersonal function is at the heart of body psychotherapy, though the specific interventions and models used are quite varied (Totton 2003). Bodywork, which focuses on breathing, sensation, imagery or movement, enhances the feedback loop from the peripheral nervous system back to the ANS. Familiarity with bodily phenomenology – changes in skin colour, muscle tension, pupil size, temperature, pace and feel of movement, conversation, etc. – informs body psychotherapy even when the therapist is not consciously formulating the process in such terms. This, as I shall argue later, is a core right-brain perceptual skill of body psychotherapy. But it is with the help of neuroscience that we can now elucidate how *any* therapeutic process, whether it is verbal or not, explicitly directed towards the body or not, has a relational and autonomic dimension/ effect.

Allan Schore's tripartite model of regulation

> Spontaneous communication employs . . . expressive displays in the sender that, given attention, activate emotional preattunements and are directly perceived by the receiver . . . This spontaneous communication constitutes a conversation between limbic systems.
>
> (Buck 1993: 266)

In *Affect Regulation*, a landmark work which spans an incredible breadth of contemporary sciences, Allan Schore (1994) links research, metapsychology and clinical data into an overarching theory of development. He makes detailed proposals linking cognitive/emotional/bodily developmental stages with radical shifts in brain organization. Sensory information from the environment is processed in a hierarchy of limbic and cortical sites which impact the ANS. Schore focuses on the amygdala, the cingulate and the orbito-frontal cortex, each acting as a representational system, and as a convergence zone for information related to learning from experience (see also Schore 2003b: 128–77).

The amygdala (active at birth) governs basic survival responses – it attributes an immediate good (safe) or bad (unsafe) valence to sensory information. The cingulate (activated from 3 months) is involved with shared pleasure, motivation, vocalization and the beginnings of self-other awareness. It stimulates and is stimulated by social interaction. The orbito-frontal cortex is much more complex in its operations, and its development parallels the critical early phase of separation-individuation (10–18 months).

Relationships between individuals and with the baby are fundamental determining factors of well-being or otherwise, which are registered as effects in the infant's body through the activation of the ANS. Body psychotherapy has focused on processes such as birth, feeding and the spectrum of early developmental reflexes as central to autonomic organization (Boadella 1987; Hartley 1995). Neuroscience has yet to fully integrate this wealth of knowledge but it has paid detailed attention to the mother's face as one of the primary vehicles of regulation of the infant's brain-body, showing that the 'mere perception of emotion on the [mother's] face generates a resonant emotional state' in her baby (Beebe and Lachman 2002: 37). In the newborn, appraisal and imitation of facial expression is fairly crude, but within months a baby can discriminate between surprise, fear and sadness, and make corresponding faces of his or her own (Meltzoff and Moore 1989). At 10 months, the infant seeks out affective information from the mother's face to help them interpret the environment. The expression on the mother's face, and her tone, body posture and touch all trigger changes in the baby's own autonomic state, the felt body feeling. The baby is responsive to every dimension of change and repeated or particularly intense transactions – traumatic or loving – become imprinted in long-term memory (Schore 1994).

A is for amygdala

Incoming sensory information from the body goes directly to the amygdala which makes a rapid first assessment of an event, triggering reflex actions such as the startle reflex. Infants have an inborn response to faces with fear or anger which registers immediately via the amygdala. This rapidly activates a strong sympathetic nervous system response correlating with states characterized by immediacy, intensity and reactivity.

Much of the new research into the amygdala has focused on the effect of traumatic events and episodes in childhood and adult life. However, Allan Schore reminds us that the last trimester of pregnancy through to 2 months of age is the critical period of maturation of the organization of the amygdala with the ANS. Early bonding within hours via smell, taste (breast milk) and touch, and subsequently via eye contact, facial expression and tone of voice, forms the basis for the earliest representation of the relationship with the mother and the basic sense of safety or danger (Schore 2003b: 155–7). Apparently unrelated trauma in later life, such as a car crash, can sometimes undo hitherto sufficient defences against very early vicissitudes in attachment.

Over-activation ('kindling') of the amygdala, accompanied by shutting down of important areas for information processing (hippocampus) and verbalizing (Broca's area), is now seen as a defining signature of trauma (Scaer 2001). It is becoming a necessary clinical skill to recognize the activation of a trauma response and the potential for dissociation in the client, detectable via autonomic changes (Rothschild 2000). An amygdala-triggered response in the client can create a feeling of being pulled into a current of intense and chaotic feelings, or a sudden explosive shift in atmosphere. This then informs the decisions the therapist can make in monitoring arousal and enabling any combination of action, discharge, contact, holding or insight that will enhance the safety and effectiveness of the therapy.

Enter the cingulate

The activation of the cingulate at 3 to 9 months, combined with rapid metabolic change in the infant's primary visual cortex at 8 weeks, ushers in a new stage which is marked by an increase in sociability (Schore 2003b: 139). The cingulate mediates contact and play behaviours, laughing, crying and making faces (p. 158). By now the infant has formed a discriminate attachment to the mother's face and the cingulate is implicated in the motivation for mother-baby 'proto conversations'. The cingulate supports co-regulation of states. Mutual reciprocal feedback through face-to-face interaction elevates sympathetic arousal, enabling increasingly heightened experiences of excitement in play and companionship. It expands the infant's intersubjective sense, mapping motor-sensory elements of the body-engaged-with-another (Trevarthen and Aitken 2001).

Attunement by the mother means being sensitive to signals for interaction, for periods of quiet disengagement, and for initiating re-engagement. At this stage the baby uses spontaneous turning away, crying or cessation of smiling to decrease contact (Schore 2003b: 158). Separation anxiety, pain and temperature regulation, and vocalization of distress are all mediated via the cingulate. Activation of the parasympathetic occurs either through the release of cortisol (hypothalamic-pituitary axis) or through the refined operation of the 'new mammalian vagus' (Porges and Bazhenova n.d.). Uncertainty and separation increase levels of cortisol which downregulates hyperarousal (sympathetic activation) but has a general inhibitory effect. Porges proposes that evolution has evolved a more sophisticated vagally-induced soothing system in humans, however, which operates through communicative interaction. Facial expression, looking, listening, sucking, swallowing and vocalization activate the parasympathetic and engage responsive attention. Touch, voice or eye contact which is soothing and familiar enhances relaxation through the release of oxytocin.

Body psychotherapists are equipped to engage in the regulation of body states through a whole variety of responses: playing non-verbally through movement, contact, making faces and voices; offering the physical warmth of a blanket, adjusting their physical proximity or actually holding the client; or just 'being there', showing interest, concern, delight and supporting the client to self-regulate through rest or interaction. In one session with a client the process moved from one of fear and rage with her kicking at me and shouting 'I want to hurt you' (amygdala) to a phase of play, laughter and relaxation where I was chasing and lightly touching her feet as she lay on her back waving them in the air (cingulate).

The orbito-frontal cortex – heart of the mind

The third part of Schore's hierarchy of brain centres regulating and representing body states has in fact two phases: the first is about the infant's capacity to tolerate high levels of excitement and arousal (sympathetic 'acceleration'); the second phase involves refining the capacity to modulate, slow down or inhibit impulses (parasympathetic 'braking'). At the end of this major reorganization of the brain, the orbito-frontal cortex will have – given optimal experience – added a new dual circuit of higher control and flexibility.

Schore calls the orbital cortex the 'executive centre' of the right-brain, because of its role in more complex assessment of and response to incoming sensory information (Schore 2003c: 21). As the orbital cortex is rapidly myelinating at 9 months, the infant becomes capable of 'joint attention', the ability to shift between an object and a person. The gradual maturation of this area allows the infant to self-regulate on the basis of experience and to manage more complex simultaneous processing.

Central to this is the regulation of feelings within the attachment relationship. The mother's synchronization with her toddler's excitement enables the orbito-frontal cortex to establish a regulatory connection to the sympathetic nervous system. This peaks at the turning point of the first year, when the infant is learning to stand and walk and needs a tremendous impetus of energy to 'get up and go', to explore and try out. In the subsequent phase of rapprochement (14–16 months), Schore notes that the connection between the orbito-frontal cortex and the parasympathetic system is being established, correlating with increasing control of bodily functions. This may be accompanied by an increase in vulnerability, disappointment and shame – the parasympathetic emotions – due to the discovery of limits to omnipotence, increasing prohibitions, and often an increase in ambivalence within the attachment relationship.

When the orbito-frontal cortex has established direct connections to both sympathetic and parasympathetic systems, there is the basis for a more refined expansion or modulation of feelings. This phase of structuralization is, like the earlier stages, highly experience-dependent. Is the infant welcome and supported in a zestful encounter with the word? Do the mother's eyes light up with joy; does her voice move in crescendos and decrescendos of encouragement and affirmation? This will develop the autonomic capacity of the infant to maintain and direct a high charge of pleasurable engagement with the world, fuelled by a cocktail of CRF (corticotrophin releasing factor) dopamine, opiates and adrenalin.

Developing the parasympathetic function will reflect how the toddler's desires for exploration and adventure are contained, and also how much safety and reassurance of love there is when the world falls apart. Are boundaries firm, or harsh, is he or she left without much guidance, or over-controlled, treated kindly or with anger and impatience? How much soothing is given, how much sensitivity is there to anxieties about separation? The repeated interactions with the attachment figure(s) may provide good experiences of calming down and/or ruptures and misattunements that provoke dreadful feelings of 'crashing', feeling deflated and rejected. These interactions will influence the transition into and experience of the parasympathetic. Parasympathetic activation affects the individual's capacity to manage self-containment, to find well-being in solitude, to tolerate difficulties, to grieve and find renewal.

The orbito-frontal cortex mediates and stores more elaborate, finely-tuned representations of qualities in its interactions with others, which are embodied in the differentiation of sympathetic and parasympathetic modes. Difficulties in the attachment relationship, absence, abuse and neglect all have an impact on the development of this dual control circuit between the orbito-frontal cortex and the two branches of the ANS. Repeated experiences of being left to cope with intense distress, especially when parents respond aggressively, inhibits the development of orbito-frontal-autonomic connections, and increases the tendency for more primitive amygdala reactions. Without this higher control – a neurobiological internalization of a good enough object – individuals are left with potentially lifelong problems in regulating affect and managing stress (Gerhardt 2004).

There is an interesting difference of emphasis between the traditional Reichian view of the sympathetic (associated with anxiety and contraction) and the parasympathetic (related to relaxation and pleasure). In Schore's work, sympathetic activation is specifically linked with engagement and parasympathetic with inhibition. Physiologically, the sympathetic is a state of muscular tension and increased arousal; it speaks of a *need* to act, to show, to be responded to, a movement towards the world (except with fear which may trigger recoil). Whether this is a joyous, hopeful experience or a state of anxious anticipation is experience-dependent. As we have seen, there are two routes and modes of parasympathetic activation. When there is sufficient stability and interactive regulation, there is a positive sense of reconnecting to self and an inner life (with good internal objects). This pleasurable state, nourished by the senses, supports rest, digestion and peacefulness. Schore, however, links the parasympathetic with the feeling of shame, when the mother signals her disapproval by reducing contact. With this the toddler is thrown back on him or herself and feels a sudden collapse in energy and painful self-consciousness, a response corresponding with a cortisol-induced sudden switch into the parasympathetic.

The implications for body psychotherapy

The reorganization of brain and body continues throughout life to be a complex response to developmentally specific (linear) and experience dependent (non-linear) processes. This outline of some of the major landmarks in very early development suggests how failures in early attachment impact basic emotional-physiological cycles and rhythms. In adult clients, feelings may be inaccessible, log-jammed or overwhelming.

With one client suffering from depression, the tension between the need to grieve and her suppressed anger and frustration maintained a chronic systemic deadlock. This reflected not just an innate divergence of motive but difficulties in transitioning through intense states. A depressed mother had meant a lack of stimulating interaction (which builds the sympathetic capacity) and an absence of comfort (parasympathetic). Janet rarely cried but my attention to bodily signs of vulnerability and the very immediate support and contact provided by my body put her in touch with new depths of sadness and longing. At another point, observing the grasping motions she was making with her hands, I gave her a cushion and suggested she let her hands do what they needed to. The physicality of trying to tear it to pieces – a motoric expressive act – enabled her briefly to tap into the fierceness of her rage. These were preliminary steps in helping her self-regulate through immediate physical contact and expression, but it was months before more complex self-with-another awareness developed.

Body psychotherapy is rich in interventions which actively and directly help the client experience, develop and transition between states on an autonomic spectrum. Another client used to stride around the room talking loudly and wanting to amplify every emotional event into a drama. In one session I had him lie down and put his hand on his chest to feel the vibration of his own voice. He spent a long time trying to connect the experience of feeling and listening to his own voice and then to take in my presence. He became aware of never having been listened to and therefore not knowing how to tune in to himself.

The attachment relationship, and later the therapeutic relationship, needs to attend to the nuance of feeling. Whilst a baby responds spontaneously to the human face, the older child and adult will often be embroiled in a more complex relationship to faces, negotiating self and other, inner and outer, past and present. In psychotherapy the therapist's eye contact may communicate understanding and acknowledgement of a range of ideas, acts and emotions. These may be explored by amplifying awareness of posture or movement, or by talking explicitly about what is being felt or feared. When therapist and client have enough working history, it may be that a prolonged gaze is itself sufficient to reorganize awareness and deepen the sense of self-with-another.

Schore's tripartite model bridges the gap between theories which focus on reflexive responses, which are relatively primitive and unmediated expressions of instincts, and theories about the internalization of an elaborate and complex social environment. Historically, body psychotherapy has been allied to the sub-cortex and the right-brain. Working with impulse, breath, movement and sensation are all effective ways of enhancing the client's self-regulation quite directly. They enhance the body's motor sensory feedback loops which can lead to spontaneous rebalancing of the nervous system and a more coherent sense of body-self. The strength of an approach to psychotherapy which engages directly with body states is that a basic level of self-regulation can be reintroduced even when defences against relational interaction are fairly entrenched. Panksepp suggests that 'all levels of information processing in the generation of emotional responses interact with each other' (1998: 33). Body-work may be a 'way in' to a process that has been sealed off from awareness, buried in muscular armour and lack of connectivity within the brain. As Boadella has put it, 'recovering motility awakens sensibility' (1997).

Body psychotherapy is organized around the perception and facilitation of emotional contact in the therapeutic relationship, often through the process of differentiating and bringing awareness to eye contact, movements of the mouth, head position, chest, arms and so on. There is a detailed understanding of the specificity of areas of muscular tension (armour) as defences against showing feelings, exploding, collapsing. There is a useful match between the neurological-behavioural-emotional attachment process outlined in great detail by Schore and the characterological map of body psychotherapy (Totton and Jacobs 2001). The amygdala-driven pre- and post-natal period correlates neatly in its timing with the schizoid stage and themes. The coming on line of the cingulate matches the oral stage, with its need for immediacy of presence, touch, play and inviting eye contact. The first phase of the orbito-frontal connection to the sympathetic nervous system fits the picture of the expansion and assertion of the psychopathic stage; and the second stage of orbito-frontal connections to the parasympathetic ties in with the masochistic stage of learning to inhibit impulses and be 'good'.

Although this outline of theory from neuroscience is structured around a hierarchy of brain sites, it's important to remember that it is in and through the body that changes in state manifest themselves. The question for the therapist is: what area of experience is being evoked right now? The more aware the therapist is of the complex, perhaps fleeting, bodily shifts in the client and in themselves, the more sophisticated will be their sense of what is needed therapeutically. Experience is what activates the necessary reorganizing of the brain and body and preliminary studies do suggest that the amygdala, cingulate and orbito-frontal cortex are all engaged and structurally modified in the course of psychotherapy (Schore 1994: 468).

Critical cortical differences

The core of the self derives from these levels of self-and-other representation involving a bodily sense (muscular patterns, autonomic regulation of states) combined with visual images, sounds etc. encoding interaction with others in a preverbal form. Figure 1.1 shows how amygdala and cingulate have direct connections into the orbito-frontal area of the right cortex, thereby providing 'the most comprehensive and integrated map of the body state available to the brain' (Damasio 1994: 66).[4] A huge shift is initiated at 18 months, however, as the left cortex starts to become activated.

The left-brain deals with language, structure and causal relationships. Whereas the right cortex is activated by novelty, the left-brain relies on sequential strategies, focus and managing routine behaviour, which enables the consolidation of learning. The shift to the left-brain coincides with a huge leap in talking and understanding words, initiating a new kind of self-consciousness. As the child matures, listening and then reading develops the capacity to take in others' voices and thoughts and to begin to manipulate concepts, symbols and abstract ideas. The left cortex is also specialized for fine motor control, attention to detail and investigation of objects and their properties, marking an increased interest in information external to the body-self. This maturational process incorporates both a fixed developmental trajectory and an idiosyncratic path influenced by object relational experiences, cultural patterns and other environmental factors. Whilst the right-brain mediates the bodily emotional experience of being-with-another, the left-brain is more concerned with what-others-think-of-me. In an adult the left-brain is normally considered the dominant hemisphere.

Left-right cortical differences have been well known for decades, but the full implications of the right-brain bodily emotional regulation in the context of the attachment relationship is only being elucidated now (Pally 2000; Schore 2003a, 2003b, 2003c). The function of the right hemisphere is to

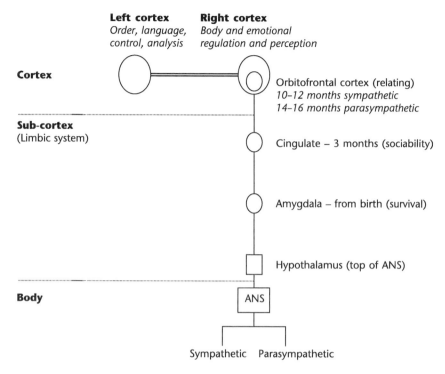

Figure 1.1   Schore's hierarchical model of affect regulation
Whilst left and right cortices process motor and sensory information for the contralateral sides of the body, it is the right cortex which receives and regulates sub-cortical autonomic and endocrinological emotional information.

maintain a coherent, continuous and unified sense of self; this is anchored in and emerges from motoric, autonomic and peptidergic regulatory patterns, which are critically influenced by the early relational environment.

When the right-brain metabolism is weak, as a result of insufficient co-regulation of states in early life, the individual is easily overwhelmed by stressful bodily states. This may manifest as dissociation: the inability to integrate bodily, emotional and relational-contextual information. Or to compensate, the left-brain may be over-active and inhibit expression generated in the limbic areas through motoric control and by constructing narratives which cover up or distort the underlying bodily information about feelings. The left-brain is an automatic interpreter, a relentless maker of links between details. When disconnected from the bodily and contextual information provided by the right cortex, the left-brain papers over the gap with logical explanations. This aids repression (see Figure 1.2).

The right-brain is activated by and regulates via eye contact, tone of voice,

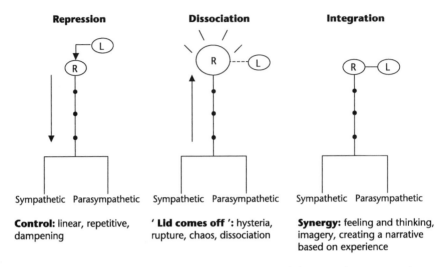

Figure 1.2 Schema suggesting what happens when the left cortex dampens regulatory processing; when the right cortex is overwhelmed; and when the two function synergistically.

strong affect, expressive movement and visceral information. In therapy, that may mean strong bodily responses (shivering, crying, kicking, somatic symptoms), intense expression of feeling or emotionally directed free association and imagery. If this process is not contained within the therapeutic relationship, there may be memories and/or emotional discharge but also a level of dissociation of the material in the here and now relationship. Trauma functionally disables the left-brain, leaving the memory encoded and accessible only via limbic and right-cortical systems (Pally 2000: 123).

Schore proposes that the right-brain correlates with Freud's 'unconscious': 'the right brain is centrally involved in unconscious activities, and just as the left brain communicates its states to other brains via linguistic behaviours so the right non-verbally communicates its unconscious states to other right brains that are tuned to receive these communications' (2003c: 29). He suggests that projective identification is the communication of intense affective states occurring during high resonance between the right-brains of therapist and client.

Containment by the therapist requires both right-cortical self-regulation (processing feelings and responses to the client) and the left-cortical capacity for detached analysis and maintaining a structure. Right-brain responsiveness means the therapist may get overwhelmed, triggered or transfixed by a client's unexpected or intense process. Alternatively, therapists may react in a defensive left-brain strategy of interpretation and explanation. The left-brain style is to verbalize, to theorize, to fall back on what is already known in order to preserve the sense of mastery.

Right-brain responses are fundamental to relationship, but activation of the left cortex also helps modify intense feelings in a therapeutic way. For the client, finding or hearing the right words or a precisely formulated insight has an immediate modulating effect. It enables connection to a matrix of previously generated and stored understanding of self-and-other. Left-cortical activity can support the right cortex through an association of feeling with thinking, experience with insight, or giving narrative coherence to a flood of feelings. It may be that the 'mind-body split' is in effect a right-left split, with left-brain activation overriding the right-brain assimilation and regulation of sub-cortically generated emotional states.

Therapist as healer, therapist as analyst/expert

The right-brain skill is in the realm of 'use of self' – presence (i.e. the therapist's ability to self-regulate strongly evoked states), awareness of subtle information relating to shifts in psychobiological state in self and other (countertransference) and the capacity to be spontaneous and relational. Schore argues that the orbito-frontal site in the right cortex is 'specifically geared towards appraising fleeting and fluctuating emotional states in the other and, simultaneously, sustaining awareness of their own internal state' (2003b: 111).

Body psychotherapists are equipped to perceive the client not just in terms of affect, but in terms of the underlying autonomic, motoric and sensory components of affect, including how it is fragmented, dispersed or deadened in the body. This perception is a fundamental anchor against the verbal slipstream of narratives organized around the client's anxieties, hopes and fears about how they are coming across to others.

The left-brain skill is in the realm of analysis and use of theory to differentiate and calibrate interventions (including bodywork) in a disciplined and strategic way. Activation of the left cortex enhances the capacity to be guided by a good understanding of theory, thereby adding structure and focus to the fluidity of intuitive right-brain responses. The therapist's own right-left cortical partnership is critical to working in a sensitive, discriminate and creative way, negotiating the tension between instrumental and relational approaches. To take this one step further, the right-brain may be the 'healer', involving deep bodily perception, tolerance and responsiveness to another's pain or joy, whereas the left-brain is the expert/analyst: knowledgeable, skilful, articulate and able to penetrate complexity.

Auto and interactive regulation

Self-regulation is the ability to flexibly regulate emotional states through interactions with others (interactive regulation) and by oneself (autoregulation) (Schore 2003c: 25). In optimal circumstances this is an intrinsic capacity which develops from the dependency of early infancy to the complex, varied and interdependent self-regulation of a healthy adult.

The organization of the brain-body is one of loops, spirals and complementary structures. Reciprocal tension between the sympathetic and parasympathetic systems manages the metabolic and emotional energy for engaging and responding, and recovering equilibrium. As we have seen, the ANS is organized largely through the tripartite hierarchy of emotion-regulating sites, which feed into the right-brain. On top of this, right and left cortices constantly negotiate or compete to optimize regulation. Vicissitudes in development are reflected in splits of all kinds (between components of experience, between parts of the self), and are reflected in avoidance of interactive regulation, and/or an inability to manage difficult feelings without intense interactive regulation (Carroll 2004). Much of therapy is about recognizing and understanding existing regulatory patterns, supporting underdeveloped resources, and challenging and helping to reformulate defensive strategies.

In psychotherapy there is an opportunity for interactive regulation which enables greater emotional intensity and the reorganization of brain-body. In an interactive regulation an unbearable state – of grief perhaps, or shame – is felt with the support of the therapist's contained but active bodily resonance. It is a process of exchange, involving a high level of coordination and contact, occurring spontaneously through the holding quality of the therapist's face-to-face empathy. The client makes sounds, words and gestures to the therapist who receives them and accepts their full impact.

Bodywork can be a bridge to self-regulation, including more awareness of the self-in-relationship. It can also become a vehicle for collusion and enactment which bypasses interactive face-to-face regulation, inadvertently recapitulating the early attachment trauma. Autoregulating strategies can be powerful unconscious and insidious mechanisms of control which have been essential to protect the client from painful feelings, but have become entrenched defences against the spontaneity and intensity of relating. This can take the form of avoiding anything to do with the body, or of a flight to the body to discharge intensity in sounds and movements which actually keep the client encapsulated in past experience.

Contemporary body psychotherapy is marked by a shift to a more relational emphasis, where explicit bodywork may be used sparingly and the body is more likely to be perceived in the context of the charged intersubjective field between client and therapist (Totton 1998; Soth 2003a and this volume; Asheri 2004). For this, the therapist needs both sensitivity to micro-changes or 'energetic' shifts in the client, and the capacity to speak to both the left (insight-oriented) and right (feeling-oriented) brain of the client. This is epitomized in the sophisticated use of countertransference. Countertransference emerges from the therapist's very rapid processing of global and micro bodily information in themselves and the client. As these impressions take some kind of form – an impulse, a metaphor, a sensation, a feeling – they can be more fully processed, leading to new in-the-moment hypotheses. This intricate left-right client-therapist brain dance inspires 'the next move', be it spontaneously strategic or strategically spontaneous (Carroll 2005).

Notes

1   Neuroscience is now a major industry, linked with pharmaceutical business, genetic engineering and even the military (Rees and Rose 2004). Many therapists fear it may only be used in service of a medicalized, pragmatic, pharmacalogical model but the field of affective neuroscience, though small, is substantiating the emphasis on attachment and growth as a complex relational process (Schore 2003a; Gerhardt 2004).

2   Self-regulation of the ANS is at the heart of body psychotherapy. Significant influences on me include biodynamic massage (Boyesen *et al.* 1980; Carroll 2002b); charge therapy as taught at Chiron by Michael Soth (this volume); Body-Mind Centering® which I learned from Linda Hartley (1995); and Somatic Trauma Therapy (Levine 1997; Rothschild 2000).

3   As well as autonomic characteristics, particular emotions are also differentiated by distinct neurochemical profiles. Molecular messengers called peptides are capable of evoking specific emotional tones and behaviours. Peptides include hormones, neurotransmitters, endorphins and growth factors. Well-known peptides associated with qualities of drive and feeling are testosterone, oestrogen, progesterone and oxytocin – the 'bonding' hormone – and the stress hormones cortisol and adrenaline. Although Panksepp has begun to map the body and brain circuits of the major emotional operating systems, it is clear that the interaction of regulatory systems of hormonal, immune and metabolic function is very complex (Panksepp 1998; Carroll 2004).

4   Whereas right and left unimodal areas of the cortex map motor and sensory information on opposite sides of body and are symmetrical, there is a marked asymmetry in the heteromodal (i.e. the areas where information from different senses is brought together) and pre-frontal cortices (involved in planning and thinking).

2 Panic, biology and reason

Giving the body its due

Peter A. Levine

The substitute tiger

My interest in the essential role played by bodily responses in the genesis and treatment of panic anxiety began quite accidentally in 1969 (Levine 1997). A psychiatrist, knowing of my interest in 'mind/body healing' – a fledging arena at the time – had referred a young woman to see me. Nancy had been suffering from panic attacks for about two years. She had not responded to psychotherapy, while tranquillizers and antidepressant drugs gave her only minimal relief. The referring psychiatrist asked me to do some 'relaxation training' with her. My attempts were equally unsuccessful. She resisted; I tried harder. We got nowhere. Since I knew almost nothing about panic attacks at the time, I asked her for more detailed information about the 'how and when' of her attacks. Nancy revealed that the onset of her first attack occurred while she, along with a group of other students, was taking the Graduate Record Examination. She remembers breaking out in a cold sweat and beginning to shake. Forcing herself to complete the test, Nancy then ran out, frantically pacing the streets for hours, afraid to enter a bus or taxi. Fortunately, she met a friend who took her home. During the following two years her symptoms worsened and became more frequent. Eventually she was unable to leave her house alone and could not follow through with graduate school even though she had passed the exam and was accepted by a major university.

In our conversation, Nancy recollected the following sequence of events: arriving early, she went to the café to have a coffee and smoke a cigarette. A group of students were already there, talking about how difficult the test was. Nancy, overhearing this, became agitated, lit another cigarette and gulped a second coffee. She remembered feeling quite jittery upon entering the room. She recalled that the exams and marking pencils were passed out and that she wrote vigorously. She became almost breathless at this point and quite agitated – I noticed that her carotid (neck) pulse was increasing rapidly.

I asked Nancy to lie down and I tried to get her to relax. Relaxation was not the answer. As I naively, and with the best of intentions, attempted to help her relax, she went into a full-blown anxiety attack. Her heartbeat accelerated further to about 150 beats per minute. Her breathing and pulse rate then started to decrease. I was relieved, but only momentarily. Her pulse continued to drop, precipitously to around 50 beats per minute; she became still. Her face paled and her hands began to tremble: 'I'm real scared . . . stiff all over . . . I'm dying . . . I can't move . . . I don't want to die . . . help me . . . don't let my die.' She continued to stiffen, her throat becoming so tight that she could barely speak. Nancy forced the words, 'Why can't I understand this . . . I feel so inferior, like I'm being punished . . . there's something wrong with me . . . I feel like I'm going to be killed . . . there's nothing . . . it's just blank.' We had rather unfortunately co-discovered, some years before it was reported in the literature, 'relaxation-induced panic syndrome'.

The session continued as follows:

'Feel the pencil,' I requested without really knowing why.

'I remember now. I remember what I thought,' she replied. *'My life depends on this exam.'* Her heart rate increased now, moving back up into the eighties.

At this point, a 'dream image' of a crouching tiger jumping through the bush flashed before me. Quite startled, a fleeting thought about a zoological article I had recently read on 'tonic immobility' or 'death feigning' prompted me to announce loudly: 'You are being attacked by a large tiger. See the tiger as it comes at you. Run toward those rocks, climb them, and escape!'

Nancy let out a blood-curdling yell – a shout that brought in a passing policeman (fortunately my office partner took care of the situation – perhaps explaining that I was doing 'relaxation training'). She began to tremble, shake and sob in waves of full body convulsions. I sat with her for almost an hour while she continued to shake. She recalled terrifying images and feelings from age 4. She had been held down by doctors and nurses and struggled in vain during a tonsillectomy with ether anaesthesia. She left the session feeling 'like she had herself again'. We continued relaxation, including assertion training, for a couple more sessions. She was taken off medication, entered graduate school and completed her doctorate in physiology without relapse. However, I realized that this was just the beginning in developing a systematic and safe (leaving much less to chance) approach to the healing and prevention of trauma.

The body has its reasons . . .

Aaron Beck and Gary Emery, in their seminal book, *Anxiety Disorders and Phobias* (1985: 188), make the point that to understand fear, anxiety and panic, the person's *appraisal* of a situation is most important. In the chapter, 'Turning Anxiety on Its Head', the authors consider cognitive appraisal to be a critical fulcrum in anxiety reactions. They argue that because anxiety has a strong somatic-emotional component, the subtler cognitive processing which occurs may be neglected both in theory and in clinical practice. Clearly Nancy's belief of the difficulty of the exam – based in part on the overheard conversation in the café – lead to her thought: 'my life depends on this', an unconscious threat appraisal. By focusing narrowly on the cognitive aspects of anxiety, however, Beck and Emery overlook the fundamental role played by bodily responses and sensations in the experience of anxiety. When Nancy drank the coffee and smoked the cigarette (caffeine and nicotine, together, can be a robust stimulant), the physiological arousal of increased heart rate both fed into and was fed by her cognitive assessment of the 'threat' from the exam driving her heart rate sharply up. Together, both assessment and physiological activation resonated with the 'imprinted' bodily reaction of being terrorized and overwhelmed, 20 years before, during the tonsillectomy. The panic attack was triggered from that synergy.

In addition to recognizing the importance of cognitive factors, systematic study of bodily reactions and sensate experience is not only important, it is *essential*. This study needs to occur conjointly with the recognition and exploration of cognitive and perceptual factors. Appreciating the role of bodily experience illuminates the complex web called 'anxiety' and connects many threads in understanding and modifying its physiological and experiential basis. In addition to turning anxiety on its head, we need also to *connect* the body with the head – recognizing the intrinsic psycho-physiological unity that welds body and mind.

Cognitive theorists believe that anxiety serves primarily to signal the brain to activate a physical response that will dispel the source of anxiety. The role of anxiety is likened in this way to that of pain. The experience of pain impels us to do something to stop it. The pain is not the disease. It is merely a symptom of fracture, appendicitis and so forth. Similarly, according to Beck, anxiety is not the disease but only a signal: 'Humans are constructed in such a way as to ascribe great significance to the experience of anxiety so that we will be impelled to take measures to reduce it'. He notes that: 'The most primal response depends on the generation of unpleasant subjective sensations that prompt a *volitional* intentional action designed to reduce danger. Only one experience of "anxiety" is necessary to do this' (Beck 1986: 188, emphasis added). As examples Beck mentions the arousal of anxiety when a driver feels that he is not in complete control of the car and which prompts him to reduce his speed until he again feels in control. Similarly, a person approaching a high cliff retreats because of the anxiety.

What is the wisdom of an *involuntary*, primitive, global, somatic and often immobilizing brainstem response (Gallup and Maser 1977)? Is it exclusively for calling the individual's attention to making varied and specific *voluntary* responses? Such an inefficient arrangement is highly doubtful. A lack of refinement in appreciating the essential nuances played by bodily responses and sensations in the structures and experience of anxiety is typical of cognitive approaches. Beck, for example, flatly states that: 'a specific combination of autonomic and motor patterns will be used for escape, a different combination for freezing, and a still different pattern for fainting. However, the subjective sensation – anxiety – will be approximately the same for each strategy'. In the following paragraph of this same article he adds: 'An active coping set is generally associated with sympathetic nervous system dominance, whereas a passive set, triggered by what is perceived as an overwhelming threat, is often associated with parasympathetic dominance . . . as in a blood phobic. In either case the subjective experience of anxiety is similar' (Beck 1986: 188).

Beck's statements reveal a significant glitch in the cognitive phenomenology of anxiety, highlighting its paradoxical nature. According to his reasoning, the same body signal is relayed to the brain's cognitive structures for all forms of threat. The 'head' (cognitive) structures are then somehow expected to decide on an appropriate course of action. This top-heavy, Cartesian holdover goes against the basic biological requirements for an immediate, precise and unequivocal response to threat. It is a view that is quite confusing because it requires that distinctly different kinaesthetic, proprioceptive and autonomic feedback be experienced as the same signal. We have tended, in the post-Cartesian view of the world, to identify so much with the rational mind that the wider role of instinctive, bodily responses in orchestrating and propelling behaviour and consciousness has been all but ignored.

Beck's statement that 'a specific combination of autonomic and motor patterns will be used for escape, a different combination for freezing, and a still different pattern for fainting' and that 'the subjective sensation – anxiety – will be approximately the same for each strategy' contradicts both evolutionary imperative and subjective experience. As one working for 35 years in what is now called somatic psychology, these statements simply do not fit the *subjective facts* and would have had William James turning over in his grave. If you ask several anxious people at random what they are feeling, they may all *say* that they are feeling 'anxiety'. However, if they are then asked the epistemological question: 'How do you *know* that you are feeling anxiety?', several different responses will be forthcoming. One, for example, could be, 'because something bad will happen to me'. Another may be that they are feeling strangulated in their throat; still another that their heart is leaping out of their chest; another that they have a knot in their gut. Other people might report that their neck, shoulders, arms and legs are tight; others might feel ready for action, and still others that their legs feel weak or their chest collapsed. All but the first answer are specific and varied *physical* sensations. And if the person who said that she thought 'something bad will happen to me' was directed to a scan of her body, she would have discovered some *somatic/physical* sensation driving and directing the thought.

If we feel threatened and assess that we can escape or fight back, we will feel one set of physical sensations. If, on the other hand, we feel threatened and perceive that we cannot escape or fight back then we feel something quite different. Now here is the key factor: both the assessment of danger and the perception of our capacity to respond are not primarily conscious. Let's look to our distant ancestors to illuminate these questions.

Instinct in the age of reason

Animals possess a variety of orientation and defensive responses that allow them to respond automatically to different, potentially dangerous, situations rapidly and fluidly. The sensations involving escape are profoundly different from those of freezing or collapse. I am in agreement with Beck in describing panic and post-traumatic anxiety states as having in common 'the experience of dread with the perception of inescapability'. What I first gleaned from Nancy 35 years ago, and later confirmed by the ethological analysis of predator prey behaviours, was that the singular experience of 'traumatic panic anxiety' that Beck talks about occurs *only* where the normally varied and active defensive responses have been unsuccessful, that is, when a situation is both dangerous *and* inescapable (Beck 1986). Anxiety, in its pathological panic form (as distinguished from so-called signal anxiety), represents a profound failure of the organism's innate defensive structures to mobilize and thus allow the individual to escape threatening situations actively and successfully. Where escape is possible, the organism responds with an active pattern of coping. There is the *continuous experience* of danger, running and escape. When, in an activated state, escape is successfully completed, anxiety does not occur. Rather a fluid (felt) sense of 'biological competency' is experienced. Where defensive behaviours are unsuccessful in actively resolving severe threat, anxiety is generated. It is where active forms of defensive response are aborted and incomplete that anxiety states ensue. *Beneath the monolithic label of anxiety are 'camouflaged' a wealth of incomplete and identifiable somatic responses, sensations, and bodily feelings.* These body experiences represent the individual's response to past experience, but also to their 'genetic potential' in the form of unrealized defensive responses. The recognition that these instinctive orientation and defensive behaviours are organized motor patterns, that is, prepared motor acts, helps to return the body to the head. Anxiety derives ultimately from a failure to complete motor acts.

Jean Genet, in his autobiographical novel, *Thief's Journal* (1987), states this premise in bold prose: 'Acts must be carried through to their completion. Whatever their point of departure, the end will be beautiful. It is [only] because an action has not been completed that it is vile' (p. 214). When orienting and defensive behaviours are carried out smoothly and effectively, anxiety is not generated. Instead, there is the complex and fluid sensate experience perceived as curiosity, attraction or avoidance. It is only when these instinctive orientation and defensive resources are interfered with ('thwarted') that the experience of anxiety is generated: I am not afraid of snakes or spiders, but of my inability to respond effectively to these creatures. Ultimately, we have only one fear, the fear of not being able to cope, of our own un-copeability. Without active, available, defensive responses, we are unable to deal effectively with danger and so we are, proportionately, anxious.

Orientations, defence and flight

A scene from an uplands meadow helps to illustrate the 'motor act' concept. Suppose you are strolling leisurely in an open meadow. A shadow suddenly moves in the periphery of your vision. Instinctively all movement is arrested; reflexively you crouch in a flexed posture; perceptions are 'opened' through activation of the parasympathetic autonomic nervous system. After this momentary arrest response your head turns automatically in the direction of the shadow or sound in an attempt to localize and identify it. Your neck, back, legs and feet muscles coordinate so that your whole body turns and then extends. Your eyes narrow somewhat while your pelvis and head shift horizontally, giving you an optimal view of the surroundings and an ability to focus panoramically. This initial two-phase action pattern is an instinctive orientation preparing you to respond flexibly to many possible contingencies. The initial arrest-crouch flexion response minimizes detection by possible predators and perhaps offers some protection from falling objects. Primarily though, it provides a convulsive jerk that interrupts any motor patterns that were already in execution and then prepares you, through scanning, for the fine-tuned behaviours of exploration or defence.

If it had been an eagle taking flight that cast the shadow, a further orientation of tracking-pursuit occurs. Adjustment of postural and facial muscles occurs unconsciously. This new 'attitude of interest', when integrated with the contour of the rising eagle image, is perceived as the feeling of excitement. This aesthetically pleasing sense, with the meaning of enjoyment, is affected by past experience, but may also be one of the many powerful, archetypal predispositions or undercurrents which each species has developed over millennia of evolutionary time. Most Native Americans, for example, have a very special, spiritual, mythic relationship with the eagle. Is this a coincidence, or is there something imprinted deep within the structures of the brain, body and soul of the human species that responds intrinsically to the image of an eagle with correlative excitement and awe? Most organisms possess dispositions, if not specific approach/avoidance responses, to moving contours. A baby chick, without learning from its mother, for example, flees from the moving contour of a hawk. If the direction of movement of this silhouette is reversed, however, to simulate a goose, the baby chick shows no such avoidance response.

If the initial shadow in the meadow had been from a raging grizzly bear rather than from a rising eagle, a very different preparedness reaction would have been evoked – the preparation to flee. This is not because we think: 'bear', evaluate it as dangerous, and *then* prepare to run. It is because the contours and features of the large, looming, approaching animal cast a particular light pattern upon the retina of the eye. This stimulates a pattern of neural firing that is registered in phylogenetically primitive brain regions. This 'pattern recognition' triggers preparation for defensive responding before it is regis-tered in consciousness. These responses derive from genetic predispositions, as well as from the outcomes of previous experiences with similar large animals. Non-conscious circuits are activated, triggering preset patterns or tendencies of defensive posturing. Muscles, viscera and autonomic nervous system acti-vation cooperate in preparing for escape. This preparation is sensed kinaes-thetically and is internally joined as a Gestalt to the image of the bear. *Movement and image are fused*, registered together, as the *feeling of danger*. Motivated by this feeling we continue to scan for more information – a grove of trees, some rocks – at the same time drawing on our ancestral and personal memory banks. Probabilities are non-consciously computed, based on such encounters over millions of years of historical evolution, as well as our own personal experi-ences. We prepare for the next phase in this unfolding drama. Without think-ing, we orient toward a large tree with low branches. An *urge* is experienced to flee and climb. If we run, freely oriented toward the tree, it is the feeling of *directed running*. The urge to run is experienced as the feeling of danger, while successful running is experienced as *escape* (and not anxiety!).

If, on the other hand, we chance upon a starved or wounded bear, and moreover find ourselves surrounded on all sides by sheer rock walls, that is, trapped, then the defensive preparedness for flight, concomitant with the feeling of danger, is 'thwarted' and will change abruptly into the fixated emo-tional states of anxiety. The word *fear*, interestingly enough, comes from the old English term for danger, while *anxious* derives from the Greek root *angst*, meaning to 'press tight' or strangle, as conveyed in Edward Munch's riveting painting, *The Scream*. Our entire physiology and psyche become precipitously constricted in anxiety. Response is restricted to non-directed desperate flight, to rage, counterattack or freeze-collapse. The latter affords the possibility of diminishing the bear's urge to attack. (If it is not cornered or hurt and is able to clearly identify the approaching human being, the bear will usually not attack the intruder. It may even remain and go on with business as usual.)

In summary, when the normal orientation and defensive escape resources have failed to resolve the situation, life hangs in the balance, with non-directed flight, rage, freezing or collapse. Rage and terror-panic are the *secondary* emotional anxiety states that are evoked when the preparatory orientation processes (feelings) of danger-orientation and preparedness to flee are not successful – when they are blocked or inhibited. It is this 'thwarting' that results in freezing and anxiety-panic.

Tonic immobility – freezing

Anxiety has often been linked to the physiology and experience of flight. Analyses of animal distress behaviours suggest that this may be quite misleading. Ethology (the study of animals in their natural environment) points to the 'thwarting' of escape as the root of distress-anxiety (Salzen 1967; Morris 1969). When attacked by a cheetah on the African plains, an antelope will first attempt to escape through directed-oriented running. If, however, the fleeing animal is cornered so that escape is diminished, it may run blindly, without a directed orientation, or it may attempt to fight wildly and desperately against enormous odds. At the moment of physical contact, often before injury is actually inflicted, the antelope abruptly appears to go dead. It not only appears dead, but its autonomic physiology undergoes a widespread alteration and reorganization. The antelope is in fact highly activated internally, even though outward movement is almost non-existent. Prey animals are immobilized in a sustained (cataleptic-catatonic) pattern of neuromuscular activity and high autonomic and brainwave activity (Gallup and Maser 1977: 345). Sympathetic and parasympathetic responses are also concurrently activated, like brake and accelerator, working against each other (Gelhorn 1967; Levine 1986: 331–54).

Nancy, in her re-experiencing of the examination room, exhibited this pattern when her heart rate increased sharply and then plummeted abruptly to a very low rate. In tonic immobility, an animal is either frozen stiff in heightened contraction of agonist and antagonist muscle group, or in a continuously balanced, hypnotic, muscular state exhibiting what is called 'wavy flexibility'. In the hypnotic state, body positions can be moulded like clay, as is seen in catatonic schizophrenics. There is also analgesic numbing (Gallup and Maser 1977: 337). Nancy described many of these behaviours as they were happening to her. She wasn't, however, aware of her physical sensations but rather of her self-depreciating and critical judgements about those sensations. It is as though some explanation must be found for profoundly disorganizing forces underlying one's own perceived inadequacy. The psychologist Philip G. Zimbardo (1977) has gone so far as to propose that 'most mental illness represents not a cognitive impairment, but an [attempted] interpretation of discontinuous or inexplicable internal states'. Tonic immobility, murderous rage and non-directed flight are such examples.

Ethologists have found wide adaptive value in these immobility responses: freezing makes prey less visible and non-movement in prey appears also to be a potent inhibitor of aggression in predators, often aborting attack-kill responses entirely (Gallup and Maser 1977: 350–4). The Park Service, for example, advises campers that if they are unable to actively escape an attacking bear, they should lie prone and not move. The family cat, seemingly on to nature's game, bats a captured, frozen mouse with its paws hoping to bring it out of shock and continue in the game. Immobility can buy time for prey. The predator may drag frozen prey to its den or lair for later consumption, giving it a second chance to escape. In addition to these aggression-inhibiting responses, freezing by prey animals may provide a signalling and decoy effect, allowing con-specifics, who are further away, a better chance for escape in certain situations. Loss of blood pressure may also help prevent bleeding when injured. An immobile prey animal is, in sum, less likely to be attacked. Further, if attacked, it is less likely to be killed and eaten, increasing its chances of escape and reproduction. In a world where most animals are both predator and prey at one time or another, analgesia is 'humane' biological adaptation.

Tonic immobility demonstrates that anxiety can be both self-perpetuating and self-defeating. Freezing is the last-ditch, cul-de-sac, bodily response where active escape is not possible. Where flight and fight escape have been (or are perceived to be) unlikely, the nervous system reorganizes to tonic immobility. Both flight-or-fight and immobility are adaptive responses. Where the flight-or-fight response is appropriate, freezing will be relatively maladaptive; where freezing is appropriate, attempts to flee or fight are likely to be maladaptive. Biologically, immobility is a potent adaptive strategy where active escape is prevented. When, however, it becomes a preferred response pattern in situations of activation in general, it is profoundly debilitating. Immobility becomes the crippling, fixating experience of traumatic and panic anxiety. Underlying the freezing response, however, are the flight-or-fight and other defensive and orientation preparations that are activated just prior to the onset of freezing. The 'de-potentiation' of anxiety is accomplished by precisely and sequentially restoring the latent flight-or-fight and other active defensive responses that occur at the moment(s) before escape is thwarted.

Jody – in a fraction of a second: An example of resolving anxiety states through completing innate defensive responses

Twenty-five years ago, Jody's life was shattered. While walking in the woods near her boyfriend's house, a hunter came up to her and began a conversation. It was mid-September. There was a chill in the air. Her boyfriend and others thought nothing when they saw someone apparently chopping wood. A madman, however, was smashing Jody's head again and again with his rifle.

The police found Jody unconscious. Chips from the butt of the rifle lay nearby where they had broken off in the violent attack.

The only recollection Jody had of the event was scant and confused. She vaguely remembered meeting the man and then waking up in the hospital some days later. Jody had been suffering from anxiety, migraines, concentration and memory problems, depression, chronic fatigue and chronic pain of the head, back and neck regions (diagnosed as fibromyalgia). She had been treated by physical therapists, chiropractors and various physicians.

Jody, like so many head-injured and traumatized individuals, grasped desperately and obsessively in an attempt to retrieve memories of her trauma. When I suggested to Jody that it was possible to experience healing without having to remember the event, I saw a flicker of hope and a momentary look of relief pass across her face. We talked for a while, reviewing her history and struggle to function. Focusing on body sensations, Jody slowly became aware of various tension patterns in her head and neck region. With this focus, she began to notice a particular urge to turn and retract her neck. In following this urge in slow gradual 'micro movements', she experienced a momentary fear, followed by a strong tingling sensation. Through following these movements, Jody began a journey through the trauma of her assault. In learning to move between flexible control and surrender to these involuntary movements, she began to experience gentle shaking and trembling throughout her body. Thus began, ever so gently, the discharge of her trauma.

In later sessions, Jody experienced other spontaneous movements, as well as sounds and impulses to run and to bare her teeth and claw at her assailant. By completing these biological defensive responses, Jody was able to construct a sense of how her body prepared to react in that fraction of a second when the hunter raised the rifle to strike her. In allowing these movements and sounds to be expressed, Jody began to experience a deep organic discharge along with the *experience* of her body's innate capacity to defend and protect itself.

Jody, through her felt sense, was able to follow her body's intentional movement. Intentional movement is non-conscious. It is experienced as if the body is moving of its own volition. Through completing the life-preserving actions that her body had prepared for at the time of her attack, she released that bound energy and realized that she had, in fact, attempted to defend herself. Gradually, as more defensive and orienting responses reinstated, her panic anxiety progressively decreased.

In Somatic Experiencing™, traumatic reactions are addressed by a wide variety of strategies. What unifies them is that they are all used in the service of de-structuring the thwarted anxiety response and restoring defensive and orienting resources. The overall picture shows how each individual's needs and resources call forth a unique, creatively adaptive solution (Gendlin 1991; Levine 1997).

3   Embodied countertransference

Michael Soth

> It is a very remarkable thing that the *Ucs.* [unconscious] of one human being
> can react upon that of another, without passing through the *Cs.* [conscious].
>
> (Freud 1915a: 194)

Introduction

The surprise in Freud's statement expresses a nineteenth-century paradigm.
Since the 1930s Reich has helped us deconstruct the mind-over-body bias in
ways which are being confirmed by modern neuroscience (Damasio 1994;
Schore 1994, 2003b; Carroll, this volume). And since the 'countertransference
revolution' of the 1950s (Samuels 1993: Ch. 2), modern psychoanalysis has
come to appreciate the patient's and therapist's inner worlds as enmeshed and
interwoven to a degree which radically deconstructs traditional assumptions
regarding the therapist's role and function (Mitchell 2002). A further recent
development is the notion of 'parallel process' (Searles 1999; Hawkins and
Shohet 2000): not only can one person's unconscious communicate itself to
the other person in the room, but the relationship dynamic between client and
therapist can unconsciously be re-enacted in another relationship, i.e. between
therapist and supervisor.

The body psychotherapy tradition has a refined body/mind understanding of transference (Reich [1945] 1972; Leites 1976; Conger 1994; Johnson
1994; Mindell 1998; Totton 2003). Modern psychoanalysis (including
relational, intersubjective, object relations and self-psychology approaches)
has a refined relational understanding of countertransference (Heiman 1950;
Langs 1981; Greenberg and Mitchell 1983; Mitchell and Aron 1999). These
traditions have grown out of classical psychoanalysis, and a (re-)integration
of their theoretical frameworks may generate a holistic phenomenology of
relationship (Fairbairn 1958; Lowen 1958; Winnicott 1971; Boadella 1987;
Schwartz-Salant 1998).

I will attempt to bring the two traditions together, without minimizing their contradictions or reducing one to the other, by formulating both transference and countertransference, internal and external relationships in body/mind terms as parallel process. I will propose several fairly large-scale extensions to the established notion of 'parallel process', with relational dynamics being embodied and reflected on different levels intrapsychically and enacted interpersonally.

This model allows us to consider 'embodied countertransference' as a cornerstone of a holistic, integral (Wilber 2000), relational framework which sees the therapeutic relationship as an intersubjective, culturally contextualized system of complex parallel body/mind processes. To make this abstract framework applicable and practical, I will focus on the therapist's stream of consciousness in relation to that system. As within any system, spontaneous processes of self-organization (Maturana and Varela 1980) are always already occurring: we can attend to the body/mind phenomenology of the integrations and dis-integrations, the transformations and repetitive patterns of the system itself and the two people within it who are both wounded and whole.

How to apprehend, understand and facilitate these systemic processes is, of course, therapy's essential conundrum. How can I do this when as the therapist I am part of these processes, including my unconscious, my subjectivity, my countertransference? How can I facilitate a system when I am part of the system?

Clinical example

I will use one clinical example throughout the chapter, as reported by a therapist.

> For several weeks, M. has been bringing issues around his job. Having talked about another incident at work, I saw M. feeling upset and felt moved. When I empathically mirrored his feeling state, he deflected by adding more detail about the story. We then got into discussing his role in the project, and he was able to consider the pros and cons of various courses of action. Throughout this, it was clear to both of us that his feelings are nothing to do with an actual lack of capability. We then establish that his sense of competence wanes at particular moments with his manager. But in exploring this, we reluctantly come to the same conclusion: his feelings cannot be explained within the parameters of the current situation. There's nothing about his manager's behaviour which would justify his reaction. However, as soon as I ask him about his feelings in relation to the manager, his eyes begin to dart about and he looks agitated and

uncomfortable. He then says he is not thinking very clearly, but obviously feels under pressure to do so. He cannot explain his reaction to his manager, and feels ashamed about not answering my explorative questions succinctly. At one point M. looks tearful, and again I reflect this verbally. He says he is not aware of feeling tearful. I feel momentarily lost and unsure how to respond to his evasiveness.

M. is familiar with the idea that current feelings have antecedents in the life story. He volunteers a story about bringing home his exam results to his dad, and how he feared his father's frustrated, intimidating reaction. This sounds like a valid and very relevant association, but throughout this I continue to feel uncertain myself. I remind myself to focus – as I was taught to do in such moments – on the essentials: what is the client feeling?

I remember my fleeting sense of his tears – it's now disappeared, but I am convinced it's the key thing. So I ask him: 'What are you feeling now?' He suddenly lashes out and accuses me: 'Why do you always ask me about my feelings? I don't know what the hell I'm feeling, and I don't think it's helping me you going on about them.' I felt helpless and confused, so I am bringing it to supervision.

This vignette is not untypical in terms of what therapists might report after a session. It contains perceptions, thoughts, feelings and fantasies about self and other – body/mind fragments of the therapist's stream of consciousness which are remembered after the session, especially for their emotional charge and significance.

Transference as parallel process

Body psychotherapy and modern analysis share an understanding of the origins of transference (Masterson 1985; Jacobs 1986; Soth 1999, 2003b): the originally wounding relationship gets internalized – as a script, a working model, a character structure, internal object relations.

Johnson (1994) provides an integrative account of the internalization process through the 'steps of character formation'. Once internalized, the wound gets projected, repeated and replicated in all relationships, including the therapeutic relationship: it gets re-externalized in the transference. There is, therefore, a parallel between the originally wounding relationship, the internalized relationship and the transference relationship. The transference dynamic then gets carried by the therapist into supervision where it is re-enacted in turn, generating what we traditionally know as 'parallel process'.

To formulate an *embodied* account of transference, we need to extend these three parallel processes into five, by differentiating the internalization process in body/mind terms. What is implied in Johnson's model and what we find phenomenologically is:

- *both* poles of the wounding relationship internalized as spontaneous process: traces of the child *and* the parent can be found embodied as a relationship between different parts of the client's spontaneous (characterologically 'given') reality;
- the client's ego countering and resisting the re-experience of the wound – here the wounding relationship gets paralleled as an opposition between 'ego' and spontaneous processes;
- a split ego (Fairbairn 1974; Johnson 1994; Gomez 1997) with conflicted and opposing parts which reflect in their relationship to each other the originally wounding relationship.

The originally wounding relationship is internalized as a body/mind matrix of three parallel relationships: between different parts of the ego; between the ego and spontaneous forces; and between physically anchored spontaneous forces in different parts of the body/mind. In short: a conflicted ego in conflict with a spontaneous conflict.

To illustrate:

> As soon as the therapist focuses on the currently painful relationship with the manager, the client's ego has a negative reaction against the immediately constellated feelings of fear. Having barely noticed his anxiety, one part of the client's ego takes a judgemental and shaming attitude, indistinguishable from the originally wounding father (ego = father, body = child). However, this is not the only way in which the originally wounding relationship can be paralleled as a relationship between spontaneous and reflective forces in the client's body/mind: it is also true to say that another part of the client's ego is as intimidated by the uncontrollable spontaneous forces as he was by his father (ego = child, body = father). It is this part of the ego which apologizes for not being able to explain himself.

An aspect of internalization which tends to get neglected in character structure theory (Reich [1945] 1972; Lowen 1958; Boadella 1987; Johnson 1994) is that *both* poles of the originally wounding relationship manifest in the client's spontaneous experience (e.g. both the wounded child and the internalized father). In characteristic holding patterns on a muscular level and throughout the rest of the body/mind spectrum, the client's body reflects – like two superimposed negatives – *both* the child's original and fixated experience *and* the wounding parent's body/mind, as perceived and internalized by the child. It is usually not difficult to find at least one physical anchor each for the various internalized objects (see Figure 3.1).

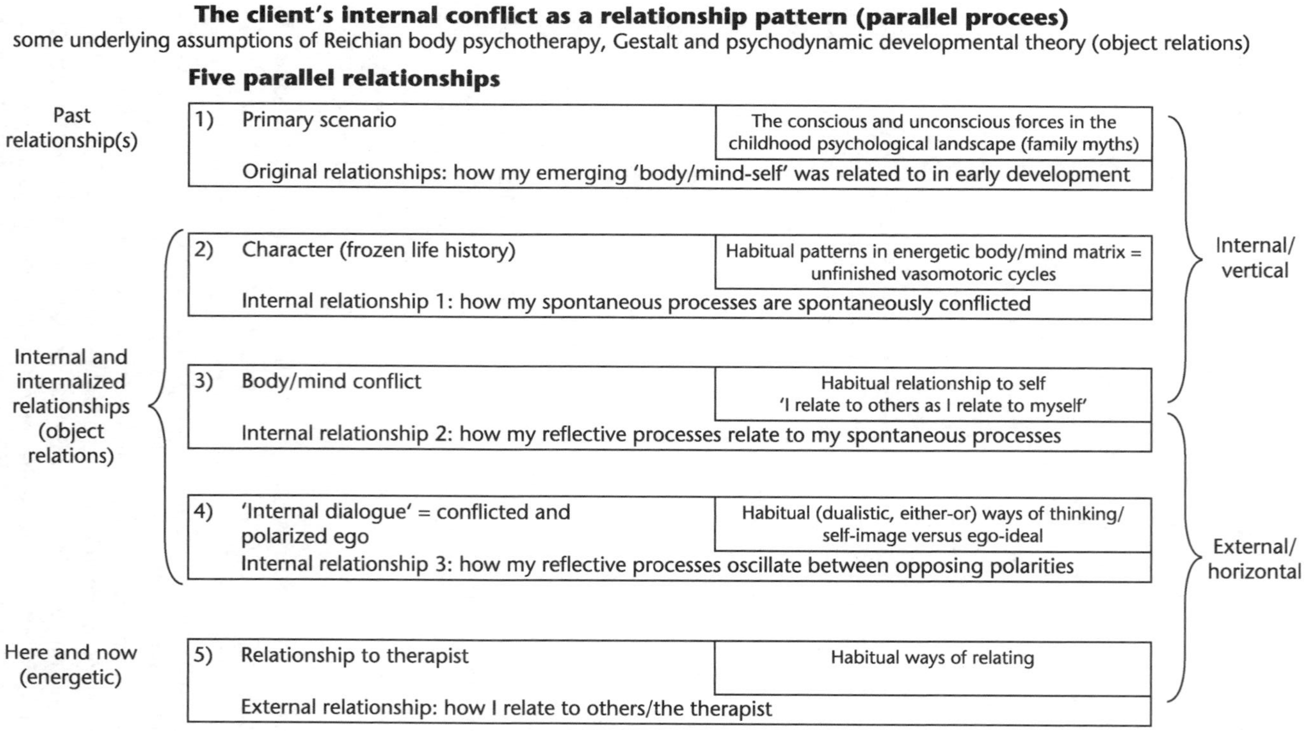

The client's internal conflict as a relationship pattern (parallel proces)

some underlying assumptions of Reichian body psychotherapy, Gestalt and psychodynamic developmental theory (object relations)

Five parallel relationships

			Internal/vertical
Past relationship(s)	**1) Primary scenario**	The conscious and unconscious forces in the childhood psychological landscape (family myths)	
	Original relationships: how my emerging 'body/mind-self' was related to in early development		
Internal and internalized relationships (object relations)	**2) Character (frozen life history)**	Habitual patterns in energetic body/mind matrix = unfinished vasomotoric cycles	
	Internal relationship 1: how my spontaneous processes are spontaneously conflicted		
	3) Body/mind conflict	Habitual relationship to self 'I relate to others as I relate to myself'	
	Internal relationship 2: how my reflective processes relate to my spontaneous processes		
	4) 'Internal dialogue' = conflicted and polarized ego	Habitual (dualistic, either-or) ways of thinking/self-image versus ego-ideal	External/horizontal
	Internal relationship 3: how my reflective processes oscillate between opposing polarities		
Here and now (energetic)	**5) Relationship to therapist**	Habitual ways of relating	
	External relationship: how I relate to others/the therapist		

Figure 3.1 Parallel process

In our example:

> The client's chest carried predominantly the inflated, bullying father, and the stomach churned predominantly with the child's fear and shame, with the diaphragm constituting the battleground between the poles.

By subdividing the internalized relationship into the conflicted ego in conflict with a spontaneous conflict, we thus arrive at a totality of five parallel relationships, manifest in the here and now between client and therapist. We can then include parallel process in its established sense, and consider the repetition of the client-therapist dynamic in the supervisory dyad: the sixth parallel relationship. It is possible to take the original dynamic back into the dynamic between the parents, and further into the inner world of each of the parents, opening out into possible transgenerational parallels as explored in family constellations (Hellinger *et al.* 1998; Schuetzenberger 1998).

Allowing transference to construct the therapist as an object

It is in the nature of parallel process that every relational experience is over-determined: it resonates with multiple other relationships *from which* the dynamic has been internalized or *in which* the dynamic has been acted out, through 'osmosis', projection or projective identification (Bion 1962a). Parallel process in the extended definition proposed here matches theoretically what experienced therapists report regarding their perception of the client: the sense of a tapestry, with recurring themes weaving in and out of a person's *psyche* and life, with multiple occurrences and resonances all the time.

This tapestry manifests within the therapeutic space and becomes accessible in the countertransference if -- as the therapist -- I can allow myself to be constructed as an object by the client's unconscious. But the multidimensional nature of parallel process implies that the answer to that moment-to-moment question in the back of the therapist's mind ('*What* object am I being constructed as?') is necessarily multiple and complex.

As we saw, most of the time I am being constructed as at least *two* objects simultaneously. By attending to parallel process, I recognize that these two objects have multiple resonances internally and externally, in the past and in the present, inside and outside the consulting room.

Which of the multiple resonances is currently relevant, accessible to the client's awareness *and* charged and significant in their unconscious? Body psychotherapy can contribute significantly to this question, from its experience with subtle and energetic perception, its habit of reading otherwise subliminal and nonverbal messages in a way which grasps the biological and physical *as* the emotional, psychological and relational. If body psychotherapists can take countertransference on board and apply their energetic, holistic perspective to their own 'internal process' when at work, they can help the 'countertransference revolution' take another quantum leap.

Charge

As body psychotherapists, we think of 'internal process' in body/mind terms, along a spectrum comprising body-emotion-image-mind-spirit. One term in use in the body psychotherapy tradition (Boadella 1987; Kepner 1987; Eiden 2002) which nicely captures the energetic and process quality of the interaction (rather than the verbal and content aspects) is 'charge'. There is some confusion in the literature as to whether this refers to:

- the vegetative 'charge' of energetic aliveness in the client's physical body (which *can be influenced* through consciously directing the breathing, physical exercises and stress positions, and is observable and even measurable from the outside); or
- the relational 'charge' arising from the subjective, spontaneous and inherent meaningfulness of the contact, internally or externally, or both.

There can be 'charge' in a therapeutic moment when, for example, the client realizes that he has spent most of his life in a contracted, paralysed position which is fuelled by an underlying fear, recognizable now in the contact with the therapist. Although there may be little sense of aliveness in his body, as he is becoming aware of his actual paralysis, there is a lot of 'charge' in the embodied, meaningful recognition and in the relational contact; although the body is not 'alive and well' at this point, there is a sense of embodiment as the client's reflection is connected to the actual condition of his body rather than to a compensatory self-image of how his body *should* be.

If we liberate the notion of charge from its predominant use in the first sense, and begin to include *both*, charge can be a suitable embodied-relational term to describe the body/mind phenomenology of transference/countertransference. It can become a crucial ingredient in the therapist's awareness and attention. Reflection on countertransference often boils down to a contemplation of charged moments in the relationship.

Three kinds of contact

We can think about charge in terms of three kinds of contact which reflect how transference and countertransference are mutually linked via parallel process. The 'quality of relating' implicit in these kinds of contact also constitutes three kinds of 'working alliance'. I mean not only the working alliance as a bond between the 'adult, healthy ego' of the client and therapist (Clarkson 1995): this rather static notion becomes questionable when we see the ego itself reflecting internalized object relations. I am complementing this with a more fluid, dynamic notion of an alliance with the client's (partially unconscious) 'spontaneous process'. This will become clearer as we proceed.

There are moments when the therapist's sense of the working alliance is:

- *Unambiguous*: the therapist has no concerns about the working alliance, as it is currently taken for granted. The transference is not constellated, active or in the foreground – the client is unambiguously using the therapist in role, or relating to the therapist as a person.
- *Ambiguous*: the therapist has a sense of the working alliance as ambivalent. The transference reality has entered the room, is constellated and active, but kept in check by, balanced by, or existing side by side with, the ego-ego working alliance. This kind of contact is a confusing mix, full of double messages, which eventually affect the therapist via projective identification. This, in turn, often leads to apparent misattunement and miscommunication.
- *Intensely conflicted*: the therapist has a sense of the working alliance being severely threatened or broken down. Usually this means the transference reality has taken over, not only in the client but in the whole relational system: always a largely unpalatable and painful experience, which constitutes both the worst and – if it can be survived and eventually contained – the best therapy has to offer. In this moment, client and therapist participate in a spontaneous re-enactment of the client's wound, for once not mediated and diluted by the client's ego. Paradoxically, re-enactment and relational transformation of the wound are two sides of the same coin (Soth 1999, 2003b, 2004).

We can apply this to our case vignette:

> At first, the therapist has no doubts about the working alliance: the client has no hesitation or scepticism and talks freely, assuming and using the therapist's support. Then, when they focus on the emotional difficulty with the manager, the wound does not just get talked about, it is also

constellated in the room. The client no longer feels or behaves as if the therapist is on his side: he feels pressurized by the therapist's questions just as he feels pressurized by the manager.

It is conceivable that the therapist communicated some urgency or impatience when asking his questions. Is the client's experience based on accurate perception, or is it transference? What's more important now than figuring this out, is the surrender to the recognition that, indeed, two relational realities are co-existing. To judge by the client's spontaneous feeling reality at this point, he might as well be sitting with the manager (who, we surmise, is a recent repetition of the same dynamic with his father). Superficially, some ego-ego alliance with the therapist remains: the client still tries to respond cooperatively to the therapist's questions (with hindsight we may recognize this, too, enacting a compliant, appeasing transference to the father).

It is when the client attacks the therapist that there is an unmistakable impression of the working alliance being lost and re-enactment taking over. The emotional impact of this is what the therapist is left with and brings to supervision. The therapist's countertransference illustrates the confusing interweaving of his and the client's reality, mixed up with attempts at processing the relationship through therapeutic knowledge.

Countertransference as parallel process: the client's conflict becomes the therapist's conflict

In relation to the client's character conflict, the therapist is in an impossible position: having conceptualized the internalized aspects of character as the conflicted ego in conflict with a spontaneous conflict, whose 'side' does the therapist take: the side of the ego or the side of the spontaneous conflict?

The ego's overall aim, in relation to the spontaneous experience of the wound, is to keep it at bay and to maintain, if not improve, the status quo. The pressure from inside, whether we conceptualize this as the re-emergence of the wound which is hoping for resolution, or in Jungian terms along the ego-self axis as the impulse towards individuation, is opposed to the status quo.

The answer of traditional body psychotherapy was largely unequivocal: Reich took sides with the 'body' against the 'ego' ([1942] 1973: Ch. 5). Psychoanalysis, through insisting on verbalization and symbolization, precisely because it appreciates the dangers of re-enactment, can be seen to be implicitly siding not exactly with the ego, but with the ego's capacities.

It is only when we fully appreciate the therapist's dilemma as *parallel process*, and see the therapist's allegiance to the two sides necessarily being as split and opposed as they are chronically in the client, that we can make full use of 'embodied countertransference'. In simple terms: the client's conflict becomes the therapist's conflict. It is only then that we get access to the paradox that *both* 'nothing has to happen' (and certainly nothing should be forced to happen) and that 'something desperately needs to happen'.

This dilemma acquires 'charge' for the therapist during the kind of contact I above labelled 'ambiguous'. Its initial manifestation in the countertransference is often as questions in the therapist's mind: What is going on? What should I do next?

These questions usually distract from the ambiguity and conflictedness of the contact. The therapist may have impulses to re-establish a clearer sense of their therapeutic position, precisely because they are in the process of losing it. These are understandable impulses, but rather than taking refuge in the trappings of the role and how we can shore it up, ideally we find some internal space for the questions: *How* am I losing my position? *What* is the body /mind and relational detail of this process? *What* re-enactment are we being drawn into?

Surrendering to re-enactment

If we accept that the wounding relationship not only enters the client's perception, nor only their experience in the consulting room, but indeed enters and affects the therapist's subjectivity as a pervasive and largely subliminal body/mind process, we are embracing the fundamental premise of the 'countertransference revolution' in holistic, embodied terms. This is equivalent to surrendering to re-enactment as emergent process. The therapeutic inevitability of re-enactment can be formulated like this:

> **It is impossible for a therapist to follow a strategy of overcoming a dysfunctional pattern without enacting in the transference the person in relation to whom the pattern originated.**

I see re-enactment and how to deal with it as the central issue of all relational psychotherapy (Soth 2004). Subjectively, from within it, it always feels 'wrong' in some way: the therapist, inevitably, is aware that this is the *opposite* of what – implicitly – the client is paying for. Attempts to structure the therapeutic space in such a fashion as to minimize the dangers of re-enactment inevitably rely on:

- creating a bias towards the ego and the ego-ego working alliance as the predominant area of engagement;
- positioning the therapist outside the danger zone of unconscious relating, and setting up a more objectifying therapeutic frame.

This is not to say that such ego-focused, objectifying work cannot be appropriate and helpful for the client. It just cannot be called holistic relational depth psychotherapy with the unconscious. Character disorders, addictions, disturbances of the self reach right down, across all the body/mind levels to the self-organizing dynamics at the root of modern western pathology. If we want the work to be powerful enough to affect these spontaneous, pre-conscious levels of being, we have to embrace re-enactment as part of the process.

Re-enactment becomes possible through the therapist – whatever their particular theory or technique – allowing themselves to be constructed as an object by the client's unconscious. Surrendering to this is difficult. In the process, re-enactment precipitates the de-construction of that object. Surrendering to this is *more* difficult. It involves meeting the full force of the client's pain and aggression as spontaneous process, without hiding behind the therapeutic role. This is inconceivable without the therapist risking their own subjectivity and being de-constructed not only as a professional, but also as a person.

If we do open ourselves and the therapeutic space to these risks, we are aware that no therapeutic concept or tool, no theory or technique in and of itself ensures that the inevitable re-enactment will not be damaging to the client. There is, in fact, not much of a guarantee beforehand that it can be worked through. All therapeutic skills, thoughts, principles and competencies can feed into re-enactment. There is no Archimedean fixed point by which we can lever ourselves onto solid ground: re-enactment is one of the essential features of a participative universe.

Having acknowledged the inevitable dangers, how can we prepare ourselves and facilitate the process so as to ethically and professionally maximize the possibilities for re-enactment to become transformative rather than more damaging?

Body/mind transformation in the relationship

As I have tried to establish, 'embodied countertransference' is necessarily a complex phenomenon, both relationally and in body/mind terms. However, it is essential for making sense of re-enactment and remaining response-able when caught in the middle of it. Here is the basic principle I have formulated for myself as to what inclines the re-enactment experience to become transformative:

> **When all the fragments of the conflict inherent in the re-enactment can be held in sufficient awareness across the levels of body-emotion-image-mind in the relationship in the 'here and now', the conflict will tend to reorganize itself.**

This is formulated deliberately from the perspective of the client-therapist relationship *as a system*. Transformation cannot be brought about by the therapist unilaterally and intentionally: it is the whole system which reorganizes itself.

It is a feature of the chronic character pattern, described as the five parallel relationships, that the client's awareness of it is necessarily partial and fragmented. Both the wound and its repression need to be kept unconscious. The whole body/mind pattern, therefore, functions to habitually keep the possibility at bay that the wound may be re-experienced acutely, in the here and now. This is ensured both through splits in the ego and the ego's opposition to spontaneous processes. Within the pattern, the ego's reflective grasp (on the level of image and thought) both of the wound and the mechanisms of its avoidance, including the ego's own functioning, is never more than fragmentary. The ego is kept chronically unaware of the complete experience and is, therefore, by definition, incapable of presenting a full account of it in the *here and now, as it happens relationally*.

This manifests phenomenologically as the client's body/mind experience being split and fragmented. The client can, for example, report intense physical sensations, without any emotional connection. Equally, they may be capable of talking about painful memories without being aware of the corresponding feelings or physical symptoms, even if these are quite strongly manifest in the here and now. Or, they may be capable of discharging strong and maybe primal feelings, as long as these have no relational context or 'other' to receive or meet them. Therapists from across the approaches will recognize the significance of these fragments coming together as a coherent and owned experience of body, emotion, image and mind.

But not only the client's awareness is fragmented: as the client's conflict has become the therapist's conflict, there is a tendency for the therapist to be drawn into similar denials and avoidances. The client's implicit fear of experiencing the wound is communicated to the therapist, who can readily identify with the impulse to avoid the actual experience of it, right here and now.

Holding all the fragments of the conflict implies, for a start, that the therapist is not seduced out of these dilemmas into a shortcut of siding with either spontaneous or reflective processes, even when under pressure. It is essential for the therapist to rest in not knowing, in ambiguity and conflict.

This especially applies to the inherent complexity of the countertransference experience: any fragment of the client's body/mind process, any object, can appear in the countertransference. The main problem is that an object does not necessarily get projected in its entirety, as a physical, emotional, imaginal *and* mental process at the same time. Particular charged fragments of it can appear in the therapist's experience, without any obvious link or reference to other fragments. For example, it is perfectly possible for the therapist to experience a stiff neck which has, as yet, no explicit relational context, long before other body/mind fragments coalesce with it into a more graspable fantasy.

This is further complicated by the fact that, as a rule, *both* object poles of the wounding relationship are communicated *and* projected simultaneously, and are both being projectively identified with by the therapist. As the two objects are usually anchored and conveyed in different communicative body/mind channels, they are also taken in by the therapist and manifest in the countertransference as fragments in different aspects of the therapist's body/mind. As a consequence, 'embodied countertransference' can never be simply a congruent body/mind experience. By empathizing and identifying with split and opposed objects, which are manifest in the client as a conflicted ego in conflict with a spontaneous conflict, the therapist ends up internalizing the client's body/mind split and its implicit object relational dynamics.

Gathering/holding the fragments

The body-emotion-image-mind fragments of the conflict and the relational fragments are, of course, only two sides of the same coin, but they do tend to get apprehended separately by the therapist. The relational fragments are apprehended more readily through a perspective which sees the re-enactment in terms of the originally wounding relationship and the steps of character formation. But as the steps of character formation reflect the internalization process, the same point could equally be formulated as the conflicted ego in conflict with a spontaneous conflict. This formulation tends to alert us more to the body/mind matrix which constitutes the experience of the re-enactment. It, therefore, is more helpful in focusing the therapist on the multitude and subtlety of charged spontaneous processes and how they are being managed, in client *and* therapist.

We understand the re-enactment in terms of a currently constellated wound. We understand that wound as layered and enacted in ways which parallel the steps of character formation in the original wounding. We understand that the enactment of that wounding between client and therapist manifests as a fragmentary body/mind matrix throughout the relational system. We also understand the paradox that whilst the client's character position affords some protection against the re-experience of the wound, it also actually perpetuates it.

In this perspective two – equally valid – universes coincide: one in which the wound is being protected and denied and one where the wound is constantly being repeated and re-enacted. The first is constituted by the all-too-real presence of a fragmented and conflicted body/mind. The second holds the potential for the wounding to be experienced acutely, but also for the elusive transformative possibility that in some unpredictable fashion the wound may finally be embraced in the context of a larger wholeness which no longer needs to deny it.

The therapist's overall presence and gesture is an embrace *both* of the potential wholeness *and* the currently fragmented dis-integration, without any habitual bias one way or the other. The ineluctable sense of potential wholeness manifests as an impulse to 'gather' the fragments, and hold them in awareness without splitting or projection. This implicitly invites the client into a universe where the wound is present, but not protected against. The therapist, having projectively identified with the various objects and thus having experienced the client's body/mind split, is inclined to increasingly hold the fragments in awareness in their own body/mind.

At this point of increasing charge, the therapist needs to understand that transformation implies a spontaneous process which cannot be forced or imposed. The 'gathering' of the fragments, therefore, is not a process which the therapist can do on behalf of the client. Unlike traditional body psychotherapy, we are not trying to unify the client's expression into catharsis, but we see the conflict between primary impulse and resistance as a parallel process to the original wounding. Any impulse on the part of the therapist to short-circuit the existing fragmentation towards his own fantasized version of transformation would need to be reflected upon as another enactment, presumably of the client's unbearable desperation, pain and defensiveness.

I am formulating the therapist's contribution to the transformative possibility inherent in the re-enactment as paradoxical: the therapist *is* co-responsible, but it is not the therapist unilaterally who is 'holding' the conflict. However, it is essential that – within the client-therapist system – the conflict is held in sufficient awareness for transformation to occur. This requires of the therapist *both* active involvement *and* the capacity to passively wait: it requires an active 'gathering' of the fragments *and* an allowing of the spontaneously emergent process; it requires drawing attention *both* to these spontaneous processes (which the client may be unaware of) *and* how they are spontaneously being resisted, by both client *and* therapist. It requires being available *both* to being constructed as an object *and* to engaging authentically, without necessarily knowing which is which. It requires *both* helpless surrender to the re-enactment *and* the authority to modulate its intensity through directive or interpretive interventions.

Ultimately, it is not the therapist who contains the client, but the experience of spontaneous, co-created transformation. Such transformation is unlikely in any consistent fashion unless the therapist can work both relationally and holistically, with the multiple resonances of parallel process as body/mind phenomena in the here and now, being *in* the relationship whilst having an awareness *of* it. Most of this is impossible without some notion of 'embodied countertransference' along the lines I have been suggesting.

In our vignette, we understood the client's experience in terms of 'embodied transference': the therapist's questions are experienced as pressurizing, and the wounding father is constellated in the room, refracted through the manager. The therapist's attention to the client's fear constitutes a re-enactment of both these relationships. The therapist correctly perceives the client's evasiveness, which – in terms of character formation – we understand as the client's survival mechanism, developed early on as a protection against further wounding. In the counter-transference, however, the therapist feels lost and helpless when his attempts to challenge the evasiveness do not succeed. This we can now interpret as the beginnings of a projective identification process by which the therapist – although also being perceived as the pressurizing, humiliating father – participates in the boy's feeling reality. As I suggested earlier, both poles of the wounding relationship tend to appear in the therapist's body/mind experience.

By taking refuge in a textbook manoeuvre which is part and parcel of his habitual countertransference (the injunction to focus on the essentials!), the therapist defends himself against his helplessness. In trying to hold on to a waning sense of therapeutic position, he loses connection with the re-enactment implicit in his questioning. As we see, this only serves to deepen the re-enactment, in a way which becomes unmanageable for the therapist. This is a general feature of re-enactment: once constellated, there is no way out of it, only a way in. Every attempt by the therapist to minimize it, even if temporarily successful, actually exacerbates it. In this case, the very object experience which the therapist was trying to get out of, i.e. feeling as lost and helpless as the child, gets re-enacted in an unmediated fashion by the client then lashing out. The client is – finally – enacting the dreaded bullying father and the therapist gets to experience the unsurvivability of this attack as the boy. This is a reversal of the enactment just a minute earlier by which the therapist was being the father, insisting on an interrogation which the client experienced as humiliating. All of this escalated under the guise of an apparent ego-ego working alliance, with the therapist apparently concerned about the client's feelings, and the client apparently cooperating with the therapist-expert.

The therapist would have needed a sense of 'embodied counter-transference' during the build-up in order to make full use of the information contained in his lostness and helplessness. This does not mean that the continued questioning did not lead to a potentially productive expression – at this point, transformation was just a whisker away. But it meant that the therapist was then not available to meet and facilitate that spontaneous expression further. This might have resulted eventually in the feeling and the relational context, the past and the present coming together. As it was, not all of the fragments of the re-enactment could be held, and the transformative potential inherent in it went unrealized, at least for now.

Conclusion

I have tried to show that by integrating the body/mind sensitivities of the body psychotherapy tradition and the relational sensibilities of modern psychoanalysis we can arrive at an embodied notion of countertransference. Making use of the full body/mind complexity of 'embodied countertransference' relies on the recognition that the therapist's experience is necessarily conflicted, torn between polarities, and that the therapist's conflict – both as a person and as a professional – frequently reflects the client's inner world as a parallel process. The therapist's subjective body/mind process therefore contains information about the 'other'. If the therapist can surrender to this, the spontaneous, self-organizing processes occurring within the therapist's body/mind constitute the construction and de-construction of the therapist as an object by the client's unconscious. The therapist is forever drawn into uncontained and uncontainable re-enactments which require reorganization and transformation of both people involved in order to stand a chance of eventually being contained. 'Containment' and 'working alliance' are paradoxical notions: they need to break down in order for them to exist.

The therapist's surrender to the constellated re-enactment is facilitated by a differentiated and attuned awareness to the multiple parallel processes resonating throughout the therapeutic relationship and the body/mind of both people involved. The therapist needs to be aware both of the overall relational pattern and of the specific and subtle spontaneous body/mind detail of 'emergent process'.

I have considered countertransference as *embodied* in contrast to the historically developed notion of countertransference – a meta-psychological context which has a good portion of disembodiment structured into it. But the systemic, parallel process view I have proposed here goes beyond the issue of embodiment. My hunch would be that in a couple of decades we will have moved beyond the nineteenth-century embodiment/disembodiment juncture into an integral-systemic-parallel process view of what I would call the 'fractal self'.

4   Articulating preverbal experience

Katya Bloom

> The experience of being bodied and the experience of being minded are inseparable qualities of the unitary experience of being alive.
>
> (Ogden 2001: 155)

Introduction

An exploration of the interrelationships between the body and its movement and psychic and emotional states is central to the work of movement psychotherapy. *Movement* in this context refers to bodily responses to internal and external stimuli. It comprises posture, gesture, position as well as movement through space; it also refers to freedom or restriction (physical and/or psychic) experienced in stillness. Movement refers not only to what one *does*, but also to a sensoriaffective registering of who and how one *is*.

In movement psychotherapy, insights can be gained through paying attention to the subtleties of the nonverbal realm, and in allowing these to inform and interact with images, thoughts and feelings. The articulation of experience is therefore rooted in two languages – that of the body in movement and that of the mind in thought. The realm of feelings belongs to both languages and can be said to link the two. It is through allowing the body to experience and speak for itself that the depths of preverbal experience can potentially be reached.

Thomas Ogden's statement above seems to mirror D.W. Winnicott's (1958) description of the inherited tendency of individuals to achieve a unity of psyche and soma. Whilst agreeing with both eminent psychoanalysts that the integration and inseparability of the psyche and the body may be an inherent tendency, it can also be said to be stunningly elusive. 'Indwelling' as Winnicott called it, can be thrown out of kilter in innumerable ways in attempting to protect the self from the vicissitudes of life, or as dance movement therapy pioneer, Irmgard Bartenieff (1980) put it, in 'coping with the environment'. We now know that the development of patterns for coping with life begins even before birth (Piontelli 1992), and can reverberate throughout the life cycle, permeating the deepest recesses of body and mind.

In this chapter I will describe my exploration into the development of primitive psychophysical patterns, and how they are represented and replicated in later life. Implicit within this is an accompanying interest in exploring the interrelationships between different realms of experience – the sensory, emotional and mental, as well as the spiritual. This exploration crystallized in the development of a psychoanalytically informed method of practice as a movement psychotherapist. I will describe the four major strands which have been woven together to form the basis for this practice.

I have used my background as a movement practitioner, movement psychotherapist and Laban movement analyst, together with my experience of psychoanalysis – as both patient and student – to develop this interdisciplinary synthesis. I have undertaken this project in order to embody my own position, which feels as if it is located on a bridge which offers interesting views of the overlapping terrains of movement – practice, analysis and therapy – on one side, and psychoanalytic object relations and infant observation on the other. Although my home ground is movement and I am not a psychoanalytic clinician, I have been deeply involved in both disciplines and have found them to be mutually supportive and enlightening, as I will discuss.

Four strands contributing to a movement psychotherapy practice

Initially, I will look at each of the four strands separately, with the intention of providing the reader with some understanding of the contribution of each to developing a method of practice in movement psychotherapy. I would also add that I am interested in what insights this exploration may have for verbal psychotherapy, where although movement is not usually the focus, the bodies of both patient and therapist are still present, sensing, feeling and containing the experience.

The four sources I draw on are:

1   Aspects of psychoanalytic theory which pertain to primitive, preverbal experience, and thus have relevance for thinking about bodily experience and movement.
2   Psychoanalytic infant observation and its contribution to illuminating and working with primitive psychophysical states.

3　Laban Movement Analysis and its value in providing vocabulary for describing nonverbal phenomena and states of mind.

4　Amerta Movement as a model of practice for discovering one's own movement vocabulary, and for recognizing, embodying and articulating direct experience in the present.

I will illustrate the material with vignettes from infant and young child observation studies as well as with excerpts from clinical work with patients in individual movement psychotherapy, which will help to describe the way in which I have made use of and synthesized the various strands. The contents of this chapter represent a condensed version of my doctoral thesis, under the auspices of the University of East London and the Tavistock Clinic, which will subsequently be transformed into a book, *The Embodied Self: Movement and Psychoanalysis* (Bloom: 2006). I hope this chapter may serve to whet readers' appetite for further reading! I wish to emphasize before describing the individual strands that it is the weaving together of all four which creates the basis for a working practice, and I hope the reader will bear this in mind.

The body in psychoanalysis

British psychoanalytic object relations, particularly as developed by Melanie Klein and by D.W. Winnicott in their work with young children and as continuously expanded and refined by their colleagues and successors, provides an invaluable theoretical context within which to understand the complexities of primitive psychological and emotional life. Movement and body psychotherapies are potentially equipped to touch and work with this preverbal level of sensoriaffective raw experience. We now know that the nature of infants' primary relationships – nonverbal and bodily based – establishes the roots of neuromuscular patterns which can become encoded for life (Carroll, this volume). In contrast to some of my colleagues writing other chapters, it is my feeling that the use of actual physical touch between patient and therapist makes working with these object relationships within the therapeutic transference more difficult: 'The more certain the patient is that the analyst will not satisfy the wish [for touch], the more free he will be to express it and to look for its transference meaning' (Quinodoz 2003: 135). I will describe non-physical 'touch', through energetic attunement when I describe Amerta Movement.

Although body-based therapies and psychoanalysis are seen by some to be almost mutually exclusive, in my view they are highly mutually supportive. Psychoanalytic theory has communicated with great specificity the ways in which infants develop and communicate their anxieties. Out of the flux of infants' sensoriaffective experience, primordial proto-thoughts and unconscious phantasies emerge. A major contribution of Melanie Klein was to begin to describe the internal psychic world. She saw it as a landscape created from introjective and projective processes – based on what comes into and what goes out of bodies. The psychic space of the internal world is seen to be populated by 'internal objects'. These are related to parental and other significant figures, but because they are internalized, they are transformed by the infant, imbued with the child's own mental impulses. I am interested in the complex links between the internal world of the psyche as described by Klein, and the physical body. I am intrigued by the question: in what ways do the relationships with both internalized and external figures get reflected in posture, gestures, facial expressions and patterns of movement?

The subtle and complex psychological processes of taking in and evacuating good and bad parts of both self and key object figures was explicated in detail by Klein. *Splitting*, an infantile process of dividing an object – initially the breast and then the mother – into an idealized good version and a persecutory bad version, was seen as a normal way for the infant to cope with intense anxiety. However, when this primitive splitting is carried on through life as a way of avoiding the pain of ambivalence and loss, contact with both body and mind are jeopardized. In the excerpt below the patient's splitting is represented bodily between her upper and lower halves. Describing a related phenomenon, Klein coined the term *projective identification*. Here unwanted parts of the self are unconsciously projected into another who, if the projections can be consciously metabolized, can return them in a manageable form (Bion 1962a). To my mind this process is not only a mental one; it is psycho*physical*. We also see a form of projective identification in the following sequence:

> A patient found it impossible to move her lower body as she sat, legs outstretched and welded together. Her arms meanwhile freely created elaborate patterns in the air, which accompanied her verbal description of having joyful feelings as she arrived for her session. In the countertransference I felt her aggressive and sexual feelings were felt to be dangerous, and were split off and projected into me, making me feel like a dangerous predator. The patient came to recognize this over time, and take back her projection, thus freeing her legs to move.

The embodied experience of both therapist and patient in movement psychotherapy can be said to form the basis for deepening clarity and communication within the relationship. Winnicott's term *transitional space* (1971) is helpful in describing the territory in which such primitive patterns can be explored and looked at from different perspectives. Winnicott described the value in achieving a state of 'unintegration'. This implied a loosening of tightly held patterns so that new sensoriaffective messages could be tolerated, making real change and integration possible. I am convinced that movement and sensory awareness can offer a powerful tool for working within a transitional space in any form of psychotherapy. The somatic countertransference (Soth, this volume) is central to the working process. Words can often bridge the painful gap between the primitive realm and a more present-day aspect of self; but at other times, words may not be possible or even necessary, as illustrated in the following segment:

> She unfolds the blanket and places it carefully, lying down on her back. She makes soft movements with her hands and seems aware of gently breathing. I am aware of feelings of depression. She rolls away from me and back towards me, curling in my direction. She seems to be in conflict. She curls away from me and stays there. I ask about her feeling or thought here. She says she could leave this place, burst out (into movement), but that she really only wants to stay. She says she can feel a tightness in her heart. I feel deep sadness and resistance in my own body. I lie on my side too. I experience sad and heavy feelings as we lie. She says she can just stay here in this stillness. I feel she is communicating an internal feeling of not being received; but she also knows we are sharing this lonely experience.

Free association in movement

The process of *free association* has been established in psychoanalysis since its beginnings with Freud; it is seen to be the best method of eliciting unconscious material. It seems to me that the process of giving voice to whatever arises during a session can be fruitfully expanded if the nonverbal experience is included, through recognition of embodied experience, whether in stillness or as expressed in movement. The body and its movement give rise to images, feelings and associations which can be voiced, and which in turn affect the body. This is a process which can be tracked and through which patterns can, over time, become more conscious. In its most basic sense, movement implies and accompanies change. The following sequence illustrates the way movement and other realms of experience flow one into another in a free associative process for both the patient and myself.

> A young woman is sitting, swaying side to side and touching the floor with her hands. She says it feels good, adding that she feels she is spreading her wings as the swaying increases; but as soon as the association is made the movement loses its energy. She continues to sway, but she has disengaged. I notice feeling as if she has temporarily stepped outside her sensation and feeling and that her focus has shifted, that it has something to do with feelings about my presence. She tells me a memory of being 10

years old, just having moved to France. Mother was sunbathing in the garden. She was beside mother and feeling very sad in this new environment. She wondered if mother felt this too; she thinks she might, but cannot ask. She seems to experience me as a possibly preoccupied internal object to whom loyalty meant refraining from spreading her wings.

I would like to underscore the importance of Klein's discovery of unconscious processes at work in her therapy with children; play was seen to be the equivalent of free association, in the sense that it revealed children's unconscious primitive phantasies. Winnicott also emphasized the value of play. I see movement as a form of expression which can touch and release unconscious feelings, thoughts and phantasies, similar to the way play functioned for Klein's patients or the way dreams function for adult patients. Using movement in this way lends itself to an ongoing process of discovery and unfolding. It does not aim for a cathartic release, as did some of the old-style body psychotherapy work. Nor does it foster a too internalized self-involved exploration as some movement approaches can. This practice emphasizes the therapeutic relationship, taking the transference and countertransference as the central elements of the work; it reflects the nuances of primitive patterns and processes, the prototypes of which were inscribed in early object relationships. In movement psychotherapy, verbal and nonverbal articulation are interwoven; thus the different realms of thinking, feeling, sensing and imagining can potentially be integrated and embodied.

Psychoanalytic infant observation

In order to get some first-hand experience of 'the articulation of preverbal experience', I participated in a series of psychoanalytic observational studies of infants and young children. I found these studies extremely enlightening as a way of observing the raw experience of earliest life. It is the nonverbal language of movement, and its accompanying sounds, which naturally provide the main means of communication between an infant and its caregivers. As a movement psychotherapist, I therefore felt that I was receiving a training in the fundamentals of nonverbal communication. I could apprehend at close range the intensity of primitive anxieties and relationships, and the variety of psychophysical patterns which were set in motion as babies' established various strategies to deal with distress and change.

The practice of infant observation was developed by Esther Bick at the Tavistock Clinic in the 1950s, where it was established as part of child psychotherapy training; subsequently it has been incorporated into child and adult psychotherapy trainings worldwide (Bick 1968). It works in the following way: the observer visits the infant at home on a regular one-hour weekly basis, usually from the time of birth to 2 years. Observers neither initiate interaction nor take notes. They are present to witness whatever happens – present as an interested party, neither as an 'expert' nor a 'fly on the wall'.

After leaving the setting, the observer writes in narrative detail exactly what she or he remembers having happened, including his or her own emotional responses. There is a small seminar group which meets weekly, led by a child psychotherapist, where a participant presents an observation for the group to discuss. Patterns begin to emerge over time in which a picture takes shape of the infants' personalities, their primary relationships and their developing bodies and minds. It is striking that each baby being presented will have a unique set of relationships, experiences and patterns, and yet each study seems to be underlined and confirmed by basic principles of psychoanalytic theory, and at times may even clarify or suggest new insights into existing theory.

I observed a baby for two years, and a young child (3–4 years) for one year, both under the auspices of the Tavistock Clinic. I then observed in an infant playgroup and at a nursery to expand my observational experience within each age range. In all settings, I was struck by how clearly children's innate qualities and characteristics as well as the effects of both internalized and external relationships were expressed in their very individual acquisition and articulation of movement vocabulary. In a group of babies, although each child found its way to standing, for example, for each it was a unique journey.

Because I was in these settings as an observer, I learned to be present in a quiet and receptive state of both body and mind. I was not there to help or provide solutions to problems. This meant I could register the psychophysical impact in a more spacious way, noting and embodying my own responses. This cultivation of the kind of receptive state required for dealing with transference and countertransference processes has undoubtedly nourished my work as a movement psychotherapist. Also, developing the habit of writing down everything I could remember after each session taught me the value of recounting things in this way. I was able to recall much more than I would have thought, and it stimulated a process of reflection. It set a precedent for how to keep regular notes after sessions with patients.

In the mother-baby group, I was interested in the ways in which the qualities of the mothers were often (though not always) mirrored in the babies' acquisition and expression of their movement vocabularies. Two mother-infant couples I will describe did share some of the same qualities, though the couples themselves were distinctly different from one another. The babies discovered very different ways to find a balance between creating a sense of safety and following their impulse to explore the unknown.

In the first pair, I had the initial impression that there was a conflict of interests between mother and daughter. Eight-month-old Sherry seemed to want to expand her horizons by entering the 'transitional space', but mother seemed unable to accommodate her wish to do so. Mother's actions seemed to imply her need for Sherry to remain a passive infant baby:

> Mum was on the floor, holding Sherry on her lap, facing outward. They looked very much alike, both with round faces, short black hair and weighty rounded bodies. Sherry seemed very alert to the space however, and mother did not. Sherry brought toys to her mouth . . . As mum held her facing out, sitting on her knee, Sherry seemed to be very active in her extremities, especially kicking her feet and mobilizing her legs. Mum turned Sherry to face her and held Sherry under her armpits so that her feet just touched the ground. She then lifted her up and held her in her arms as if she were a younger baby, cradling her head. Sherry seemed to struggle against this, making some sounds. Mum said, 'Are you tired?'
>
> I felt uncomfortable and wondered why mum seemed to want to keep hold of Sherry. Sherry then pressed her feet strongly against mum's thigh, sending energy right through her body. This seemed to give her a firm contact with mum as well as exerting her ability and desire to use her weight. Her intention seemed to be to move. Mother continued to cradle Sherry on her lap.

On another occasion some weeks later, mother placed Sherry in front of the mirror before leaving the room for the usual tea break:

> Sherry held a blanket to her mouth and looked at herself in the mirror. She also watched things going on behind her in the mirror. She seemed content like this for quite a while.
>
> Here we can see what might be a preference for a flat surface view of the world, a two-dimensional view, rather than having a sense of actually being present in a three-dimensional space. It was as if she had not been weaned onto the liveliness of the outside world, as if mother could not receive and metabolize the projective identification.

A different approach was seen in baby Rodney, also at about 10 months. He could not get away from mother fast enough. This mother, although attentive, appeared quite highly strung:

> Mum put Rodney down and he was off. He spent most of the hour moving round the room from object to object, never spending more than a few seconds with anything. He crawled near Winnie who held a soft toy dog. He pulled it away from her and she pulled back, recovering possession. He moved on. I had the feeling when watching him that there was no sense of planning, just a constant moving on. Pushing with his feet,

he seemed to dive into the floor with his head, as he moved among the toys. He had a very manic and intense approach and there was lots of seemingly self-satisfied grunting.

Something seemed to impel Rodney to rush forward. He seemed caught up in an imaginary state of omnipotence and control, though he kept bumping his head against the harsh reality, in this case the floor.

In observing the babies, I wondered if I was watching patterns being set in motion, so to speak, which might last a lifetime. Because, as I have suggested, this preverbal level of experience can be tapped into through movement, movement can potentially provide a medium for working through early trauma or gaps in development, for altering dysfunctional patterns and out-moded coping strategies. Although my work to date has primarily been with adults, observational studies have certainly been of help in apprehending and attending to the early primitive level of distress which underlies many patients' material. I feel that observational studies of this kind could be of great benefit for trainees in body and movement psychotherapy.

Laban Movement Analysis

Nonverbal experience, by its very nature, is hard to pin down or describe.

Rudolf Laban (1879–1958) was a pioneer in the field of movement obser-vation, analysis and research. His perceptive curiosity led to the formation of a detailed vocabulary for describing human movement (Laban 1950). Laban Movement Analysis (LMA) allows for great subtlety and specificity in dis-tinguishing between a wide range of different components, both quantitative and qualitative. It is currently recognized worldwide in the fields of dance movement therapy and the performing arts as a common language for com-munication about movement.

I find LMA especially useful for describing states of mind and patterns of habit and of change – both in the client's material and also in the therapist's experience of the countertransference. Having access to a language for describ-ing experience in terms of nonverbal communication can help to deepen the experience of what is actually happening in present time within the therapy relationship, in identifying moments of transition; but perhaps most import-ant is its value in reflecting on the changes and trajectory of the work over time. (Like the use of any theory, including psychoanalytic theory, if LMA is used prematurely, it can serve the purpose of providing distance from the emotional impact of being with the patient.) Patterns may be recognized in terms of specific use of the body – its gesture, posture and positioning, in terms of dynamics of movement or in the patient's use of space (*vis-à-vis* the therapist in individual work, and *vis-à-vis* other members in a group).

Effort theory: the dynamics of movement

The Effort theory of LMA is a means for describing the role of movement in motivating and/or reflecting psychological and emotional states. Laban delineates *weight, space, time* and *flow* as the four basic dynamics of movement. Though they are all always present in movement, they can be explored in terms of which ones predominate in an individual's experience, which are the key motivating factors and how and under what circumstances the predominance may change. Internal and external object relationships can be seen to be reflected in terms of movement vocabulary, and the effort elements are of great significance in describing this.

The element of *weight* (*strong* or *light*), relates to the physical sensory world, the literal, material substance, both surface and depth of the body itself and the sense of touch. In bringing this aspect of experience to life, through making it conscious, one develops the *intention* to work with, to do something with, the body. Often this something is done in relation to others who are either available or not to our intentions toward them. (If you stretch your muscles or touch your skin, you are tuning into this realm.)

The element of *space* (*direct* or *flexible focus*) relates to one's experience of the external world, one's perspective, one's perceptions and points of view. It implies a space for reflection and thought, and is therefore related to the mental aspect of experience. (If you feel your eyes and let them absorb the view around you, you enliven this quality.)

The element of *time* (*accelerating* or *decelerating*) relates to the experience of the rhythm, the impulse, the natural order of events and change. It is an *intuitive* aspect of human experience. It is inherent in making (conscious or unconscious) choices and transitions. (If you notice the rhythms of your breathing and heartbeat, you will experience a relationship to time.)

Finally the element of *flow* (*bound* or *free*) relates to the control or release of feeling, the experience of emotion in the body. Flow is related to the freedom or restriction of breath, energy and life force. (If you close your eyes and become receptive to the felt sense of emotion in the body, you will experience the quality of flow.)

Taken together, the physical, the mental, the intuitive and the emotional aspects can all be observed and experienced in the therapeutic relationship. Knowing which elements predominate can contribute to the recognition of internal and external object relationships.

If we consider the infant-mother pairs in the previous examples, Sherry seemed to start out using a vigorous combination of strong weight and direct space punctuated at times by an acceleration in time as she exerted her own will; but she then adapts to her mother's resistance and by the second excerpt we see her motivated by a binding of flow and staring blankly into the mirror;

time and weight have receded as motivating factors. Space and (bound) flow create a mood called the 'remote state' which aptly describes Sherry's state of mind. Rodney on the other hand is clearly motivated by the flow of feelings and by the element of time. This state is called the 'mobile state'. The stability associated with weight and space are not motivating Rodney. The Effort vocabulary differentiates quite clearly between the characteristics of different psychological and emotional states. Consciously or unconsciously, we tend, in various situations, to be motivated by certain basic effort elements rather than others. Laban's description of the six states (combinations of two effort qualities) and four drives (combinations of three qualities) can be explored in other literature (e.g. Bartenieff 1980; Maletic 1987).

Space Harmony is the name for the other major aspect of Laban's work. It concerns the body's relationship to, and orientation in, the surrounding space. He defined the space around one's body as one's personal reach space or 'kinesphere', and he described the dimensions, planes and diagonals within this personal space as they related to the centre of gravity of the body. As psychoanalytic object relations theory emphasizes the context in which events happen and the primacy of relationship, this part of Laban's theory also has resonance with psychoanalytic thinking. There is not scope here for further explication, but readers wanting to know more about this aspect of the Laban vocabulary can explore the references listed above.

Amerta Movement – an object relations approach

The work of Suprapto Suryodarmo, an Indonesian movement teacher whose non-stylized movement practice derives from his relationship with the natural world, offers valuable insights for understanding how to recognize and use movement as a psychophysical process. It is my feeling that this approach has much to offer in thinking about practice in movement psychotherapy, especially because of its resonances with psychoanalytic object relations: 'Prapto uses his own body movement as a diagnostic tool, a barometer, to sense what is evolving or trying to emerge in a person's life, or in the interaction between people of different cultures' (Kemp Welch 2001). His sensitivity to the energy of interrelationship has much to offer in fine-tuning the experience of transference and countertransference.

Through responding to both internal and external impulses in movement, students of Amerta Movement are encouraged to be in the here and now, finding the time and space which embodies not only the present, but is also acknowledged to incorporate and reflect the mover's background. Students acquire 'response-ability' – the ability to respond to these impulses, through discovering the movement vocabulary which embodies their own sensory, perceptual and emotional experience from moment to moment. For

Suryodarmo, movement provides a 'bridge to understanding' and growth. This process has much in common with the psychoanalytic technique of free association.

Without guiding patients directly, I can enquire into their recognition of physical experience; I can enquire into abrupt transitions – between speaking and moving, or lying down and standing up, for example. This supports a more conscious embodying of movement and the development of vocabulary for patients, as well as clarifying my own countertransference experience.

Over time, students become increasingly 'articulate' in movement which derives from their developing relationship to both inner and outer experience. Suryodarmo speaks of finding safety through discovery of the right proportion in the relationship to space and time, not too big or too small or fast or slow to feel comfortable and present. He distinguishes between the body itself, the *organism*, which is rooted in the world of nature, and the human mental and imaginative processes which he speaks of as *organization*, which are rooted in *human* nature. One aim of the movement practice is to recognize these as two aspects of the self, which can be integrated through movement. One could describe it as the embodiment of thoughts and feelings.

Suryodarmo does not refer to his work as therapy; rather, he has referred to himself as a 'gardener'. He describes the garden as being a space in between the protected world of home and the outside world of society. The area in between is a space where there is potential for creativity and play to take shape. This description mirrors Winnicott's notion of 'transitional space'.

As Suryodarmo moves with students, he supports them in dealing with whatever is arising, in their efforts to become 'in-formed' by what they are doing – through recognizing and embodying, expressing or containing their feelings, wishes and needs. This is very much like the way a therapist uses his or her experience of the transference and countertransference stirred by the relationship to receive the patient's phantasies and states of mind. With Suryodarmo, this is usually a nonverbal process which he has described, when things are flowing, as a process of 'irrigation'.

Amerta Movement could have a place in the training of movement and body psychotherapists as well as verbal psychotherapists. It offers a skill which is often overlooked – how to make one's own bodily experience more conscious as a resource, to sense oneself as a three-dimensional container, able to receive and reflect the transference, projective identification and countertransference more fully. This work could support an exploration of what happens when therapists become enmeshed, overwhelmed or unconsciously absorbed by interactions with patients.

The following excerpt recounts a session in which a young man has a hard time moving on from the knowledge and grievance about not having received what he needed as a child. Although this was true in many ways, it stood in the way of taking in anything good. This was expressed in a feeling of being unable to use the therapy, and of our relationship lacking what he needs. We both acknowledged this in the session and then found a way to move through it and onward. In this session I instinctively felt it was necessary to take the initiative to move first, so as not to collude in the feeling of lifelessness and failure.

> He sits curving forward, holding his knees in the usual way. I notice I feel rejected and I really take that in. I say he seems to have a feeling of giving up on me. He nods. And yet, I say, he is able to come, and to acknowledge it. I speak of its longstanding presence – that I have not been any good, that it just doesn't work here. Sensing his pent up energy, I say these are strong feelings. I begin to breathe and move a little as I digest this material and suggest he might be able to express his feelings in a way that gives them some life. I go on working with it in my movement and he gradually does move from his intractable position.
>
> I feel his hesitation and resistance; he shifts forward and back from squatting, but with a sharp directional intention to move forward. I stay on roughly the same level as his and move alongside, in my own way. This evolves slowly until we are really attuned and working with the energy we experience from each other, yet each following our own line. We move through different levels, no longer always at the same time. There are spells of him starting to disengage, as he goes on half-heartedly. I slow and tune in to that and just feel it; he seems to be drawn back into moving. At one point I put my feet down strongly, just walking with this sound and release. He walks with subtle articulation of his feet – he seems involved; not a pussyfooting around. Not copying. Just contained, quiet, focused.
>
> He goes to the floor and I follow that. There is some sound which escapes from him at times as he stretches – it is really authentic, as if despite himself. He comes to sit and I do too.
>
> He seems to go back to his starting state, sitting in the middle of the space. I sit against the side wall. He is opaque, looking down. I say this feels like where we started today, as if nothing else just happened. He says yes, that one thought he had was that I have a programme in mind and I want him to follow it. I say it's hard to hold onto anything else if he feels I'm someone who just wants him to follow my plan, and he feels he's given in. At least before, he could assert himself by resisting doing anything.
>
> He lies down and stretches. I feel this is very poignant. I move to lower myself, folding, stretching. Little sounds escape from him now and then. I say I'm aware of the sounds – how natural they are, how small they are, that they sound like it's a relief to let them out. He says it is a relief.

In this sequence, few words were needed for a 'dialogue', in which this patient gave up a position of firm conviction that no one perceived to be in a 'parental' role could offer anything good. There was pain as well as relief for him in moving on.

Conclusion

I have described a method of working as a movement psychotherapist which draws on my first-hand experience of four distinct but related disciplines. The synthesis of these has informed, illuminated and deepened the development of this practice. The influences of psychoanalytic theory, psychoanalytic infant observation, Laban Movement Analysis and Amerta Movement have been interwoven. The result is a fruitful integrative approach to movement psychotherapy. It is a process which has evolved over many years, and continues to evolve. I have learned that while sharing basic human qualities, each patient is unique, and this is reflected in the way they make use of movement as part of the work of therapy, to contact and articulate early experience, which is often found to have its roots in the primitive, preverbal stage of life.

5 Dilemmas concerning the ethical use of touch in psychotherapy

David Tune

Introduction

At one extreme, within some schools of psychotherapy, touch has been associated with the expression of adult sexuality, or with an unwanted provocation or contamination of the therapeutic relationship; whilst other humanistic, existential and Reichian psychotherapies have actively sought to incorporate touch as an integral part of the therapeutic relationship and within specific techniques. The subject still provokes controversy and debate, though the use of touch is moving much more towards centre stage for many therapists and trainings.

It is useful to take a brief look at some of the history surrounding touch in psychotherapy, and the origins of the current controversy. These centre around issues including a perceived need for the therapist to remain a 'blank screen' in the relationship, prevailing social and cultural norms, the risk of erotic stimulation, fear of litigation, and the meaning of touch to the client. Within this debate it will be appropriate to explore issues for practice in the ethical use of touch, and I will present arguments from those practitioners who favour a set of guidelines for using touch, as well as those who wish to incorporate touch within the subjective phenomenological field of the relationship. Findings from current research will be presented, and their implications for practice discussed.

History, theory and current controversies

The history of touch in psychotherapy is one of controversy, confusion and taboo. Freud certainly touched his patients in his early work with hypnosis, though he abandoned it in psychoanalysis and argued fiercely against analysts using touch, on the grounds that it would gratify the patient, break the rule of abstinence, and thus interfere with the transference.

Freud's justification for this was that by frustrating the patient's instinct-ual desires, the unconscious material would push through into their thoughts, feelings and fantasies toward the analyst, and thus be available for interpret-ation in the transferential relationship. As these desires found words so they would become conscious. This was Freud's theory of the working through of unconscious material.

Mintz (1969) identifies the factors that led to the taboo against touch in psychoanalysis as the social context, demands of a positivistic science, and Freud's break with hypnosis. Working in the social context of the repressive sexual attitudes of Victorian Europe, Freud sought respectability for his theor-ies: based as they were on unconscious sexual and aggressive drives, they were controversial enough as it was!

However, the centrality of the body when working with early attachment disorders and trauma is currently being re-evaluated by practitioners from a variety of theoretical backgrounds (Rothschild 2000; Carroll 2002b; Orbach 2004), including some psychoanalysts. One such is Reuven Bar-Levav (1998: 53), who provides a powerful argument for using touch when working with early attachment trauma:

> But how do we address and change such preverbal 'knowledge'? Surely not by talking from our cortex to the patient's. It is done by repeatedly establishing exquisite contact with the distrustful and scared infant within the adult patient. We persist until the fragile inner baby begins to feel safe in the therapeutic setting.

In this context, when working at the pre-oedipal level, associating the patient's need for holding with sexual transference is difficult to argue, as any yearnings for the therapist's love are more likely to be an expression of a much earlier longing to be mothered safely. Bar-Levav argues that to deny the patient the possibility of a developmentally reparative experience at this time is difficult to defend on a theoretical basis alone: 'Forbidding touch on the basis of the possibility of stimulating an erotic transference essentially reflects the fears of the therapist. Though it is often expressed as a generally accepted fact, such an assumption is also theoretically incorrect' (p. 55).

Humanistic psychotherapy has adopted a different position towards touch. Humanistic approaches ascribe qualities of openness, spontaneity and con-gruence to its use. In accordance with the client-centred value base of the humanistic model, and its rejection of scientific and positivistic theory, touch is not employed as a technique, or seen within the context of either the client's developmental stage, or any transferential dynamic within the relationship. The rejection of the medical model, the analyst-patient power relationship, and the dehumanizing effects of behavioural methods, led the 'human potential movement' to increasingly place the genuine person to person encounter as the primary impetus for growth. Authenticity and spontaneity were advocated by Rogers (1970) who opened the way for humanistic therapists to experiment with touch, taking the person-centred core values into the realm of the physical and moving the work forward to a more holistic way of being that still places the client as the central agent for change.

Attention to the energy of the physical body is of interest in some areas of humanistic psychotherapy. There is a developing emphasis in person-centred therapy on what Rogers called 'presence' in the therapeutic encounter. This is difficult to accurately define, though it seems similar to what Gendlin (1981) called 'felt sense', or an inner awareness of energetic movement within the body. In the same context Cameron (2002) refers to ancient Chinese and Indian concepts of *chi* and *prana* in her work with the 'subtle body'. In her practice she explores the concept of an energy that bridges the link between psyche and the physical body. Whilst touch is not necessarily employed in these concepts, the exploration of a more embodied and relational approach within the energetic field of counsellor and client is the basic premise. This is a way of being that takes conditions of empathy, congruence and acceptance away from simply words and gestures to a deeper embodiment within the energetic field of the therapeutic relationship: 'by asking if the whole body, the whole organism, can learn something the mind does not know, or only learns later, Rogers emphasizes other modes of intuitive perception' (Cameron 2002: 66).

Touch can also be used in Gestalt and psychodrama approaches, though it is not specifically a part of these theories. Touch plays an important role in facilitating emotional catharsis. In the role-plays used in psychodrama the 'protagonist' may be invited to express him- or herself in many ways that involve touch towards the other 'actors' in the drama. Pushing away, holding onto, leaning on for support, are just some of the many ways in which the role-play can be embodied, in order to recreate and work through the original scenario. 'Sculpting' is a technique sometimes used in family work, which involves exploring body language and touch to demonstrate, in a physical way, the family dynamics of the client.

In Gestalt, emphasis is placed on 'awareness in the moment' and completing the 'energetic cycle of discharge' or the 'Gestalt'. Many direct and subtle ways of touching are often used by Gestalt therapists to help their clients to gain awareness of their feelings in the moment, or to discharge the blocked energy from some 'unfinished business' from their past and complete the cycle. Smith (1985) pays attention to where a client 'self-interrupts' in the cycle of contact and withdrawal. He describes four tasks of the body-orientated Gestaltist: to *facilitate awareness, facilitate breathing, melt body armour* and *stop retroflected action and interaction* (i.e. turning feelings for others against the self, or doing to the self what one would like others to do).

Of course touch is used in body psychotherapy approaches, though by no means all the time, or with all clients. (Reich [1945] 1972; Keleman 1975;

Lowen 1976; Boadella 1987; Pierrakos 1990). However, it is important to distinguish the use of touch within the context of a psychotherapy that has at its core a theory of body-mind integration, from other approaches that have incorporated touch into their model at a later stage (or are in the process of so doing), or value it as an adjunct to other interventions that are more central to their theoretical position.

The main point here is that in Reichian approaches touch is not only legitimized, in that it is the major mode of interaction, but also formalized into a system of techniques. As such, therapeutic touch should not come as a surprise to a client, but would have been discussed as an integral part of the therapy, much as it would be for someone seeking massage, reflexology or osteopathy.

The body psychotherapist may use touch in a variety of ways to release chronic holding. Direct pressure on a particular part of the body is one method. Inviting a client to adopt a position that puts stress onto a specific area of the body to facilitate release is another technique, used in bioenergetics (Lowen 1977). Various forms of massage, and working with the breath are also commonly used.

Current controversies

There is of course a risk of employing these techniques in an objective, directive and mechanistic way, and I can remember in the earlier days of my own practice not paying sufficient attention to the relational aspects of my work, focusing instead on the client's physical and psychological defences, and then wondering why the therapy became 'stuck'. Thinking back I can liken my relationship to my clients at that time to one of a sports coach, encouraging and supporting them to go the 'extra mile' towards mind-body integration, but paying insufficient attention to the dynamics of our relationship. This was not Reich's intention, however, and his use of touch went alongside analysis, working with the relationship within a psychoanalytic paradigm.

There are of course dangers in working with the body in an objectified way, and one such danger is that this can impose a pressure upon the client that has the opposite effect to the intention of the therapist. The client can start to see their defences (as they are physically manifested) as a 'bad part of themselves' that must be eliminated, and this can reinforce the mind-body split. I would also argue however that verbal therapies that focus on 'the problem', rather than taking a more holistic view, probably do the same. Michael Soth in a conference paper recently pointed to the dangers of 'negatively objectivizing' the body in this way. He suggested that by focusing exclusively on the physical character structures, the therapist runs the risk of colluding with the client in relating to their body as 'alien', and as such may be re-enacting the original traumas that resulted in the need to defend and split: 'As long as I am talking about using the body in an objectifying fashion, I am not identifying with it, thus perpetuating disembodiment' (Soth 2004).

Many body therapists work less with hands-on techniques however, and work to enable clients to breathe more fully, and experience themselves at a deeper level within the relationship. Nick Totton (2002: 24) describes this approach: 'The central focus of embodied-relational bodywork, then, is on re-establishing a fuller, more spontaneous breath – not by efforting, but by gradually letting go of our need to protect ourselves from feeling by not breathing'.

So while the history of the use of touch in psychotherapy contains many disparate views and prohibitions, which are sometimes reinforced by theoretical positions, and often at odds with them, the fact remains that many therapists of all theoretical persuasions use touch at certain times, with some clients, in different ways and for different reasons: 'It may be that the touch taboo is not deterring many therapists from using touch, but is strong enough to keep them from admitting it to one another' (Wilson 1982: 24).

In an update of an earlier study on touch (Tune 2001), therapists reported numerous spontaneous and reciprocal expressions of touch at the beginnings and endings of therapy, on meeting clients on the stairs or in the hallways, or other places that they considered 'out of the therapeutic space'. I believe that this split, perceived as 'therapeutic space' and 'social space', is a manifestation of the conflict within therapists between the rule of abstinence and the objectification of the patient inherent in a positivistic psychotherapy. Lindon sees the prevalence of abstinence as the norm in much of psychotherapy practice as 'not quite a law of nature, it is unconsciously taken as a given in psychoanalysis' (1994: 551).

Over many years I have heard clients speak of their need to have a genuine person to person engagement with their therapist, and I have seen therapists who have suddenly become more relaxed and 'natural' with clients when therapy ended. I do not believe that this is always evidence of poor boundaries, or necessarily transferential issues that are not worked through. It is equally possible that this is the energetic connection between two people that is suspended during therapy. While many therapists can be authentic and in contact with the physical dimensions of the therapeutic relationship, others would seem to reconcile this dilemma through abstaining from an awareness of the corporal self.

This is difficult to reconcile within the energetic relationship that develops between two people occupying the same space (whether it is acknowledged consciously or not). As Susie Orbach says, 'there is no such thing as a body, only a body in relationship with another body' (2004a: 28).

Issues in practice

My motivation for undertaking research into the use of touch in psycho-therapy has its origins in my own practice. I have tried to engage with the issues presented by touch, in a way that is congruent with what I feel to be in the therapeutic relationship while mindful of the clients history, character structure and transferential phenomena.

My work some years ago with one client, who I will call Mary, provided me with the impetus to explore the issue in greater depth. Mary was a woman in her twenties who had initially self-referred in order to look at her pattern of losing her enthusiasm for relationships, jobs and other activities after a fairly predicable period of time. She was preoccupied with her physical appearance and had suffered from a period of anorexia in her teens. After some weeks of working together she asked me the question, 'Do you touch your clients?' I was acutely aware of wanting to give her an authentic reply on the one hand, while wanting to explore the meaning of the question on the other. As my position as a psychotherapist is that of trying to hold to humanistic principles and values, while paying attention to any transference dynamic, my reply to her was '*sometimes*'.

Not surprisingly this response was the subject of many more sessions of work with Mary. As we explored what touch meant to her, she also challenged me to look at my thoughts, feelings and decisions concerning issues of touch in greater depth. Although I was trained as a body psychotherapist, there were times when I did not use touch at all with some clients, and with others I used a bodywork approach throughout. Certainly it was more of an intuitive 'gut reaction' that prompted my answer to Mary, than any clearly thought through decision-making process. What interested me was the process by which I came to make these decisions, and subsequently how other therapists approached the issue.

As argued earlier, simply avoiding touch does not necessarily avoid the issue of touch in the therapeutic relationship for the client or the therapist. While there has been little enough written about touch in the transference, until recently it is has been even more difficult to find literature on the counter-transference and touch. In the interviews I conducted in my own research (Tune 2001), 20 examples were given where touch did not actually occur but it was still perceived as an issue in the relationship, either because the therapist had *not* touched the client, but on reflection thought it would have been a more useful intervention, or because the client had *wanted* to be touched and the therapist had declined. These decisions emerged from a number of differ-ent motives. However, a conflict was evident between 'external injunctions' such as the rule of abstinence, negative messages from training or supervisors, fear of ethical violations, or more commonly a general confusion about touch on the one hand, and the 'felt presence' of the therapeutic relationship at that moment on the other.

Frequently, questions come up about *how* to touch, when discussing touch in psychotherapy with colleagues and trainees. For example, 'What is the best ways to use touch?' or 'Which clients should I use or not use touch with?' Often a set of guidelines for touch seems to be required. As a trainer I welcome open debate about touch. However, I believe that touch, like any intervention, cannot be prescribed, and should be embodied in the relationship and context of therapy, guided by the therapist's own energetic awareness.

Having said that, it is worth noting some basic rules on the use of touch at this point. It should be clearly stated that touch should never be aggressive, sexual, against the wishes of the client, or to gratify the therapist's own needs or wish for power.

On the last point, therapists who are thinking of using touch would do well to reflect on *who initiates it*. If the client initiates, how does the therapist feel about responding? How does their body react? Perhaps they welcome the invitation to touch the client, or do not want to, but go along with the request anyway. Conversely, they may be clear immediately that this is something they do not want to do and decline. If the therapist initiates touch, what are their reasons? And even if it can be put down to spontaneity, how does the therapist process this on reflection? These questions apply to any intervention, but given the power of touch, and the myriad of meanings associated with it, they should not be ignored. Whilst this may seem self-evident to any competent practitioner, the evidence from my own research is that the processing of touch issues in the therapy session or in supervision is patchy, and largely dependent on the theoretical background of the supervisor and therapist, on therapists' perceptions of supervisors' reactions to touch and on messages from training.

Though my research study was small-scale and the issue merits further investigation, it was interesting to note that the incidents or issues of touch that were discussed in supervision were more likely to be those initiated by a client than those initiated or contemplated by the therapist. This could be indicative of perceptions about who has permission to touch in the relationship, which has implications for the empowerment of clients. Hunter and Struve 'strongly advocate that power should not be ignored or avoided. It is essential that therapists facilitate the process of making power dynamics conscious and intentional' (1998: 69). The same authors claim that the cultural and social context is vital to understanding dimensions of power. The gender, ethnicity, religion, class or disability of a client may influence their perception of the power of the therapist and their use of touch, just as much as any individual subjective meaning.

Status and role can be conveyed by touch. Reciprocal touch promotes intimacy, while non-reciprocal touch reinforces positions of dominance or distance. Culture and ethnicity determine norms about touch, and there can be a wide range of differences about its meaning between different groups. One study (Journard 1966) observed couples talking and interacting in a café in different societies. In Latin American and Mediterranean countries the couples touched between 110 and 180 times in an hour. In England and the USA they touched no more than twice. Maybe the use of touch has changed since the study was done, but there are clearly considerable cultural differences concerning touch.

Gender is another dimension relative to touch. Holroyd and Brodsky (1977) noted that female therapists tended to touch their clients more than male therapists. Henley (1973a, 1973b) noted that men tended to initiate touch to women more frequently than women initiate touch to men. While there are numerous studies that contradict one another on this topic, given the power of gender role socialization it would be foolish to ignore the implications of touch between and within genders.

Therapists must ensure they use touch in a consciously intentional way. Though touch can have many meanings, some of the intentional functions are:

- *To provide containment or grounding:* this may take the form of holding, offering a hand or giving a client something to push against. Making eye contact while suggesting a client breathe can have the same effect.
- *To help the expression of feelings:* some of the techniques of bodywork may be used to help someone to kick or hit out at a cushion, for instance, or to make a noise where the client is blocked in verbal expression.
- *To provide nurturance:* by offering affection or support that was missing in the parent-child relationship. This can revitalize a client who has become 'cut off' from physical sensation (for a number of vignettes on nurturing touch read Breckenridge 2000).
- *To provide real contact:* in order to reinforce the immediate I/thou physical and psychic presence.

Some of the functions of positive touch can therefore be evocative, stabilizing, nurturing and relational.

Whatever the intention of the therapist regarding the issue of touch, it is the processing of that intention that is crucial:

> the question may not be whether therapists should touch their patients, but rather how touch is utilized and processed in therapy. That is to say, if a therapist decides to touch a given patient, he or she must do so in a thoughtful manner and must be willing to accept responsibility for the patient's interpretation of the touch. Likewise if the therapist decides not to touch, there must be a similar willingness

> to accept responsibility for the meanings that the patient will assign
> to the absence of a natural form of human contact.
>
> (Kertay and Reviere 1993: 16–35)

Mistakes in interventions are as important as successes. In my own work I know that I will not always 'get it right' and that no amount of self-awareness, training or sensitivity to my client will prevent me from sometimes making an intervention that is in energetic disharmony with where he or she is in their own process. If that intervention happens to be touch, no matter how well-meaning my intention, my client's negative reaction will be felt at a somatic level, even if this is not conscious or verbalized. If I ignore this useful information, or admonish myself for taking the risk in the first place, I miss a therapeutic opportunity to process the meaning for me and my client, which may give us valuable insights into their 'body-mind' relationship to others.

Geib (1998) reiterates the point made by Wilson (1982) that the taboo concerning touch doesn't prevent many therapists from touching their clients, but it often makes them feel sufficiently guilty and secretive not to discuss it with colleagues and supervisors. Geib interviewed ten female clients who had worked with male therapists and received non-erotic physical touch (defined as not sexual either in intent or content). She was interested in establishing what made touch a positive or problematic experience for these clients, and concluded that there were four factors that influenced six of the clients' experience of touch as positive:

1   The therapist provided an environment where the client was in control.
2   The therapist was clearly responding to the client's needs and not their own.
3   The therapist encouraged open discussion of the contact.
4   The therapist made sure emotional and physical intimacy were congruent in time and space.

The factors that made touch a problematic experience for four of the clients were:

1   Being touched made them feel loved and worthwhile, but it was consequently difficult to mention negative feelings.
2   They felt guilt about expressing their anger at the therapist.
3   The therapists were perceived as needy and vulnerable and in need of protection from the client's feelings.
4   The therapy re-created the original dynamics of the trauma, and did not help resolve it.

Interestingly, the positive factors seem to correspond to Rogers' therapeutic conditions of client-centredness, respect, empathy and genuineness.

Ethical considerations

There are other reasons why a general prohibition against touch has developed that are not related to psychotherapeutic theory, notably confusion over the ethical use of touch and fear of litigation. It is not uncommon for therapists to be concerned that when using touch their intention may be misinterpreted, and while it is a fundamental professional principle that therapists should wish to cause no harm to their clients, their intention is a factor of considerable importance to malpractice insurers and professional bodies. The British Association for Counselling and Psychotherapy has a 'professional liability policy' which makes a clear distinction between 'deliberate acts' and unintentional harm caused by misunderstanding. The policy includes the following exclusion clause: 'Liability for any injury loss or damage deliberately intended by the insured, but this exception shall not apply to liability attributable to any breach of professional duty' (Litton 2004: 4). As Litton points out, 'you cannot accidentally have sex with a patient'.

So while misperceptions and conflicting meanings concerning touch in psychotherapy may arise, and may in a minority of situations lead to scrutiny by ethics committees, provided the therapist is clear that their intention is ethical, the fear of litigation is probably exaggerated.

Hunter and Struve (1998) argue that much more attention needs to be devoted to the ethical use of touch by training organizations, supervisors and professional bodies, and that leaving these decisions to the lawyers may move therapists away from their clinical goals.

The worry that physical contact may lead to sexual contact has, as I have already stated, been around since Freud. The evidence paints a different picture however. Holroyd and Brodsky (1977) found no evidence that touching patients *per se* made sexual contact any more likely. They did find that differential touching (gender-specific touching) of opposite sex patients was more likely to lead to erotic touching. I would expect this differentiation to be far less likely to occur with practitioners who are trained in the use of touch, or who have integrated it into their overall practice.

Sexual attraction towards clients is not correlated with using touch. Pope *et al.* (1986) and Bernsen *et al.* (1994) found four out of five psychologists and social workers in a national survey reported experiencing sexual attraction towards at least one client: 'Yet simply experiencing the attraction (without necessarily even feeling tempted to act on it) causes most of the therapists who reported such attraction (63 percent of the psychologists and 51 percent of the social workers) to feel guilty, anxious, or confused about the attraction'

(Pope *et al.* 2001: 171). Unfortunately, the discomfort this evokes may have contributed to a lack of attention to the issue in training courses, professional books and discussion with supervisors and peers.

The body psychotherapist and trainer Tree Staunton offers a useful debate on the subject, and on the issue of prohibition and desire asks 'and what of isolating physical contact and imbuing it with all the power and allure of the erotic?' (Staunton 2002: 72). She goes on to challenge the abstinence rule, and the implication that making physical contact sexualizes the relationship:

> I would argue the contrary. If the analytic frame of abstinence and distance was designed to increase transference, including the erotic, then it follows that a more natural ease of relationship which focuses awareness on the bodily reality will decrease or defuse the erotic charge, bringing the client more into a 'related' state with regard to their body; the body does not equal the erotic but includes it.
>
> (2002: 75)

A list of guidelines for the ethical use of touch in psychotherapy has been drawn up by Hunter and Struve and is repeated here. My own research and practice experience leads me to believe that sensitivity to the embodied thera- peutic relationship, and giving time to process the meaning of touch for client and therapists, is the most efficacious ethical approach. I find one particularly useful technique is to imagine that I am discussing my practice with a group of peers, and to notice if there is anything I would prefer to avoid. If there is, then that is the issue or situation I should take to my next peer supervision group meeting.

The following guidelines (Hunter and Struve 1998: 138–46) may offer useful clarification in the ethical debate. It is appropriate to use touch in psychotherapy when:

1 The client wants to be touched.
2 The purpose of the touch is clear.
3 Touch is intended for the client's benefit.
4 The client understands concepts of empowerment (they can say no).
5 The therapist has a solid knowledge base about touch.
6 Boundaries are clearly understood by both client and therapist.
7 There is enough time in the session to process touch.
8 The therapeutic relationship has developed sufficiently.
9 Touch is offered to all types of client (there is no differentiation on the basis of gender, age or sexual orientation for instance).
10 Consultation is available and used.
11 The therapist is comfortable with touch.

My own research into the use of touch

Many of the issues in Hunter and Struve's guidelines evolved as themes for the therapist in my own research on touch. In my study, I interviewed 23 therapists from a range of theoretical backgrounds, who were all qualified and had been in practice for at least two years. Two were male, and 21 female. I realize this gender bias may have influenced the material I collected and this is an area for future exploration. As this was a qualitative study I asked a range of fairly open-ended questions about the therapists' use of touch (or non use/ avoidance) in psychotherapy. The majority (17 out of 23) initially said 'no' they did not use touch in their work. However, when given a prompt to include *any* form of touch between therapist and client all 23 answered 'yes' to this question. There were 69 examples of touch discussed in the interviews, and when they were asked to include occasions when touch did not occur but they felt it was an issue in the relationship, then a further 20 examples were given.

A number of themes and sub-themes emerged which are relevant to the issues already presented in this chapter, and I will now mention them briefly.

Many of the examples of touch that were given were considered by the therapists to be in a 'social space' – for example, hugs at the end of sessions, handshakes or physical contact in the waiting room or hall, and not 'part of the therapeutic process'. For this reason they had answered 'no' to the first question. Touch also often occurred at the end of sessions or at the end of therapy, and so it was not usually discussed again.

Processing emerged as a major theme. Incidents or issues of touch were only discussed with clients on 19 occasions (out of 89), and 8 of these were by the two body-orientated therapists in the research. Many pointed out it was not possible to process the physical contact as it had happened at the preceding session, and they did not come back to it in the next, or else it had been used in the very last session and therapy had then ended. While I understand the wish to acknowledge the achievement of the therapy with some physical contact at the end, I think it important to raise the question about what this may mean to the client. In particular, one danger may be that if touch has been denied or withheld throughout therapy, then could the unconscious communication be that a 'different kind of relationship is now possible'? Janet Sayers (1996: 120) is critical of touch at endings and beginnings in therapy, describing one of her own experiences:

> He came for one last session – just before his holiday. As he stood up to leave I put out my hand to shake farewell. Our hands touched. Immediately he shuddered. Then froze. In his job he must have shaken hands innumerable times with his fellow professionals. But

with me the intimacy was too much. It evidently felt tantamount to abuse.

If therapists are only touching at endings, and consequently unable to process the effects of this, this raises the question as to whether they are discussing the issue in supervision. Of the 89 examples of touch given, 33 were mentioned in supervision, 17 of these by the same three therapists. Most of the therapists thought there were negative connotations with discussing touch and it was a subject that they did not usually mention with their supervisors or colleagues. Many thought that their supervisor would disapprove. One said she had mentioned it but was simply told 'don't do it' by her supervisor.

In relation to training there are clearly issues for consideration. Despite the prohibitions against touch, and the references to the dangers of its unethical use in professional codes of practice, only two therapists reported touch being discussed in their training other than being warned against it, and none of the therapists had an experience of touch playing any significant part in discussions about practice in their training. Only the two body-orientated therapists had received any training input on the ethical use of touch.

Some themes and sub-themes emerging from the research are as follows:

- A split is evident between what is considered the therapeutic space and social space. Touch at the end not seen as part of the process.
- Whilst 'No, I don't touch' was given as the first response in all but two interviews, when further explored numerous examples emerged.
- Touch would seem to be more accepted when the therapist initiated it than when the client initiated it (as identified in the feedback on supervision), though this is an area which needs further exploration.
- The processing of touch in therapy sessions is very limited, which may be in some part because touch is frequently introduced at the end of a session or at the end of therapy.
- Touch was not often mentioned in supervision (either as a form of contact in therapy or as an issue).
- Uncertainty about touch in practice generally was evident.
- Touch is frequently 'hidden' (from process, supervision and the interview initially), and debate seems to be avoided in training.
- There seems to be a 'mind-body split' among therapists in their choice of interventions, with factors influencing choice being:

Therapeutic model
Intuition
Ethics
Anxiety regarding litigation
Confidence with touch

Own needs
Confusion concerning intention

In summary, the conflict between different messages regarding touch often left the therapists unclear about why they chose many interventions, and they frequently found it difficult to integrate touch into other motivating factors. Negative messages from training, theoretical prohibitions and a climate of anxiety regarding professional issues all seem to have contributed to touch being avoided in supervision and processing in many instances. Though these findings are tentative and merit further investigation, they indicate an unhealthy atmosphere of taboo and secrecy about touch in the profession, especially among those practitioners for whom it is not a part of their training or theoretical orientation.

Conclusion

There are many historical and current prohibitions against touch. These are justified by theoretical constraints, fear of litigation, uncertainty about how and when to touch ethically, and are fuelled by an attempt to create a modernistic science of psychotherapy. The reality would seem to be that a great many therapists do touch their clients and in a variety of ways that include social rituals, technical interventions and spontaneous expressions of the energetic connection within the relationship. Historical taboo and a more general uncertainty and confusion concerning the place of touch in psychotherapy would seem to have contributed to a difficulty in acknowledging its use in a variety of contexts across the profession, in supervision and in discussion with colleagues, in the processing of its meanings within the therapeutic relationship, and in the exploration of its ethical use in training. It is my hope that the current renaissance of the debate about the ethical use of touch will lead to a reiteration of its place in psychotherapy as a form of meaningful human expression worthy of consideration and more widespread integration.

PART 2
New Dimensions of Practice

6 Recovering and eliciting precursors of meaning

A psychodynamic perspective of the body in psychotherapy

Yorai Sella

Introduction

In working within a psychodynamic framework one is frequently challenged by patients who experience the therapy as 'meaningless'. Despite having gained substantial cognitive insight they are frustrated by what they experience as an elusive quality of unreality. In trying to define this quality they refer to the therapist's not being 'present', to their own experience of 'not experiencing themselves', not feeling their bodies, not feeling, not being aware of their sensory inputs. For some, these experiences will lead to a premature termination of the therapy. Others will retrospectively describe the agony of not having met with any physical attributes of the therapist's presence: not having been offered a cup of tea, not having been greeted by a handshake – and feeling confronted by unbearably long instances of silence. The therapist's image would not take hold in their mind – for, in order to create an image an experience is necessary, which, due to their experience of the therapist's 'unpresence', was not provided. We may surmise that, for such patients 'the analyst's every casual . . . gesture or movement may . . . assume an importance far beyond anything that was realistically intended' (Balint 1984: 18). Deprived of the physical aspects of what is in other ways an intimate interaction, the entire dialogical situation is experienced as meaningless.

The term 'meaning' habitually connotes a cognitive conceptualization, which lends an organizational framework to actions, behaviours, emotions and ideations. It is a conceptualization which renders them 'meaningful' or 'significant' – in that they are interpreted to be a 'sign of', a symbolical event, rather than crude, concrete happenings. Thus, the psychodynamic and analytical schools are reliant on the meaning-giving attributes of verbal interpretation, perceiving them to be the basis of insight and its attendant emotional resolutions.

The joint impact of humanistic thinkers and of presymbolical and prelinguistic formulations within the psychodynamic world, of neuropsychological research, and of Oriental (particularly Buddhist) psychotherapeutic philosophies is generating an erosion of these long-held beliefs. In clinical practice it is becoming widely recognized that interpretations may be not only 'incorrect', 'inadequate' or 'inappropriate', but may serve to obscure some aspects of experience that patients perceive as meaningful, thereby frustrating therapeutic progress (Balint 1984). Generating prejudice as well as sincere debate, these innovative inputs are infiltrating and influencing the mainstays of psychodynamic theory and technique as regards the use of physical intervention and the verbal exploration of concrete phenomenological experience.

In this chapter I shall propose that the precursors of 'meaning' are embedded in the bodily-sensorial reality and that the roots of 'knowledge' are closer to the biblical-carnal-corporal sense of the word, than to intellectual cogitations. I shall suggest that there may be specific physical events and processes through which the sense of 'meaning' is derived and formulated. I shall try to demonstrate the relevance of this approach to the categorization of 'meanings' in the clinical practice of effective therapy within a psychodynamic framework.

I initially encountered the elusive nature of the term 'meaningful' in working with adult patients with residual manifestations of 'attention deficit disorder'. It became clear to me that normative social cues often conveyed no 'significance' to these patients, as the methods in which social 'signs' or 'signals' are commonly sensually displayed were not normatively apprehended by them (Dodge and Frame 1982; Grennel *et al.* 1987). An illusive discrepancy in the interpretations of, or responses to, varying input modalities seemed to prevail – for example, a handshake would be felt to be threatening, overly clinging or avoidant, due to an incorrect evaluation of the accompanying facial expression. This created a breach in the capacity to formulate meaningful links across experiential modalities, and/or between these modalities and cognitive functioning. The sense of a painful and pervasive discrepancy between verbal communication and the attendant gestural, sensory and energetic communication used by the 'verbal', psychodynamic or behavioural-cognitive therapist, often brought these patients to seek a more integrative form of therapy as 'a last resort'. Gradually I came to see the same frustration of common-sense congruence in patients presenting with a wide variety of diagnoses, involving varying forms of defensive 'splitting' and dissociative symptoms.

In order to create what is ordinarily meant by 'meaning' the structures underlying the capacity to attain symbolical representation must be formed. One must be able to accumulate experiences and to establish the recognition of an experience, and at least some of its basic attributes: is it internal or external? Pleasant or otherwise? In order to realistically formulate ideas and metaphors one must have individual perspective, ownership and agency – all dependent upon the temporal and spatial context of the body at a given instant (Damasio 2000). Yet the acquisition of sensory-sensual-bodily precursors of meaning seems to require a system of categorization, based on links between the experiential and verbal domains, which the patients I am referring to had never fully developed. It would seem as if their life experience has taught them to distrust verbal communications and their derivatives in the form of associations, connotations and elaborations (Sella 2003).

Conversely, aspects of physical reality – such as physical distance from objects, body and room temperatures, or the therapist's perceived level of energetic intensity, are conceived of as tacit or explicit communicational signs and signals. A perceived incongruity between these 'communications' and the verbal ones will serve to confabulate the communication, render it meaningless or, at times, suggest that it be *intentionally* baffling or threatening – in its supposedly intentional inscrutability. It is as if the psychodynamic therapist, when reliant on the solely verbal aspects of the therapeutic interaction, is intentionally withholding the most important and meaningful aspects of themselves so as to thwart the patient's very attempt at cohesion and cohesive communication. A state of continual frustration and 'envy' ensues.

The establishment and maintenance of a sense of meaning is dependent upon a bodily and energetic experience which has gained an internal cohesiveness and is 'sensual, bodily and reliant upon the various uses to which the infant might put his sensory organs' (Briggs 2002: 8). The crucial building blocks of communication need to be established experientially time and again, in order to gain a sense of reality, spontaneity and coherence. Gradually, an organizational framework is established through the employment of patterned 'constellations' constructed sensorially and cross-modally through the invariant attributes of shape, intensity, hedonic tone etc. (Stern 1985: 67). We may thus think of a 'meaningful' occurrence as one in which a sense of cohesive meaning is subjectively attained by a 'good enough' sensory congruence of internal or external events. This congruence serves to organize experience in a way that is subjectively meaningful – i.e. promotes a sense of internal cohesion, provides direction for energetic output and facilitates viable and rewarding interactions. These will be consciously or unconsciously established or replicated in therapy, and may be explored through the transferential relationship, and through paying close attention to the somatic registers in the countertransference.

It is with these initial proposals in mind that I would like to suggest that in order to be able to conduct useful therapy with people presenting with these characteristics, one must be able to formulate an understanding of what I would call the precursors of 'meaning'. Particularly, one must be able to communicate with, and to relate to, unverbalized aspects of the psychic reality.

The role of environmental sensory provision

It is the environment's role to provide a sensorially 'good enough' continuum of stimuli so as to enable the infant to usefully organize them. The provision of congruent, 'good enough' stimuli may be defined by the individual's (infant's) capability to allostatically respond, rather than be overwhelmed by them. Alternatively, an incongruent stimuli pattern may cause the infant to become reactive rather than spontaneous in their gestural or vocal response, thereby compromising their own integrity. Since a true self is formed of an accumulation of spontaneous gestures and 'good enough' reciprocations, constituting a 'summation of sensori-motor aliveness' (Winnicott 1960: 149), overwhelming and incongruent interaction, typical of periods of stress or of developmental trauma, will be deleterious to development and functioning. In evoking primitive defensive strategies such as dissociation, these experiences will be 'split off' from the sense of emerging sensory-motor aliveness, thus rendering these interactions 'meaningless' to the 'true' aspects of the self.

It is suggested that the sensorially, bodily-based 'meaning-giving-function' follows Piaget's (1954) immortal model of cognitive development. Inherent in this model is the idea that the establishment of meaning entails a sensory reorganization, so as to facilitate a mode of accommodation that may enable integration. In 'infantile' psychic reality this implies a 'frantic search for an object – a light, a voice, a smell or other sensual object' (Bick 1968: 2) that will fulfil the organizing function. Inevitably, reorganization implies a change in homeostatic equilibrium, leading to perceived and real tension – in muscle tone, for example. Freud (1915b) proposed that the capacity to muscularly effect a distancing from a stimuli is the prototypical precursor for the cognitive perception of 'internal' and 'external'. Bick's contribution shows that the same may apply to the capacity to sensorially engage or disengage.

In trying to physically and sensorially reorganize, a period of tension ensues which is accompanied by a change in directionality of attention, so as to engage or disengage with the object, accommodate and sensorially resolve the tension. Since 'experiential perspective not only helps situate real objects but also helps situate ideas' (Damasio 2000: 145), shifts in perception inevitably result in conceptual change. The fact that concepts and cognitions are not intellectually defined but exist within a global contextual field has far-reaching clinical implications.

Touch is a good example: tissue structure in and surrounding a place that is touched undergoes change; it has a different structural organization than the one it had hitherto. At the same time, of course, it has other organizational impacts, since touch is always imbued with a context comprising sensational, emotional and cognitive correlates. In this way, actions which originally had a causal instinct-based pleasure-driven motivation become, *ipso facto*, 'object relational' actions which serve to fortify the emerging sense of 'meaningfulness' and capacities of 'organization'.

Since the experience of establishing 'meaning' and the constitution of the psychic structures that derive meaning from experience are environmentally dependent, it is implied that the ideal environmental or therapeutic provision is:

- *Attentive and non-imposing*: the energetic input must be attuned to the receiver's capacity to make use of it so as to avoid over-stimulation. On the other hand, it must carry far enough so as to reach beyond the 'borders' of sensory thresholds, in order to be usefully meaningful. An input is perceived as of organizational value if it allows one to use it with some freedom of choice and movement, in responsive and creative play, rather than in reaction to concrete, realistic demands.
- *Adequately fitting to the level of energy available to the receiver*: this necessitates that the receiver (patient) have available 'energy' at his or her disposal and assumes that the processing of the input is not energetically exhausting.

In pathological development, the piece of the conglomerate of experience that language relates to is so distant from the original experience that a cruel choice must be made at every juncture as to what aspect of reality conveys 'true' meaning – and which must be compromised or given up as 'false'. This will engender a situation, familiar to therapists attentive to bodily processes, in which some patients have a sense of leading a dual life: 'their original life as nonverbal experience, and a life as a verbalized version of that experience' (Stern 1985: 174). In the instance of 'good enough' sensory and cognitive provision, the global experience may remain as such, with language refining the capacity for the description thereof, thereby enriching and rendering the shared experience all the more meaningful. Hence the third attribute of environmental or therapeutic provision:

- *Simultaneous on a multi-faceted array of reality experiences*: i.e. bodily, energetic-sensational, emotional and cognitive. This is because the experience of communication on one level, coupled with a non-existent one in others, may be felt to be as traumatic as the total absence of meaningful communication.

The rationale for using the body as an object within the subjective field of psychodynamic psychotherapy

Using the body as an object within a psychodynamic context would seem to present an inherent contradiction. It defies the disparaging contention of the body as being a primitive residue of 'primary processes' and the exclusivity of a definition of psychoanalysis as an interaction that avoids any muscular effort and sensory input that may distract the mind from mental activity (Freud 1904). It seems to defy the ideals of abstinence and of professional integrity in the face of the temptation for 'need fulfillment' (Casement 1986).

However, some psychoanalytical theorists now attest to the fact that, in certain instances, apparently 'encapsulated' (McDougall 1989) somatic symptoms seem to defy the relational capability of the analyst using orthodox verbal technique. This necessitates a resort to 'techniques like damp packing . . . rhythmic rocking, body to body contact . . . and so on' (Anzieu 1990: 73). It is the budding understanding *within* some schools of psychoanalysis that psychoanalysis can no longer regard 'respiratory difficulties, intestinal rumblings and muscular contractions . . . as null' (Anzieu 1990: 68) that has led relationally-oriented psychoanalysts to perceive of a 'two body psychology' as an elaboration of, rather than as a contradiction to, a 'two person psychology' (Aron 1998: 14). The divergence from orthodox neutrality may thus be enriching: recognizing what is apparent and obvious through use of the senses, although not verbally transmitted, would seem to be an obvious contribution of body psychotherapy to the capacity described by Bion (1962b) as 'reverie'. Elaborating on the concept of 'reverie', Mitchell and Aron (1999) note the emphasis on what may seem irrelevant, mundane and trivial, as a gateway to the patient's internal world.

It has often been my experience that, through the function of 'reverie' I was able to notice physical aspects of appearance that patients have long held to be private and secret. One patient experienced a substantial shift in the ability to relate after I, rather naively, asked whether she had ever noticed a difference between the left and right sides of her face; another was moved by the close attention I paid to her narration of various nuances of physical pain in her foot.

Another point to be considered is that communication is a global function, which includes verbally explicit messages as well as projections (Heiman 1950), rhythmic oscillations (Hammer 1990) and enactments. Paying specific attention to verbal gestures seems to defy the demand from the therapist of providing a neutral, free-hovering type of attention (Freud 1900). In acknowledging that inducing the therapist to 'act in [a] predetermined way . . . may be the manner in which . . . a thematic isomorphism is created between the ordering of the [patient's] subjective and interpersonal fields' (Atwood and

Stolorow 1988: 92), enactments are redefined as acceptable communications. In this instance, being true to the requirement of neutrality seems to require a capability to make use of the countertransference evoked in and through a therapeutic rapport which includes sensory and physical transmissions.

The creation of meaning by the bodily precursors

The process in which meaning is created – and recreated in therapy – in and through the body, may be divided into the following three aspects:

1   The birth of the sensorial-bodily self, struggling with marginally bearable friction, the resolution of which involves attaining a nascent sense of direction and control of distance and space.
2   The structuring and formation of emotional and cognitive meanings through interactions that involve stimulation, tension and reorganization. 'Meaningful' resolutions are achieved through movements that 'mould' and shape the environment and through encounters with shapes that help define one's bodily contours and form.
3   The search for an attuned rhythmic fit, often involving anxiety and confusion, resolved by a sense of 'going on being' and a continuity in space and time.

These themes will be elaborated in the following pages.

The birth of the sensorial-bodily self: the experience of direction and the structure of space

The sensorial-bodily self is born in the fluid environment of the uterus, takes form through aggression directed at the uterine wall, and finds a meaningful resolution in the plunge, head first, through the birth canal, to the next phase in life. Patients' and therapists' accounts of altered consciousness experiences, the reconstruction of birth experiences in therapy, research as to the long-term effects of birth processes and myths relating to the passage through dire straits all point to the significance of passage through the 'narrow strait'. This may be seen as a prototype underlying life issues involving a sense of direction and directionality despite inevitable resistance and friction. A sense of resolution may often be experienced as 'the light at the end of the tunnel'.

Additionally, meaning is embedded in the embryo's movement from and towards the wall of the uterus, in what Winnicott saw as the prototype for aggressive movement (Issaroff 1989). This type of movement receives its organizational impetus from the level of tension in the uterus, which is determined, partially, by the mother's internal state: the uterus walls are highly responsive to both sympathetic arousal (Challis and Smith 2001) and to neuropeptidal stress indicators (Pennefather *et al.* 2004). The baby then carries on using this 'meaningful' experiential learning as a blueprint in initiating movement throughout the birth process, and later in life 'this pattern . . . becomes one of the templates that are placed onto each successive experience of contact' (Alhanati 2002: 133). The tension experienced in these interactions with the environment may serve as a blueprint for the amount of friction and tension sought in later interactions (Odent 2002) and its personal 'exegesis'.

Conversely, patients' experience of a failure in establishing a sense of direction is one of feeling stuck and immobile, claustrophobic – and being under unbearable pressure. In extreme cases, patients will describe these experiences as being akin to a feeling of a violent suffocation, a crushing of the body – experiences they may describe as a prescient experience of death.

In other instances, where urgency is not experienced, a sense of 'stupor' might indicate an internalized state of overwhelming stimulation, friction or stress. For some this will presumably represent a replication of a stupor experienced at an early developmental stage – at birth in some instances. The original meaning of the word stupor relates to a stuporous state, in which one may feel 'stupid' or 'stupefied' – dazed or amazed at a perceived gap between the experience of reality and one's capacity to contend with the experience (Ian-Paul 1997). The experiences patients may relate at this stage are ones of obscurity, fogginess and a loss of a sense of direction. They will demand that I verbally 'direct' them, that I provide strong and clear physical stimulation or, conversely, that I provide a protective, warm and enveloping environment. At this point in therapy verbal communications will not be comprehended, since they 'are not experienced by the patients as interpretations' (Balint 1984: 18), and if attempted will meet a barrier of 'dumbness' that may well feel like a mutually resonant experience shared by the therapeutic dyad.

One of my patients, an extremely intelligent and sensitive woman, frequently oscillated between two highly differentiated states. In what I see as a 'stuporous' state, she would wrap herself up in a blanket, her eyes shut fast, hearing but hardly able to comprehend anything other than sensorial or tactile messages. Alternatively, instances would arise in which, spontaneously, she would manoeuvre herself to meet my physical resistance. In these instances, I was manipulated to create such 'friction' that would streamline her movement. This resulted in a type of motion that had a clear 'forward' *direction*, displaying strength, clarity of purpose and physical expressiveness – allowing her an exit from an unbearable sense of stupor and verbal 'dumbness'. At times, the repetition of these sequences seemed to be crucial in establishing a significant and meaningful communication between us, and to be a prerequisite to the renewal of a normative mode of communication with the environment. She came to regard these enactments as significant steps in regaining a capacity to set her own goals, and direct herself towards them.

For other patients, friction and resistance are interpreted as constriction, whereas attribution of meaning is dependent on an experience of spaciousness. One patient suffered a sense of constriction and a 'loss of meaning' and of inspiration in moving from her home, in the open desert plain, to the city. She attributed this sense of loss to the lack of space. In therapy it emerged that this feeling resembled a feeling verging on 'unreality' and depersonalization, that habitually made its appearance each morning before her first bowel movement. The experiences of a lack of internal bodily space, the sensation of a constriction of movement in space, and the 'loss of meaning' were all felt to be part of the loss of a global-spiritual experience promoted by the 'boundless' desert plains. Initially many sessions were conducted wandering through the streets or sitting in a park. The working through in therapy (whilst roaming the streets and the parks) utilizing, interpreting and reflecting back the experience of a global physical-sensory-emotional Gestalt, gradually lent meaning to her life. Her morning bowel movement improved. She came to see a correlation between a sense of choice and freedom and a loosening of physical constrictions. The perceptual capacity came to include symbolical and ideational representations of spaciousness, which she added to the internal repertoire of 'meaningful' experience, originally limited to actions performed within a concrete physical space. Eventually, she was able to feel as comfortable in the clinic as in the outdoors and accommodations to the normative clinical setting declined.

The shaping of forms and of objects: providing meaning through touch and movement

Having looked at the contribution of the perceptions of 'direction' and of 'space' to the provision of meaning, we shall turn to look at two additional prototypical substrata in meaning formation. One is the process in which the body learns its own shape and boundaries; the other is the experience of physically, creatively, shaping one's environment. Through these sensorial experiences with objects, the earliest forms of organizing and organized experiences are formed (Ogden 1989).

In orthodox psychodynamic therapy, the boundaries within the therapeutic interaction may be felt to be frustratingly inflexible, as the therapist will not surrender to 'being shaped' by the patient. Alternatively, some patients experience the neutral tone of the interpretations, coupled with their weighty emotional inputs, as hard, penetrative objects acting on the skin and entering the viscera (Sella 2003). Insistence on 'neutral' verbal communication and blindness to the substrata of physical precursors of meaning may, paradoxically, encourage these patients to project, provoke and ultimately rely on nonverbal communication (Ryle 1994).

Creating the boundaries for containment of the bodily intima
The neonate entering the world is not dissimilar to 'an astronaut who has been shot out into outer space without a spacesuit' (Bick 1986: 66). In order to create a 'me not me' differentiation the neonate must experience touch in a way that will assist them in delineating the contours and boundaries of their own body, without carrying within them too much of an imprint of the 'toucher's' body. This point may need some clarification, because standard 'intake interviews' within conventional settings, that include allusions to touch and tactile experiences, are not specific and accurate enough. Often it is only through a careful study and a reconstruction of early experiences of attachment, in therapy, that we may learn whether early tactile stimulation and handling was adjusted and 'good enough' – or otherwise.

Many patients reconstruct and describe having been held and handled by hands which they – literally and figuratively – felt to have been cold. It is those sensations which serve as precursors for feelings and concepts of deprivation, longing and frustration (Ogden 1989).

Rather than give up the prospect of warmth, the body which forms itself in relation to the cold hands of the 'object' may well be moved to create warmth of its own accord. Thus we might meet patients who blush or experience flushes, who complain of persistent cold or heat, who use every opportunity to cuddle up, or to approach the French windows in order to steep in the sunrays. The thwarted need for a benign physical encounter may manifest in the constant 'rising of energy', causing sympathetic hyperarousal (Schore 2002), and manifesting as sensations of heat, heartburn, sickness or choking. In psychoanalytically-minded settings these symptoms easily lend themselves to a standard, but often erroneous, interpretation of 'somatic expressions of anger'. In my experience, these manifestations display, more often than not, the strivings of a body unwilling to resort to withdrawal and solitude – seeking encounter, 'expanding' so as to meet an external 'shape', a hand, an 'object'. It is in this manner of a frantic, unconscious search for 'shape' and 'form' that immunity is sought from the experience of 'a return to an unintegrated state' or 'falling forever' (Winnicott 1963) into 'an endless shapeless void' (Rosenfeld 1984).

Faced with a lack of an adequate 'shape' that will respond to touch and movement against which one's boundaries and form gradually define themselves and emerge, a constant demand for touch may be pertinent. 'Acting-out' does not in these instances represent a defective mental apparatus lacking in impulse control, but rather the way in which brittle individuals strive to 'sustain the structural cohesion and continuity of a . . . sense of self' (Atwood and Stolorow 1988: 94). Since the lack of physical contact is perceived by these patients to be tantamount to an invalidity of experience, their 'enactments' may indicate their experience of a suspension of the ability to deduce significant meaning from verbal 'signs'. The therapeutic dialogue will proliferate in descriptions of a 'lack of skin', a sensation of 'leaking' into the environment, loss of sensation in parts of the body and sensations of 'holes' or 'voids' in some parts of the body. These may take verbal form in the mantric, supposedly manipulative-demonstrative 'I cannot exist without you'. Declarations of this nature may signify that, in the patient's subjective experience at that time, all of the above sensations (dis-integration etc.) lie closely and ominously in wait, and will inevitably reappear with the withdrawal of the object's (therapist's; lover's) bodily presence.

At the other end of the spectrum lie those instances in which bodily boundaries are ruptured or impinged upon. Over-stimulation is registered as penetrative in a manner that constricts the sensory, skeleto-muscular and internal organ systems, leading to 'psychic deadness' (Eigen 1998). Autonomy and self-agency are compromised. Briggs (2002) describes the environment's misattunement in interactive function in these instances to be 'convex' – i.e. penetrative and invasive. This encourages the individual to prematurely designate his own boundaries, forming a 'bodily armour' (Reich), or a 'second skin' (Bick).

A patient with whom I conducted integrative, psychodynamic, body-oriented psychotherapy insisted that my manual manipulation be strong and penetrating. He described his only recent experience of 'vitality' to have been due to the employment of very strong pressure by a close family member on a particular point on his hand. In attempting to implement similar pressure, however, I found myself hesitant in imitating the manipulation, which, I felt, would cause him extreme pain. It was in delving into the frustration he felt regarding my refusal to 'give shape' to his body that he ultimately began learning of the assertive and aggressive manner in which his own body was 'given form' in his childhood. In continuing to seek this external environmental toughness that enabled him to 'feel' he embarked upon an extremely stressful and high-risk secret-service career (in lieu of the painful, penetrative handling). This perpetuated his experience of his body as a taut (but vital) and painful entity. It gave his life a sense of being meaningful and significant. When not intensely stimulated, he tended to experience both vegetative and self-deprecatory ideational depressive symptoms. Vigilantly walking through a hostile village raised his sensory threshold and general bodily tension to a range in which he could begin to register a sense of 'being alive'. It was from this sense that he derived the significance of his mission and his service.

Shaping the environment – a struggle for creativity

At the other end of the continuum lie those prototypical experiences in which the precursors of meaning are explored and discovered through self-agency in the shaping of the environment.

The ability to shape the environment is partially determined by the level of metabolic energy at one's disposal. Physique, muscular strength and coordination, upon which the ability to physically manipulate the close environment is dependent, form a significant depth structure, defining experience, perception and conception. These innate capabilities interact with the environment – the ability of the infant to 'correctly' manipulate the mother's nipple and body to his adapting needs is the psychodynamic prototype for this capacity (Winnicott 1953). A transitional capacity mediates the generalization of experience from the narrow prism of the manner in which one experiences and 'moulds' the physical shapes and surfaces in infancy to their function as templates of subjective conceptual reality. Similarly, Ogden (1989) proposes that the early sensations – such as softness – are much later associated with *ideas* such as protection, soothing and affection.

Winnicott (1958: 95) demonstrates this form of interaction in the following therapeutic vignette:

> A patient dug her nails into my hand at a moment of intense feeling. My interpretation was 'ow'. This scarcely involved my intellectual equipment at all, and it was quite useful because it came immediately (not after a pause for reflection), and because it meant to the patient that my hand was alive, that it was part of me, and that I was there to be used.

One of the most moving experiences I have had in my work was in therapy with a child suffering from perinatally-caused brain damage, who, at age 10, was a victim of peer abuse: children would bully and exploit him and then – supposedly in mutual play – painfully bend his arm. Try as he might, he was unable to affect this interaction in any way, since his own actions were ineffective. It took two hours of psychotherapy for me to teach him to effectively and *meaningfully* bend arms. His growing proficiency in the technique through which he could 'shape' his peers' arms, enabled him to creatively (and honestly) regard their invasive touch as 'mutual play'. For the first time in his life he was able to experience physical interaction in a social context as involving vitality and lightness – as well as the familiar avoidance and incomprehensibility. What had been experienced as impenetrable and alienating had been re-established as common ground for the creation of meaning through the newly-found efficacy and significance of his actions.

Attuned rhythmic fit – 'going on being' in space and time

Many patients seek to resolve a feeling of meaninglessness through the pursuit of a physical regimen – often accompanied by the practice of a spiritual discipline. The dual pursuit often represents an intuitive understanding of the close relationship between metabolic life-sustaining processes – the pulse, regular breathing etc. – and the ideational-spiritual capacity for sustaining a sense of regularity and continuity of existence (see Epstein 2001 for an elaboration of this theme). In this context, the tendency to regard the physical-meaning-giving aspects of existence as trivial in psychodynamic therapy may be detrimental to the very neutrality of empathic attention: when vital bodily rhythms form an essential part of the meaning-giving Gestalt, it is the therapist's job to focus on them in order to sustain the continuity of experience – i.e. imbue the therapeutic process with the longed-for meaning. The continuity of empathic attention is dependent on the ability of the therapist to be aware of (and in certain instances to participate in) the creation of a continuity of corporal experience. Acknowledgement, mirroring and interpretation may not suffice – as suggested by Anzieu (1990: 66): 'It is essential . . . that the interpretative function of the psychoanalyst . . . be preceded by the exercise of a presymbolic function, which ensures intersensorial connections and contact in the form of mental representations belonging to different registers (sensory, motor, rhythmic, postural, mimetic and emotional)'.

I became acutely aware of this through seeing a patient who, in addition to being a practising Jew, undertook extensive martial arts training. Very early on in the course of therapy he expressed frustration at the therapeutic endeavour, which he described as meaningless. Having sought therapy in order to help him experience continuity, he felt unable to form and retain imaginal 'pictures' of concrete experiences and of our interactions from one session to the next. For a duration of months in therapy he felt nothing to have been created or remembered. It was as if he were meeting me anew in each consecutive session.

His mood swings were extreme – oscillating between depletion and depression on the one hand and states of high excitation on the other, during which he experienced breathlessness, extreme restlessness and extreme muscular tension in the chest. During one session, a few months into therapy, he stood up and walked about the room in frustration. He sped up and down, exuding physical tension, occasionally coming up against the walls of the clinic with force. When I was moved to physically constrain the painful collision, the constraint evoked erratic arm and leg movements and shallow, rapid breathing, accompanied by a sensation of choking – all reminiscent of an infant in distress.

It was through a process of slow unravelling that I began to be able to decipher the communication encoded in the 'acting-out'. I learned to acknowledge the effect that his rhythmic transitions were having on my own vital functions. I also learned the usefulness of keeping a certain certitude of my own well-being, through the maintenance of regular respiration, monitoring of the pulse and attention to the ingestion of saliva. The care with which I attended to my autonomic vital functions seemed to aid him in containing the persecutory attacks on the self (projected onto the clinic walls and myself), gradually enabling him to establish an experience of 'going on being'. This, in turn, eventually allowed for the gradual accumulation of experience based upon image formation. At this stage he was able to consistently attribute meaning to his experience, and conceive of an ability to constructively make use of his internal world, in interacting with his environment.

The perception of a continuity of life from one moment to the next is in no way trivial. It is deeply dependent on the unconscious maintenance of rhythmic continuity, through the life-preserving functions of the hindbrain, and the rhythmic movements of the internal organs. It is the life-sustaining functions of the respiratory and vascular systems that form the basis of the experience that Bion terms 'linking' – the way in which things connect and interact coherently and continuously when unarrested by the invasive panic which Williams (1997) describes as the 'heart-stopping' moment, equating it with Bion's (1962b) 'nameless dread'.

It would seem that the frequent disruptions of rhythmicity in our age and culture (Sella 2003) are the motive force behind patients' struggle to re-establish – through rite, ritual, dance or spiritual commitment – the inter-action with cosmological and seasonal sequences that modulate the reciprocal resonance between the rhythms of the exterior and the interior. When – due to trauma, impingement, stress or cultural constraints – this resonant capacity is breached, we find ourselves trying to reconstruct the rhythmic 'precursors of meaning' in the clinic.

Conclusion

Psychoanalytic theory and psychodynamic therapy has come a long way since the days in which Freud expressed concerns that physical interventions would inevitably lead to 'petting parties' (letter to Ferenczi quoted in Jones 1955). Yet episodic contributions in the form of direct use of the body within psycho-analytical practice, such as Winnicott's (1949) participation in birth re-enactment have, for the most part, been regarded anecdotally. The recognition that 'memory traces may be preverbal . . . sensorimotor . . . nonmodal . . . and mostly somatic' (Krystal 1997: 146) has not to date been reflected within a theoretical framework committed to the assumption that 'words would lure bodies back' (Phillips 1995 quoted in Cornell 2003).

In this chapter it is suggested that, in gradually recognizing the organiza-tional attributes of 'somatic and visceral experiences . . . as well as organized motoric actions . . . that direct and integrate emotional life . . .' (Bucci 1997: 161), psychodynamic therapy now stands to compromise and reformulate some of its early assumptions. Within those new assumptions, internal reality and its associative verbal disclosure are no longer given absolute precedence over action, in the attribution of meaning within the therapeutic discourse (see Snelling 2001 for the underlying philosophical debate). This may have significant influence over the terminology and nosology of psychotherapeutic clinical discourse.

The fact that the concept of 'meaning' can no longer be exclusively relegated to verbal definitions and communications also has clinical and technical implications. Allowing the subjective communicative experience to override the 'objective' linguistic communication in the psychoanalytic encounter, Hammer relates: 'my mental posture, like my physical posture is not one of leaning forward to catch the clues . . . but of leaning back to let the mood come to me, to listen to the music behind the words' (1990: 99). Employing the concept of bodily signifiers and precursors may lend theoretical validity to techniques such as this – already intuitively implemented. In the light of this line of thinking, traditional axioms such as 'free hovering attention', meaningful communication and the implications of complete 'abstinence' may be re-evaluated.

Finally, I would suggest that, clinically, understanding and utilizing the concept of 'precursors of meaning' may enhance understanding of the global nature of experiences – such as 'loss of direction', 'friction', 'continuity' etc. In this way, some of the gaps between conceptualizations and applications of physical interventions in the 'body psychotherapies', and the abstention from using the body as an object in psychodynamic therapy, may be bridged.

7 'In my flesh I shall see god'
Jungian body psychotherapy

Gottfried Heuer

For my wife Birgit Heuer, with love, on the occasion of celebrating the 25th anniversary of our relationship.

There is only one temple in the world
and that is the human body.
Nothing is more sacred than that noble form.

(Novalis 1798)

Introduction

In this chapter I shall briefly describe the origins of the body/mind split in western philosophy, religion and culture, in order to contrast it with a new and alternative paradigm of body/mind unity. I shall argue that body became shadow as it renders us powerless *vis-à-vis* the vicissitudes of desire, ageing and death, and was split off from the higher-valued immaterial aspects of human experience. Thus excluded, that which is not becomes evil. This bias continues to flourish in analysis: in clinical practice the aim is to touch the soul – yet never the body. Here, I propose to bring the body back from the outer edges of experience, and re-enthrone it in its rightful place – married to self – at the very centre of experience: body as 'the stone which the builders rejected' (Matth. 21:42), that needs to become the cornerstone. My contribution considers the issue from a threefold perspective: the philosophical background in the history of ideas, the historiography of analysis, as well as the theoretical and clinical issues involved. The latter will include clinical vignettes as well as practical suggestions towards working with the body in the context of Jungian analysis.

The body/mind split

> And if the body were not the Soul, what is the Soul?
>
> (Whitman 1891)

In his contribution to 'the mind-body problem' in *The Oxford Companion to Philosophy*, Jaegwon Kim concludes: 'One thing that is certain is that the mind-body problem is one of the deepest puzzles in philosophy, and that it will continue to test our philosophical intelligence and imagination' (1995: 580). It is interesting to note that in this volume of over a thousand pages 'one of the deepest puzzles in philosophy' should deserve barely more that a single page.

For Kim, the problem starts with the Cartesian split, as if the concept of an alternative, of a healed split, were philosophically inconceivable. Yet, considered from a perspective outside of the dominant monoculture, we can see that this 'problem' is by no means inherent in nature but particular to culture, *our* culture. In a number of non-western cultures 'the notion that mind and body can be separate . . . is quite foreign' (Clarkson 2002: 3). Even our own culture did not start in that way: 'In Greek thought, soul and body were generally indivisible' (Hillman 1978: 207). The rupture in our cultural perspective seems to have started with Plato, as Antony Flew observed: '[t]he literature on the philosophical problems of body, mind, and death begins, effectively, with Plato' (1971: 3).

Knowledge and recognition of the unity of mind and matter, soul and body in western tradition could only exist underground, in the mystical traditions of the desert religions. To ensure that it stayed there, dissidents were persecuted – as for example Giordano Bruno (1548–1600), who 'explained in his *De Magia* that there was no soul without body, since by necessity soul is always embodied' (Samsonov 1995: 21). Bruno responded to the Catholic judges sentencing him to death: 'Your fear in pronouncing this sentence over me is probably greater than mine who is receiving it' (Schoppe 1600: 468). He was burnt at the stake in Rome in 1600. Clearly, the issue has both a spiritual as well as a political dimension.

It is almost as if the biblical Fall from Grace reflects a development that later culminated in Descartes' *'Cogito ergo sum'* (I think therefore I am) with its implicit denigration of the body: the beginning of knowledge seems automatically linked to shame and horror about our corporeality. Culture and nature are seen as at war with each other. Does 'eating from the fruit of knowledge' truly mean that we have to differentiate all we see into good and evil, as we tend to do with soul and body? Can there be no organic thinking, in the sense of a thinking that grows out of and is rooted within the body? It may just mean that it is usually too difficult for us to conceptualize a unity that embraces opposites.

How could the body/mind split have gained such prevalence? Where does it come from, this desire, in our perception, to split asunder what nature – or God – clearly has put together? Could it ultimately be a terror of closeness, of intimacy, a fear of bridging the gap of traumatic bodily separation at birth – or spiritual separation at conception, if we want to consider a spiritual dimension? Is that the reason that body and soul have to be kept apart?

In the growing awareness of a body/soul unity, Cartesian-structured language appears to severely limit what we are able to conceive of. Hence the sometimes convoluted and paradoxical language of mystics and alchemists. Thus, at present, I see no other way than speaking simultaneously of a psycho-physical unity on the one hand, and an ongoing continuous dialectical process between the two poles of this unity, between psyche and body, on the other. This reflects the struggle of consciousness, itself an aspect of our immaterial nature, to conceptualize the nature of a paradox.

It might be useful in this context to consider the nature of light. Christ's saying, 'thy whole body is full of light' (Luke 11:34) is at present confirmed by physical research (McTaggart 2003: 48–73). In spite of Aristotle's rule that two contradictory statements cannot function in the same system, physicists have to live with the paradox that sometimes light is observed as particles and at other times as waves. This means nothing less than that at present we seem unable to fathom the nature of light which somehow unites these opposites. What is the relationship between particles and waves? Can we imagine one of mutual influence? Einstein believed 'that the next stage of the development of theoretical physics would "bring us a theory that light can be interpreted as a kind of fusion of the wave and the emission particle theory" ' (Cooper 2000: 12). Clearly, what is needed is a new 'paradigm that looks upon psyche and soma as aspects of each other' (B. Heuer 1998: 93).

The body in analysis

> The reality of the body is not given
> But to be made real, to be realised.
>
> William Blake

Wilhelm Reich (1897–1957) brought the body into analysis. He discovered that the respiratory system regulates the expression of feelings and that repressed feelings are stored in the body by patterns of muscular tension that he called 'character armour'. Following Freud who, in 1894, had spoken of the existence of an energy 'which is spread over the memory traces of ideas some-what as an electrical charge is spread over the surface of the body' (1894: 75), Reich discovered a bio- or life-energy that he called 'orgone energy'. Aware of the political implications of his work, Reich partly identified with Giordano Bruno. He 'remains unique in combining all three perspectives – the "mental", the "bodily" or organismic, and the social – in one' (Wilson 1995: 24). Even before Reich had to flee Germany and before his books were burnt by the Nazis, he had been made an outcast by the psychoanalytic establishment. He was declared insane by his former colleagues and his books were no longer mentioned, as if, by tacit agreement, they had been struck off the official canon. In analytic literature, that ban largely lasts to this day (Heuer 2002). In 1934 Reich was expelled from the International Psychoanalytic Association because as a known anti-Fascist he was intolerable for an organization that was trying to make 'a deal with the devil' (Lothane 2001) in Germany and did not want to alienate the newly-elected Nazi party (Nitzschke 1999; Goggin and Goggin 2001). In the USA in the 1950s Reich was jailed for contempt of court because he maintained that scientific discoveries could not be judged by a court of law. His books were burnt again and he died in prison.

These violent reactions seem to indicate that with the body/mind split we are not just dealing with a philosophical issue. Could Reich's radical politics truly have been the only reason for such a powerful reaction? Although this has to be pure speculation, I wonder whether there was not another factor that played a role here: he saw body and soul as one, saying, 'It would be wrong to speak of the "transfer" of psychological concepts to the psychic sphere, for what we have in mind is not an analogy but a real identity: the unity of psychic and somatic function' (Reich [1945] 1972: 340). In his therapeutic work he refused to work with one half of that unity only. Was Reich's unpardonable sin that he demanded a return of the repressed by introducing the body into psychoanalysis and discovering ways to successfully work with the organismic basis of the psyche?

It is highly ironic that just months after Reich's expulsion from the Psychoanalytic Association in 1934, Freud should have said to one of his patients, 'Analysis is not everything . . . So long as the organic factors remain inaccessible, psycho-analysis leaves much to be desired' (Wortis 1963: 111).

In the years since Reich's expulsion, mere tentative inroads have been made towards including bodily aspects into psychoanalysis and his pioneering work remains unacknowledged there. Examples include Margaret Little's description of Winnicott holding her head during analysis (Little 1985: 20), Theodore Jacobs' work (e.g. 1973, 1994), and Guy da Silva's 'Borborygmi as markers of psychic work during the analytic session' (da Silva 1990) – the latter a remarkable parallel development to Gerda Boyesen's neo-Reichian work of *Biodynamic Psychotherapy* (cf. Boyesen 1987; Boyesen *et al.* 1980, 1995; Boyesen and Bergholz 2003) that she developed from the mid-1960s onwards in London.

In the development of analytical psychology, there is no comparable practical engagement with the body in clinical terms, except in Jung's association experiments in the early 1900s in which bodily reactions to words were measured, a concept that ultimately contributed to the development of the lie detector. Jungian psychology seems marked by a theoretical ambivalence towards the body, whilst mostly ignoring it clinically. Jung himself, for most of the second part of his life, immersed himself in the hermetic countercultural traditions of alchemy. From these studies, Jung developed some of his most important theoretical and clinical contributions – I am thinking here of his *The Psychology of the Transference* (1945), his concept of the psychoid, the subtle body, synchronicity, the ultraviolet/infrared spectrum from energy to matter, *et al.* All of these are only thinkable from the assumption of a basic interconnectedness of body and mind, matter and spirit. 'Indeed', writes Birgit Heuer, 'the deeper one delves into classical Jungian theory, the more it appears that body and being already have an intrinsic place within it, ready-made and waiting to be more explicitly developed' (1998: 96).

One central goal of the alchemists in their work was the discovery and/or creation of the Philosopher's Stone, a paradoxical, mystical marriage of opposites, a *coniunctio oppositorum* in a *mysterium coniunctionis*. In the rich symbolic imagery of alchemy, this has often been depicted as the union of male and female. The alchemists projected their own difficulties with this into the nature of the process itself and spoke of it as being an *opus contra naturam*, a work against nature (Samuels *et al.* 1986: 78). Jung adopted this thought for his psychology of the individuation process, revealing a rather antagonistic attitude towards nature: what other concept of nature would regard a maturational process of coming into one's own as being against nature? This negative take on nature with intent to divide and conquer is a war that cannot be won.

From alchemical woodcuts, Jung abstracted his famous diagram of dialectical relating (1945: 221) (see Figure 7.1). Jung himself and analytical psychologists may well understand this diagram primarily in terms of the relations between conscious and unconscious, interpersonally as well as intrapersonally. Yet, especially if we remember the alchemical concern with

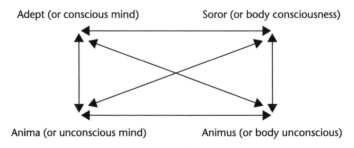

Figure 7.1 Jung's diagram of dialectical relating

soul and matter, as well as Jung speaking in this context of two *substances* coming together, a process in which both are affected towards change, then this diagram contains a further dimension of relating, that of corporeality: it can be understood not only in external terms as the marriage of the above with the below, but also internally as that of mind with flesh, soul with body. (I have added my own terms relating to this perspective in brackets on the diagram.)

Yet Jung himself remained highly ambivalent about this dimension, going as far – in the same text – as finding a caveat necessary for his readers when, in the series of woodcuts illustrating the alchemical opus, it comes to the consummation of said *coniunctio* in the flesh, i.e. of graphic depictions of a couple making love. In his commentary, Jung (1945: 250) warns: 'As to the frank eroticism of the pictures, I must remind the reader that they were drawn for medieval eyes and that consequently they have a symbolic rather than a pornographic meaning'. This is an almost grotesque leap into surrealism, reminiscent of Magritte's mid-1920's painting of a pipe with the caption '*Ceci n'est pas une pipe*' ('This is not a pipe')! Are we truly to understand from Jung's comment that there is no alternative other than that between the symbolic and the pornographic? Sadly, that would hardly leave any space for bodily erotic pleasure in loving union. Just as Freud, Jung saw culture as opposed to nature and sexuality.

In the development of analytical psychology, opportunities to truly heal the body/mind split in the sense of actually including the body and its functions into clinical considerations were mostly missed: Jung's encounter with Otto Gross, who saw that 'each psychical process is at the same time a physiological one' (Gross 1907: 7) ended acrimoniously (Heuer 2004). Jung seems to have taken no notice of Wilhelm Reich's work. Both Gross and Reich after him envisioned a culture not at odds with nature and sexuality. Just as Jung dismissed Gross as schizophrenic and ignored Reich, the post-Jungians have only rarely engaged with the body in their theoretical and clinical work and mostly continue to dismiss Reich, who was alluded to as a 'crackpot' by the keynote speaker of the most recent large international congress of Jungian analysts (Hillman 2004: 6). Some exceptions to this rule are Bosanquet (1970), Mindell (1998), Ware (1984), Conger (1988, 1994), Greene (1984, 2001), McNeely (1987), Wiener (1994) and Wyman-McGinty (1998). But in terms of any broader influence and/or an acceptance of working clinically with the body, these authors remain voices in the wilderness.

Only in a few areas of (post-)Jungian theory, the body/mind split appears as healed. Clinically, body is sometimes being seen as a vehicle for expressing the vicissitudes of soul – but is body ever considered as the primary agent in this supposedly dialectical relationship that forms the unity? Can soul be changed by body? In clinical practice there seems to be a clear bias for psyche and against physis.

In recent years, dance and movement therapeutic work has become somewhat accepted by (post-)Jungians. Other Jungian authors have written of psychosomatic concerns and linked Jungian psychology with homeopathy and neuroscience. Although these endeavours certainly have to be welcomed as indeed focusing on the body, it needs to be noted that (neo-)Reichian body psychotherapy, in its working directly with touch, focusing on specific areas of the body, is taking place in a completely different dimension of immediate corporeality.

From theory to clinical practice

> I know that touching was and still is and always will be the true revolution.
> (Nikki Giovanni in Montague 1986: XIII)

Under the present paradigm in contemporary clinical practice, biodynamics and psychodynamics – working with the body and working with the transference – seem mutually exclusive: clinicians either work bodytherapeutically – and not with the transference – or psychodynamically – and then not with the body. The two rarely meet. The erroneous assumption of even an incompatability of simultaneously working with the body as well as with the transference has recently been explicitly stated by Ray Holland (2004: 11). So the quest is on for a *coniunctio* of the two sides as the Philosopher's Stone of cutting edge clinical practice. I shall suggest a paradigm shift by exploring ways in which the two can indeed be married not just in theory but also in the clinical practice of working both psychodynamically (i.e. with transference and countertransference), and biodynamically (i.e. directly with the body). Eckart Tolle states, 'in the end you will always have to return to the body, where the essential work of transformation takes place. Transformation is *through* the body and not away from it' (1999: 98).

Considering that 'words account for as little as 7% of the perceived message' (James in Ukairo 2004) a *cure* exclusively relying on *talking* is an impossible endeavour indeed. 'The one-dimensionality of the word becomes a substitute for the richness of the multidimensionality of the senses, and our world grows crass, flat and arid in consequence', Ashley Montague writes in the preface to his authoritative book *Touching* (1986: xiii). The way I work with the body in analysis is an attempt to bring the other 93 per cent into conscious awareness, to bridge the gap between unconscious perception and conscious understanding.

In my clinical practice, the 'one-dimensionality of the word' does indeed get 'enriched by the multidimensionality of the senses' that represent 'the organic factors' that Freud found so sorely missing in analysis. In other words, feelings and their expression are a central focus of my work. *Everything* that happens in the session has an emotional dimension. And feelings are either expressed or blocked by the body. Thus 'the organic factors' do become comparatively easily accessible by paying attention to and working with the body – both my own as well as that of the patient. There are three ways of giving the body its due: attention, permission and invitation to move, and touch.

Where in a dream lies the strongest emotional charge? What is the emotional content of what is being said? Is the facial expression congruent with what is being said? What is the body posture, what are the movements and gestures as we speak? Are there any impulses visible towards a stronger movement that might be amplified? For this attention I need to be aware of my own responses of feeling and sensation.

In the traditional setting, the Freudian analysts largely deprive themselves of the visual: from the perspective at the head of the couch, behind and above the patient, not much of the facial features can possibly be adequately observed. Ethologists put a great importance on bonobo monkeys' face-to-face love-making in terms of how close to humans this gazing into each other's eyes makes them appear to be (Blackledge 2004: photos and caption facing p. 179). The king and queen of the *Rosarium*, the alchemical series of woodcuts upon which Jung based his pioneering work on transference and intersubjectivity, are always looking into each others' eyes, whether standing opposite each other or making love. Freud has stated that in analysis, 'essentially, . . . the cure is effected by love' (Freud and Jung 1974: 12–13). How can such a cure be possible when the participants are deprived of looking into each other's eyes? Allan Schore has demonstrated how the gazing into each other's eyes between mother and baby patterns the infant's brain by the baby using its mother's brain as a template (1994, 2000). If psychotherapy/-analysis is attending to or analysing soul – Hillman speaks of 'soul-making' – then the eyes of both therapist and patient as windows of the soul, as fundamental possibilities for contact from soul to soul, are vital bodily organs for our work.

A frequent argument against working with emotional expression is that in a rather restricted way it is regarded as acting-out. But, actually, there is a great difference between the unconscious expression of a feeling in acting-out and its consciously intentional expression in enactment. Here are two examples.

A patient comes late to his session because he lost time looking for his mislaid car keys. When I interpret this as an attack on our work, an unconsciously having been angry and not wanting to be in the session, he explodes with the anger that I understand was already there before he left home. His misplacing the keys can be understood as an acting-out.

A patient tells me in a neutral voice that she feels like killing me. I respond by asking, 'Can you say this in such a way that I can believe you?' After a brief pause, she yells at me with such force that it literally makes me jump in my chair. I understand and acknowledge this as an important cathartic enactment of held-back feelings.

Intention, context and witnessing play an important role in working with the body in analysis. There is a huge difference between a patient punching a pillow that in this moment represents a parent and someone punching a punching bag during a workout: the former can be an important part of dealing with a long held-in rage, the latter may amount to nothing more than a letting off of steam. If the punching of the pillow in the session is not verbally and intellectually integrated, it may remain mechanistic too, and there is a danger of the activity deteriorating into a meaningless ritual that can be repeated *ad infinitum*. There is also a considerable difference between the secret expression of a feeling and the shared or witnessed one. In terms of the adequate dealing with a feeling – and that includes respecting and honouring it – it is almost as if a feeling expressed in secret or isolation has not been expressed at all, as in the riddle of the tree that falls in the forest: if no one hears it falling, is there a noise? I understand this in relation to interpersonal and intrapersonal communication: almost as if what I cannot express in relation to another I cannot truly own myself either. Wyman-McGinty (1998: 252, 256) compares

> witnessing . . . with . . . aspects of the mirroring relationship inherent in the infant-mother dyad, in which the mother is able, through words and bodily responses, to communicate to the infant an understanding of his [or her] internal world at a bodily level . . . essential for the establishment of a secure body image and growing sense of identity

I work with what I call *negotiated touch*. This means that when appropriate, I may suggest touch to the patient, for example in order to further the expression of an emotion, and I am asking permission to do so. Afterwards, we discuss what feelings and thoughts my touch has brought up. Such negotiation can most fruitfully continue over time. Here is an example.

In her initial session, a patient who has heard that I am a trained body psychotherapist as well as a Jungian analyst, asks me to confirm the former. When I do and ask why she wanted to know, she replies that it was important for her to know that bodywork including touch was a possibility in our work. Yet, when in connection with separating for a break the issue of shaking hands in saying goodbye came up, she expressed fears that such touching might easily lead to sexual abuse. We were able to explore the mixture of fear and desire that led to a phantasy like that and our work has continued for years since then. We have never shaken hands nor has there been any other kind of touch, yet from time to time we refer back to this exchange and the feelings involved. I understand this as continuing work on this issue that is being negotiated both internally as well as externally between us in the transference/ countertransference relationship.

Among practitioners of the 'talking cure', there are two great fears in particular that surround touch. Both seem rooted in the puritanical culture produced by the body/mind split that also pervades the helping professions. These are first that touch unleashes elementary forces in both analyst and patient that then may prove impossible to control, and, linked with this, that touch may be experienced as gratification.

The first fear seems to assume that abuse is first and foremost of a physical nature and only secondarily is it verbal or emotional. Although this is a very complex question, in my view the decisive element is to do with intention, conscious or unconscious, rather than how that intention manifests. If we are that uncertain about our intentions, we may need to ask ourselves whether it is safe at all for another person, irrespective of their gender, to be alone in the same room with us. But just as it is possible to speak about sexual intimacies without that unavoidably leading to intercourse, it is, in my view, equally possible to touch in ways that are experienced as helpful rather than as a breaking of sexual boundaries and constituting abuse.

As to the other fear, that of gratification: why should touch raise the degree of gratification to intolerable levels when we gratify our patients anyway by giving them our fullest possible undivided attention in the session, something they may never have had before? Again, if we wanted to avoid gratification at all costs, maybe we should not work therapeutically at all, as working towards healing is always gratifying, even when painful. Certainly, deprivation needs to come into the transference/countertransference relationship. Yet the view often seems to be that it has to be an either/or, as if inviting deprivation into the therapeutic relationship completely excludes gratification. In my view it is possible to work in such a way that there is time and space to consciously include both.

Bodywork can also become an important and reliable tool in supervision. Here also I am paying close attention to the feeling aspects of voice, facial expression, gestures and body posture of my supervisee, trusting that consciously as well as unconsciously in a form of parallel process the body of the supervisee can be understood as the carrier of the emotional expressions of the patient we are discussing. So I may say, in response to my supervisee directly quoting a key sentence their patient has said, 'Content-wise, the words were quite friendly, but the tone of voice and the facial expression with which your patient – i.e. you in this moment – spoke them suggest an entirely different feeling.' My supervisee confirms that, at the time, he has observed the very same discrepancy in his patient. Here is another example.

A supervisee speaks of an injury her patient has suffered on his hand. In terms of a different right-hand/left-hand symbolism I ask, 'Which hand did he injure? The right one or the left one?' My supervisee does not remember. But I have seen her left arm and hand make a small movement as if frightened or startled. I voice this observation, saying, 'My guess is that it was the left hand.' In the next session, my supervisee confirms this.

There are three direct and practical ways in which even an analyst/ therapist untrained in body psychotherapy can start to include the body in their work even if not by way of touch: breathing, movement and peristalsis.

Reich discovered the link between *breathing* and emotional expression: no breathing, no expression. This is why we immediately take an inbreath and hold it when we get hurt. We irrationally hope not to have to feel. I say irrationally, because in actual fact the pain is held together with the breath. It is, for example, easier to tolerate pain during a dental treatment if we can continue to breathe deeply. In therapy, when I see a patient close to tears, then catching their breath and hold it, I gently suggest, 'Breathe.'

Movement can mean both gestures and movement of the whole body. Traditionally, gestures are understood as underlying/illustrating the spoken word. Actually, recent research has discovered that the relationship between speech and gestures is a much more complicated one: gestures can help us to find words in the first place (Begley 1998; McGinnis 2002). It is as if, in part, the body knows first, then helps us to find the appropriate word. Also, gestures and movement can help with the expression of feelings, especially when I invite the patient to amplify either. Here are some examples.

I may see a patient speaking in anger and reaching for his neck. I ask, 'What's happening there?' 'I've got such a pain there.' 'Who is a pain in the neck right now?' In this way, the physical symptom may lead both to a discovery in consciousness as well as a cathartic abreaction when I ask, 'How does this anger want to be expressed towards the person who is a pain in the neck?'

A patient may be clenching her fists whilst speaking in anger. I may ask, 'What is it that your hands want to do?' This may lead to me inviting her to punch a pillow.

Movement may also mean movement in the consulting room. A patient has dreamt, 'I am standing there very rigidly in the middle of this clearing in the woods.' I may respond by asking, 'Do you feel like standing just like that here in the room?' This will lead to a more immediate re-experiencing of the dream situation in which the feelings are included as well. Richer associations both in words and images may be possible.

In a patient grieving for a parent that has died many years ago, I see small movements in both arms that may indicate impulses of expressing loving and longing. After having enquired in a low voice – almost as in an aside – whether this might be appropriate, I offer a large pillow to let the patient's hands explore by direct touch what her arms and hands might want to do. This leads to gentle stroking of, then embracing of, the whole pillow. This triggers a flood of tears, uncried for decades.

Peristalsis is the movement of the digestive tract to transport its contents. These movements produce peristaltic noises, called 'borborygmi' in medical language, 'tummy talk' in everyday language. Neo-Reichian body psychotherapist Gerda Boyesen's pioneering discovery is of a direct link between muscular tensions that store repressed feelings and peristaltic movements: each release of a muscular tension is echoed by a peristaltic movement. On this basis, Boyesen has developed a series of massages that are continuously monitored by stethoscope and thus allow the reception of a (bio-)feedback directly from the organismic core of the body in the form of peristaltic noises. The digestion of feelings and thoughts that we may metaphorically refer to is thus intimately linked with a bodily basis. Independent from Boyesen, yet much later, as well as independent from each other, two psychoanalysts, da Silva and Freeman, have tentatively thought in a similar direction. More recently, Boyesen's findings have been confirmed by the research of Michael Gershon, who discovered what he calls 'a second brain' in the bowels that for our well-being needs to be in harmony with the brain in our head (Gershon 1999; for the parallels with Boyesen's work see Bartuska 2001, 2002).

Correspondingly, in the analytic session I understand peristaltic noises from the patient as a spontaneous commentary or feedback relating to what is happening. Sometimes they occur as if in response to an interpretation I have offered – in which case I regard them as bodily confirmation. At other times they may occur right after the patient has spoken – in which case for me they are an organismic emphasis, underlining the importance of what has been said. In silences these noises help me to understand the silence: when they occur, I feel I can rest assured that this particular silence is one needed for digestion – as opposed to, for instance, one of passive aggression. In the latter instance, there will be no psychoperistalsis, until some of these feelings are expressed. It has also happened that a psychoperistaltic dialogue has occurred: noises in my body have been responded to by those from the patient and vice versa. In such a situation, I feel that words would only be an obstacle to the dialogue happening on a deeper corporeal level, although, of course, after a 'conversation' of that kind, we may need to try to understand and integrate intellectually what has happened.

Another form of dialogue can unconsciously happen on a bodily level via gestures, movements and, once removed, so to speak, via clothes: I may notice my patient repeat a gesture or movement of mine like, for example, scratching the back of my head or crossing or uncrossing my legs, or I may find myself unconsciously imitating my patient in such a way. What does this mean in terms of the transference feelings we have for each other in that moment? Can they be brought into consciousness in order to understand and integrate them? Or I may notice that a patient wears clothes or a piece of clothing similar in style or colour to what I am wearing, or have worn in a previous session. Or, conversely, I observe an impulse, for example, to wear clothes that match the colours my patient has worn in the previous session. What does that say about my countertransference to them?

Conclusion

Starting with some observations of attitudes towards the body and the resulting body/mind split in western culture, in this contribution I have briefly sketched the corresponding history of the body in analysis in order to argue for a paradigm shift in therapeutic work to include the body so that a holistic healing towards a body/mind unity can take place. I have offered a description of how I work with the body in my clinical practice as a Jungian training analyst and have concluded with some examples of how the body can begin to be clinically integrated into the analytic and therapeutic work of colleagues who have not yet had a training in body psychotherapy. Restriction of space has only allowed me to hint at the political and religious dimensions that are both deeply involved in as well as affected by such a shift. For me, psychotherapeutic concern for the body and the urgent necessity of reclaiming it for analysis is the matter that matters most, as the body itself is not simply the matter closest to us but the matter that, in fact, we *are*!

Acknowledgements

I would like to thank my wife and colleague Birgit Heuer for inspiration and support, Gerda Boyesen for suggesting 30 years ago that I might consider becoming a therapist, and friends and colleagues Monika Schaible, Jochen Encke, Jan-Floris van der Wateren, Richard Wainwright, Diane Harris and Dr Keven Hall for our discussions that I have greatly enjoyed.

8 Developmental Somatic Psychotherapy

Developmental process embodied within the clinical moment

Ruella Frank

Introduction

In contributing to *New Dimensions in Body Psychotherapy*, I am pleased to be part of a project that brings together diverse and novel explorations within the field of psychotherapy. A prerequisite for any work to be labelled a new dimension is that *new* parts have been integrated into what is already known in such a way as to create a different and unique whole.

This is certainly true of Developmental Somatic Psychotherapy. Inspired by the work of somatic/developmental practitioners and theorists, this new dimension is a relational and movement-oriented approach to psychotherapy within a Gestalt therapy framework. In pulling together these dynamic strands, a template for understanding and working with early psychophysical blocks as they arise within the here and now of the adult therapy session has emerged.

In any process-oriented, present-centred therapy, embodying developmental theory within a session must be firmly grounded in the data of experience, the world of phenomena – what we see, what we hear, what we sense and what we feel. What was *then and there* is an abstraction or cognitive construct and can offer relevant and viable information only if observed in the *here and now* of therapy. Developmental Somatic Psychotherapy provides a comprehensive system of phenomenological analysis for practitioners to diagnose and treat their clients through explorations in developmental movement patterns. Simply put, it is a new way of observing and working with the unfolding, moment-to-moment unspoken dialogue of therapy. It is only by understanding *how* early experiences arise through a variety of phenomena within the client/therapist relationship that we gain access to them.

Developmental Somatic Psychotherapy is not only an expansion of Gestalt therapy – a novel approach within its theory and practice – but also can be quite usefully combined with other psychotherapy models, even those which do not attend to movement processes. It offers a framework for understanding clients' preverbal experiences that are often overlooked or misunderstood and left unattended. Thus, existential issues with roots in early life surface with great immediacy. These issues would not emerge as easily, if at all, in other psychotherapies. Fleshing out the greater background from which present behaviours arise enhances the narrative developing within each session, as well as throughout the course of therapy.

Developmental roots

The origin of my work is in the mid-1970s, when I was introduced to Bonnie Bainbridge Cohen. An occupational therapist with a background in dance and movement, Cohen spent years studying and working with developmentally delayed infants. Her keen eye for movement analysis led to unique observations of infant patterns. She then applied her observations to their treatment. Knowing that early infant movements also underlie movement possibilities for adults, Bonnie taught her work to dancers and movement therapists, analysing and working with their movement patterns to provide integration and balanced alignment (Cohen 1993).

At the time, I was teaching dance and developing a private practice in movement therapy. I was so intrigued with developmental movement that I taught the patterns to my students and private clients, many of whom were Gestalt psychotherapists. They were equally fascinated and reported a variety of changes in their emotional, physical and psychological states that were difficult for them to verbalize. Interested and encouraged by their reactions, and wanting to make further sense of what was happening, I enrolled in a Gestalt training programme. From what I had read and from my personal experience as a client in Gestalt therapy, I believed its holistic approach and use of experiment would enable an almost seamless inclusion of infant developmental patterns within its practice. My intention was to integrate developmental patterns within the psychotherapy session as a means to facilitate insight and change.

After my four years of training were completed, I continued my studies with Laura Perls, co-founder of Gestalt therapy, along with her husband Fritz Perls and Paul Goodman (Perls *et al.* 1951). In Laura's weekly group, we focused on the central and unifying concept of Gestalt therapy theory: contacting – the quality of being in touch with ourselves and our environment. Laura taught that the processes of contacting were primarily and fundamentally supported by coordinated movements (Perls 1993). Contacting could not occur without accompanying sensorimotor support. The quality of sensorimotor support influences the quality of contact and vice versa. Both exist simultaneously and are the essential structure of experience. This was my

'Aha!' moment. I now understood that infant developmental patterns, which underlie all possible movement, are also primary supports for contacting.

In the 1980s, Daniel Stern (1985) and many other researchers and theorists brilliantly observed parent-infant interactions in detail. Whereas former psychoanalytic thinking described infant development in discrete stages, these researchers described the emergence of self as a co-creation – a relational event occurring throughout the course of a lifetime. The organizing self arises in overlapping waves and is dynamic. Past continually interacts with present, shaping and being shaped by it. This process-oriented approach supported Gestalt therapy's original assertion that self is the interaction of individual and environment in ongoing sequences of creative adjustment, that self is, in fact, co-created by individual and environment.

Almost a decade later, another important piece came together as I discovered the work of Esther Thelen, a motor-developmental psychologist (Thelen and Smith 1993). Thelen challenged a former understanding that had dominated the field since the 1950s – that infant movement patterns were a product of brain development alone – a genetically-driven perspective. Creating elegant infant experiments, she demonstrated that early movements arise in relation to the environment – gravity, earth and space – as well as the infant's biomechanical potential, and physiology in relation to tasks the infant was exploring and accomplishing. The brain was one of many subsystems that contributed to these developing patterns, no one more important than any other. Thelen believed that infant patterns of perception and action – developmental patterns – were fundamental to the evolution of the childs's mental and social life. From this, I added that the tasks infants explore and accomplish are generally in relation to their primary caregivers and through such dynamic interaction patterns the infant's *body* takes shape – breathing, gesture, posture and gait – reflecting and expressing that relationship.

My work since then has expanded Laura Perls' (1993) concept of sensorimotor support within the client-therapist field with a new emphasis on its developmental roots within the infant-caregiver dyad. Based on the findings of a variety of contemporary researchers, I elaborated the theoretical basis for support from a developmental and relational perspective and have explored its relevance within the client-therapist field. A new approach for psychotherapy emerged, an approach rooted in human development, attending to actual phenomena and drawing on the richness of direct experience: Developmental Somatic Psychotherapy.

It is impossible to go into a detailed explanation of Developmental Somatic Psychotherapy within the confines of these pages, yet this chapter may give the reader some idea of its primary concepts and theoretical underpinnings. The case study at the chapter's end demonstrates theory into action. (For further information please see Frank 2001.)

Developmental movements: primary patterns of response

If you carefully observe an infant and caregiver relationship, you see the grace-ful and fluid emerging of ongoing nonverbal interaction. Subtly, yet power-fully, each partner influences the other so that every exchange builds upon that which has occurred just moments before. Patterns of movement begin to form from these creative, spontaneous connections. Each pattern that develops *between* the partners has its own unique rhythm and style, a kind of improvised dance, reflecting the nature of every interaction. There are as many varied rhythms and styles of movement pattern, as many dances, as there are different relationships.

Developmental patterns are seen most clearly in a variety of transitions in functioning – sucking to chewing, grasping to releasing, sitting to creeping on all fours, toddling to walking. They organize within the daily tasks of caring for an infant: carrying them from one place to another, feeding, hugging, rocking, changing nappies, playing with etc. Such fundamental exchanges between baby and caregiver contribute to the physiology of the infant and manifest in his or her individual pattern of breathing, gesture, posture and gait. And because movement patterns are social by nature – meaning that they emerge in relation to one another – they accompany the infant's evolving psycho-social experience. Every developmental pattern that emerges, therefore, is a primary response within the relational field and expresses a dominant need at the time of its emergence. *The infant's developing psychological functioning is experienced and expressed through movement.*

Movement patterns form in overlapping sequences throughout develop-ment. Earlier patterns do not appear, then disappear, but rather serve as sup-ports for later patterns to surface. One pattern integrates another, creating larger and larger supporting structures contributing to the whole experience. The earlier pattern remains, therefore, part of later and more highly organized experiential processes – sucking provides the foundation for chewing while crawling underlies and supports walking. What came before provides the background for what is next to come. In this way, each developing movement appropriates the structure or internal coherence of the earlier pattern, as well as lending its structure to the forming of the next. Because the infant (and adult) can move from chewing to sucking or walking to crawling at any given moment, background patterns continue to be available and ready for use.

Spontaneously emerging movement patterns become essential supports for contacting and are integrated into the developing nervous system – the quality of being in touch with one's body (me) and the environment (not me). Contacting is not possible without underlying sensorimotor support, and the sensorimotor system functions only in contacting. They are an indivisible unity. Throughout the process of early development, a newly organizing experience of self – including the differentiation of me and not me – gradually comes into being through movement. It cannot be otherwise.

Patterns take their own form and shape through rhythms emerging over time. Rhythms are seen in the visible changes in bodily tensions (Kestenberg-Amighi *et al.* 1999: 24) as the infant (or adult) moves, and are heard through changes in breath and patterns of speech. Individual rhythms articulate patterns as they develop dynamically within the relational field. Rhythmic patterns that arise between infant and caregiver create emotions as well as characterize them.

We can look at an infant's developing rhythm and style of moving and learn about their contacting style or how they organize experience. We are able to see their preferences for either high or low intensity of stimulation; how they will live through and express their emotions, how their emotions are sustained and how they dissipate; how the infant will move toward or away from that which they prefer or do not prefer; their sense of personal space, their preference for relational space; and the energetics (the flow and quality of outward moving energy) they use in relation to the task they perform.

Fluid functioning and patterns of disruption

When the relationship between infant and caregiver is well matched, such that each partner is sufficiently met often enough, movement patterns emerge as graceful and fluid. This does not mean that every infant and caregiver dialogue goes smoothly. Times of difficult adjustments are vitally important in allowing both parties a function in co-creating their relationship. For the infant, especially, these moments of discomfort provide the opportunity to exercise newly-developing functions. This may be learning to tolerate a moderate amount of frustration and accompanying anxiety. The infant also learns something about how to signal their needs most effectively to another and how to cope when they are not met. The caregiver gains similar skills and learns to tolerate their own levels of frustration and anxiety in adapting to the infant. For both parties, these mildly difficult adjustments are an essential aspect of learning, so necessary to the process of growing.

When too many difficulties occur within the relationship and neither partner is satisfied enough of the time, the infant's emerging movement patterns begin to demonstrate anxious, troublesome disruptions. They appear awkward and less effective in achieving the task at hand. Even in the seemingly simple patterns, for example, rolling from back to belly, the infant cannot easily find the coordination between one part of their body and the other, and in relationship to the environment. The patterns that emerge during these chronically difficult encounters disrupt the infant's maturing neuromuscular system and inhibit their capacity to be in touch with their body and the environment. When the infant-caregiver field does not sufficiently mature over time, the inharmonious patterns that develop overpower the infant's newly-emerging and highly sensitive system.

Because all patterns are supports for one another, the disrupted pattern comes to dominate the preceding pattern, and influences subsequently emerging patterns. The impediments to movement echo at every level of functioning as contacting episodes emerge without sufficient support. This can appear as diminishing sensory experience, repressing and displacing of affect, inability to regulate emotions, distortion in perception and difficulty in organizing meaning.

Developmental patterns and the adult therapy client

Looking – once more – at Laura Perls' (1993) notion that sensorimotor supports (or coordinated movements) underlie contacting, it becomes clear how rhythmic patterns organize within the infant-caregiver dyad. Patterns provide flexibility for creative adjusting over time. Similarly, we see how patterns organize in chronic disruptive infant-caregiver fields and produce inhibition and fixation.

Developmental patterns are the foundation for all possibilities of movement, and form not only the body of the infant but are also present in the structure of adult experience. Watching adults move, therefore, gives us much the same information as to their adult organizing capacities as directly observing infants gives us knowledge about theirs. In fact, with a thorough understanding of how infants develop through movement, we can know something profound about how adults assimilate experience in the here and now of therapy. Because patterns organize relationally, they provide psychological material for investigation within therapy. With this knowledge, the therapist now has sufficient ground to understand how his or her clients' movement patterns have emerged in infancy and how they have adapted over time.

When therapists apply this relational and developmental approach, they analyse subtle, rhythmic patterns that continually arise within the client-therapist field. They notice not only the client's fluid and alive movements, supporting clarified and spontaneous experience, but also those movement patterns that do not complete themselves easily, inhibiting experience. Therapists have the ability to not only observe, but break down movement patterns into their most basic components and utilize developmental patterns as experiments within a session.

This opens the possibility for a variety of explorations. Attending to the incomplete pattern, the client's primary style of contacting is revealed and the function of the chronically fixed pattern becomes known. For example, how does this disrupted pattern support some belief the client has concerning themselves in the world? In the discovery process, the habitual disruption, initially taken on by the infant or child as temporary assistance, becomes available for use. The existential issue that accompanies the fixation of pattern moves to the foreground to be worked with and through. And when the client explores a more fluid variation in movement pattern, another choice in contacting is made available. How does the client experience the novelty in contacting – with what degree of curiosity and excitement and what degree of anxiety? In each case, the client's psychological organizing reveals itself through the primacy of movement.

All patterns continue developing in the here and now. They are fundamental to contacting and are present in all experience, forming the present/past and present/future.

Developing supports for contacting: rhythmic diagnosis – the story of Jenny

To carry us into the moment of the therapy session is to pull us away from the *concept* of what is done into the *actuality* of how it is done. This case study has been distilled from my recollection and detailed notes taken after each session.

These sessions were part of an intensive where my client Jenny and I worked for one and a half hours daily for five days. Six months prior to this series of sessions, we had done another five-day series. In general, my psychotherapy practice is conducted on a one hour per week basis. As Jenny lived in Europe and I in New York City, this was certainly not possible, so a change in format was necessary. These meetings were the first time that we had seen each other since the autumn series. Jenny had come to work with me only months after the sudden, accidental death of her adult daughter. The reader will notice that each of Jenny's movements that emerge during our sessions – her breathing, her gestures, her gait, her posture – express some meaning and communicate how she lives within her world.

In our initial phone conversation, Jenny told me that although her husband and colleagues were very willing to comfort her, she was not experiencing their support. At a loss for words, Jenny wanted to work through the language of her body. 'I just can't talk about this any more,' she said. 'I have to do something else.' 'Well, we will have to experiment and see what happens,' I told her.

Day one of the intensive

> As the session begins, I take a moment to focus on my body and sensitize myself to my breathing, the level of my muscle tension, any organic stirrings, my state of alertness etc. All these experiences will become

supportive background to the developing session. In placing the locus of attention on myself, my sensory system fine-tunes and allows me to move into a state of readiness – able to flow in any direction with my client. Only now do I turn my attention to Jenny.

Sitting, Jenny appears motionless. Her arms gently rest on her lap. When she moves them, the action is from her wrists and hands alone, while her forearms and upper arms remain sedate. As Jenny breathes, each shallow inhale carves a slender, vertical path from the base of her breastbone upward to her collarbones. Her exhale is even less perceptible. The movement of her abdominal area appears held on both inhalation and exhalation. (Fluid inhalation begins at the navel and simultaneously expands upward and outward to the collarbones and downward and outward into the abdominal cavity. Fluid exhalation simultaneously condenses inward and downward from collar bones to navel and inward from pubic bone to navel.) Now aware of increasing tension in *my* chest, I take several deeper breaths.

Jenny tells me of an image from a dream that she had after our last series of sessions. Although the dream was many months ago, the image has stayed with her. It is that of a red suitcase. I ask Jenny if she might like to unpack her suitcase in order to discover what might be within it. Jenny closes her eyes and slowly moves 'inside' the image and 'inside' herself.

After some time, she tells me that she can visualize the lining of her suitcase. It is 'Sort of red. The walls are red, but I can't touch them. They seem far away.' Jenny's arms reach out as if to touch the walls on either side of her suitcase. With a perturbed look she continues, 'I can't touch them.' I watch as she rubs the pads of her fingertips with each of her thumbs in a constant and easy rhythm.

I invite Jenny to become acutely aware of this motion. 'Put all your consciousness into this experience,' I say. As she explores her patterning, eyes closed, I notice that her head gradually circumscribes small, subtle circles in the air. Within moments, her lips appear to purse and release, purse and release. I ask her to notice the movements of her lips and, if she is interested, to exaggerate them. At first, Jenny opens and closes her mouth almost imperceptibly, then more boldly. Her tongue stirs and I say, 'If you want to, you might include more of your tongue in this motion,' and she does.

We sit there for what seems to be quite a while until Jenny's feet begin a pulsation – she broadens and condenses the surface of her soles and her toes stretch and flex. After some moments, Jenny's torso and pelvis become part of the action and begin to twist and compress – one upon the other. Now, a whole-body phenomenon has emerged. Again Jenny says, 'I can't touch the lining,' sounding more and more frustrated – more and more strained. I notice that her breathing is held or bound on the inhalation and she begins to gasp. While I sit at the edge of my chair, Jenny lives at the edge of her experience.

I have the impulse to reach over and offer my physical presence as a container. I take a few breaths to make sure that this is not my need alone and then take the risk. Moving to the edge of my chair, I place my bare feet on either side of Jenny's feet, giving her a boundary that she can press into. My wordless intervention is welcomed. 'Please don't leave me,' Jenny cries out. I move out of my chair and crouch on the floor in front of her. I hold the outside of her lower legs with my hands, while my feet remain on either side of hers. Now sobbing Jenny repeats, 'Please don't leave me.' 'I'm here. I'm not leaving,' I respond. She moves towards me and we embrace. Her heaving sobs are punctuated by several sharp, staccato inhalations. I feel as if her heart might break – and my own. 'I'm here. I won't leave you. I promise.' Jenny and I hold onto each other until our breathing has steadied. Only then do I return to my chair as she settles into hers.

Jenny monitors her breathing rhythm and notices that it is now without her familiar gasping. She tells me that the gasping that she felt just moments ago, when she was crying, had been with her all her life. When she was a young child, a teenager, and young mother, she suffered panic attacks. And even now, when she feels unsteady, the gasping returns.

She tells me that on two occasions, one when she was approximately 7 months old and the other during her early childhood, her mother had been hospitalized for some months. At that time, Jenny was left with her aunt until her mother was well and could return home. And when her mother was home, Jenny experienced her as critical and distant. 'Your gasping pattern seems to be similar to that of an infant or young child who has been left for too long and is terrified,' I say. Jenny says that the experience of not feeling the lining of the suitcase was, indeed, terrifying, and although she did not have the words to really describe what was happening at the time, this experience was familiar to her.

With both arms around her, Jenny holds herself tight. I bring this to her attention. 'Now you are providing the kind of container that I provided for you,' I say. Jenny rubs her hands up and down her arms in a soothing rhythmic way, breathes deeply and whispers to herself, 'I won't leave you.'

Structural analysis

The work looked as though it was intuitive on my part, but it was merely my attending to what became most obvious within the relational field. The emerging rhythm told me what went before and what will be next – what has been and what will come. I kinaesthetically attuned to the field and waited for the rhythm to clarify and to pull me inside itself.

The first rhythmic patterns to clearly grab my attention were observed through the steady, circular movements of Jenny's fingertips and hands, the circling motions of her head, the almost imperceptible opening and closing of her mouth, a stirring/reaching action of her tongue, joined by the broadening and condensing of her feet.

At first, the movements' rhythm was even in its flow, had a low intensity to it and appeared graceful. Then its intensity heightened and the rhythmic flow lost the even quality and grew abrupt and strained. Jenny's breathing became shallow and tight. She gasped repeatedly and I felt my concern build. I sensed where the rhythm was moving and intervened non-verbally, providing support for the next relational step to emerge. In other words, I met and contained her anxious reach and offered her my resistance – something/someone to press into. As Jenny accepted my support (my feet on the outside of each of her feet, my hands placed on the outside of each of her legs), the relevant existential issue underlying the repetitive rhythm spontaneously expressed itself – *now that you are here with me, I can feel my terror of your not being here.* She then sobbed and continued gasping.

Jenny's primary pattern – sucking/swallowing/breathing – that emerges immediately after birth with its accompanying predominant need (to be met, to incorporate, to feel soothed) was often left unsatisfied in an earlier relational field and, predictably enough, restated itself in the present. It is, in fact, the present/past. As in the infant, the pattern originated at her mouth and spread to her head, hands and feet which expressed a similar rhythmic flow.

The frequent loss of Jenny's primary caregiver now expressed itself as a pattern of reaching/straining with the mouth, hands and feet, gasping for air and, alternately, holding her breath. The breathing pattern, set early in the client's history, *was* the primary adjustment. Over time, a pattern of depression, punctuated by moments of panic, emerged as a repetitive, 'preferred' rhythm. Jenny's movement pattern reflected some deficiency in the satisfaction of sucking/swallowing/breathing. The rhythm restated the world again and again, 'I cannot feel *you*, touching *me*, touching *you*.' The redundancy shaped and shaded a habitual emotional tone – terror. This emotional constancy forged identity – something to hold onto in an unsteady world. With the repetition of pattern, the entirety of the earlier environment came back each time. Behind this adjustment, the prior waves of panic collided with an exhausted depression and expressed that which had not been adjusted to – a devastating abandonment.

Jenny, now stroking her arms and breathing deeply at the session's end, was able to give herself the support that had not been provided by the prior, historic environment and that was essential for her to move through her grief-filled present situation – the accidental death of her daughter.

Day three of the intensive

Jenny begins the session with a familiar, agitated depression. 'I don't know why I came here . . . after all . . . I always return to this experience . . . my depression . . . it's always the same . . . I feel so heavy . . . and weighted down.' Each phrase seems to drift out of her mouth and suspend in space.

The recent and devastating loss of her daughter has brought the earlier experiences of abandonment and the accompanying sensations of depression and panic to the foreground. With a lighter, steady, gradual rhythm and firm tone, I tell her, 'Of course you're depressed. It seems so natural at this time. As you work through your earlier losses, it will help to heal this recent loss of your daughter. And, as you mourn her loss, it will help to heal your prior losses.' I say this with conviction, having been through a similar process.

Jenny looks directly at me. 'I believe you,' she says, and appears to take heart. She reports that now she has a light and airy feeling inside her chest and abdomen. 'I'd like to follow these sensations,' she tells me, and closes her eyes. Jenny stays with the novelty of lightness/airiness and reports feeling both excited and 'a little scared'. Moments pass and I watch as her mouth begins a sucking/reaching movement; her hands/ fingers, feet/toes join in the process as they flexibly expand and condense in a gentle, even rhythm; and her torso wriggles as if looking for some- thing to snuggle into. Jenny's movements are flowing and graceful. I roll up several thick, cotton blankets and tuck them along either side of Jenny's torso, giving her something to resist. 'This feels right,' she says.

After some time, Jenny's arms, which were held close to her body, start to reach out to either side and behind her. She moves forward in her chair and now reaches in my direction, her eyes remaining closed. I have the impulse to extend my hand and meet hers, but wait until I know that it is not my wanting to make something happen, but rather my being part of a larger happening. I move to the end of my chair and grab onto her hand. At that same moment, she also moves forward as if to rise, and we both use each other to pull ourselves onto our feet. Standing, we hold each other's hands and begin to sway side to side. It is unclear which one of us began this rhythmic movement. What is clear is that we both enjoy it. As we sway, I experience the tension held in Jenny's shoulders in my hands.

I now include my feet (separated from each other by about 24 inches) in the sway, and shift my weight from one foot to another, exag- gerating and slightly changing the movement's rhythm – lift/drop, lift/ drop. Then I stamp each foot onto the floor – lift/stomp, lift/stomp, mak- ing the movement more of a march as I draw my feet closer together.

Jenny opens her eyes and joins me in this different beat. Letting loose our hands, we march away from the chairs and into the studio to use the larger space.

Marching consists of an even up-down rhythm in the vertical plane. I notice that Jenny's march has much more emphasis on the down rather than the up-beat. This creates intensity to the rhythm and gives it a held rather than free quality. Once brought to her attention, Jenny exaggerates this downward movement and finds words for her experience. 'I won't. I won't,' she shouts. Jenny realizes that she is saying this to the mother of her childhood. 'I feel such defiance when I say this. It's very familiar. This describes my relationship with her,' she says. I ask her to pay attention to her throat as she shouts 'I won't' and she senses a familiar tension there – part/whole of her pattern of defiance.

I invite Jenny to try something different. I ask her to give more emphasis to the up-beat while she marches. This will make the pattern more even and free-flowing. Jenny practises this new pattern and soon 'I won't' changes to 'No!', which she speaks with a newly-freed energy. Now there is no holding in her throat.

In a prior session, Jenny told me how difficult it had been to express the depth of her grief about her daughter's death to her colleagues and friends. She would start to tell them how *she* felt, and soon would begin to worry about *their* needs, putting her own in check. I found a phrase that might serve as her mantra – '*Right now, this is more about me than about you.*'

In this session, I ask Jenny to march right up to her colleagues and friends and repeat her mantra. '*Right now, this is more about me than about you,*' she says several times and with great enthusiasm. Jenny then decides to say this to her mother. This time she not only enjoys the statement, but the presence of her mother as well.

Structural analysis

The first rhythm to organize our relational field was Jenny's vocal pattern of drifting/suspending – I don't know why I came here . . . I always . . . my depression . . . it always . . . etc. I chose not to echo what I sensed was habitual, but rather to influence the pulse of the relational field by creating a different rhythm (and tone). I met the low intensity of her drifting/floating rhythm with one that was lighter, steady and gradual. This shifted Jenny's experience from 'heavy and weighted down' to 'light and airy'.

Following this experience, Jenny moved into a flowing rhythm of sucking/swallowing/breathing that moved throughout her entire body. Her reach extended beyond the environment of her body, and towards me. I reached back, offering leverage and assistance. For a reach to emerge as fluid, there must be an appropriate source of response. We grasped onto each other, pulled ourselves up and out of our chairs, and easily fell into a swaying rhythm with our arms – side to side. Jenny had moved smoothly from the earlier suck/swallow/breath rhythm of an infant to the later soothing swaying rhythm of a young child. Sensing the tension in Jenny's shoulders, I took the initiative to start a different rhythm – the march.

The even up/down vertical rhythm of the marching pattern has its roots in the chewing or dental aggressive pattern (beginning in the sixth month to the 24th–30th month). It is a pattern of differentiation – **push**/*release*, **push**/*release* (Kestenberg 1965). I thought that the chewing/marching pattern would more clearly diagnose the interruption that I noticed in Jenny's sway – her unaware and held shoulders that prevented her feet from fully contacting the earth and supporting her – and it did. Jenny's emphasis on the downbeat of the march demonstrated a lack of rebound (**push**/*release*) in the pattern. There was much intentionality in the intensity of the rhythm's downward stroke.

When she experimented with the emphasis on this downward stroke, her defiance emerged. It was not merely a chronic physical pattern, but rather part of the entirety of experience – the mother-daughter dyad of her childhood which was reinforced with her every step. As Jenny balanced the upward/downward stroke, the pattern lightened in intensity and became more symmetrical (her push was now freed). Defiance transformed into a more fluid 'No!' A change of rhythm changed the quality of the whole and a new relation emerged.

Postscript

At the end of our five-day series, Jenny stated that she would not be coming back to see me. She had accomplished what she had wanted to do, and believed that now she could do the remaining work of her mourning with friends, family and colleagues. And I agreed.

9 Embodying the sense of self
Body-Mind Centering® and Authentic Movement

Linda Hartley

Introduction

The first movement of life is the rhythmical expanding and condensing of the fertilized cell as it absorbs energy and nourishment, and releases wastes. The rhythmical movement of expansion and condensation, filling and emptying, underlies the basic pulse of life; the beating of the heart, the pumping of the lungs, cycles of activity and rest in daily life, giving and receiving in relationships, bringing to birth and letting go in death, all reflect this fundamental pulsation between moving out and moving inwards, and health and sickness depend upon it. If we block the natural cycling of energy, trying to hold to one arc or the other, imbalance is created and somewhere in the body-mind the seeds of disease are planted.

In my practice of Authentic Movement, a discipline which has its roots in dance movement therapy, Jungian psychology and mystical practice, I found myself exploring over many months and years a gesture of opening, of reaching out. I discovered many aspects to this gesture: I could reach in longing or fear, reach to touch with tenderness, to hold onto in need; I could reach out to offer, to give; I could reach out to surrender and receive. The movement stories evolved over a long period of time until there was a moment when I simply stood, hand held out in front of me with upturned palm, simultaneously offering and receiving. How simple, yet how complex it actually is to allow ourselves to offer and receive freely. The web of conditioning, prohibition, rejection and punishment, which interweaves throughout our formative years, forms a veil obscuring this free exchange of energy.

Interruptions of our basic impulses to open out to the world and move back in towards ourselves will be reflected in the body as patterns of muscular or organic tension, weakness or flaccidity; in cardiovascular, respiratory and digestive cycles, sexual function and the immune response; and in the quality of holding, permeability, rigidity and responsiveness at the cellular membranes. Physiologically this balance is regulated through the autonomic nervous system, with the parasympathetic branch stimulating internal processes of digestion, rest and recuperation, and the sympathetic branch enabling us to attend outwardly to challenges, goals and potential threats. Within the psyche an intrinsic need to periodically turn inwards for renewal and deepened connection to self, then outwards for self-expression and growth, also regulates cycles of inward and outward focus. Keleman writes: 'If you want to know yourself, slow down. Stop what you are doing. But if you want to grow, if you want to form yourself, you must actively express yourself' (1975: 124).

As the embryo and foetus develop, various functions evolve which mediate cycles of inward and outward flow. The nervous system begins to develop at an early age, but only as nerves myelinate (become covered in a fatty insulating sheath) can they function with precision and efficiency. Motor nerves, which travel from the inner core of the brain and spinal cord to the body peripheries, myelinate before sensory nerves, which complete the cycle by returning from periphery to centre. First I move, I express myself, then I receive sensory information about that movement, and thus I come to know myself (Cohen 1993: 118). I also come to know the world as I touch, taste, bump into and fall against its surfaces: 'We can never touch just one thing; we always touch two at the same instant, an object and ourselves, and it is in the simultaneous interplay between these two contiguities that the internal sense of self is encountered . . . By rubbing up against the world I define myself to myself' (Juhan 1987: 34). This is how the foetus and infant begin to learn about self, other and the interplay between them. Through this play the infant lays a foundation for the way they will balance movements out into the world with returns to centre, to self and self-knowing.

A number of specific movement responses, *primitive reflexes*, are also developing. A specific stimulus will, if the infant is in a receptive mood, elicit a specific response. Primitive reflexes mediate movement towards or away from the stimulus, and these movements underlie *bonding* and *defence*, both of which are essential for the infant's survival and offer a neurophysiological basis for the way they will learn to negotiate their relationship to others and to life (Hartley 2004: 110).

Cohen describes movement as a sensation, and movement and touch as the first senses to develop (1993: 114). They form the foundation for growth, learning and engagement with the world. From the earliest days of life in the womb, experiences are imprinted within the foetus' developing nervous system from self-generated movement, the sensations this creates, and information coming to the foetus from outside. This process continues throughout infancy and indeed throughout the whole of life. This information colours the sensory-motor patterning that is being laid down in the developing neuromuscular system, and will affect how the infant births herself, how she feeds, bonds, learns to crawl, to reach out, how she plays and socializes. It will be reflected in the movement patterns that emerge and the postural attitudes these patterns

coalesce into. Layers of experience will accumulate upon early learning processes which begin in the womb, and all areas of development – emotional,
social, intellectual and spiritual – will be supported or influenced by underlying cycles of sensory-perceptual-motor response, the inward and outward
flow of energy, information and desire.

Movement and touch in psychotherapy

Because the process of early learning and psychological development is so
intrinsically embedded within somatic process, the use of touch and movement in psychotherapy can offer a potent entry into the realms of perinatal
and preverbal experience; here the early roots of disturbances can be explored.
I draw upon the theory and practice of Body-Mind Centering, an approach to
somatic movement therapy developed by Bonnie Bainbridge Cohen (Cohen
1993; Hartley 1995), and Authentic Movement, originated by Mary Starks
Whitehouse and further developed by Janet Adler, Joan Chodorow and others
(Chodorow 1991; Pallaro 1999; Adler 2002).

Both of these approaches invite dialogue between consciousness and the
unconscious through movement, body awareness, touch and dialogue. Creative expression through dance, artwork, writing and voice may also be used to
integrate into consciousness experiences accessed through the body. The process of giving language to somatic experience reflects the development of the
sense of a verbal self. As the infant begins to master language, some areas of
experience become difficult to communicate. They may be experienced as
threatening or unacceptable, and become relegated to the shadows, forming
the *private or disavowed self* (Stern 1985: 228). Through bringing into creative
form and language the experiences encountered in movement and bodywork,
we can begin to heal the rift created between 'interpersonal experience as it is
lived and as it is verbally represented' (Stern 1985: 162). But first let us return
to the beginning, to preverbal and perinatal processes, and to birth itself.

Infant movement development

The process of *infant movement development* is a foundation of body-mind
centering practice. During development the foetus and infant embody a series
of movement patterns inherent within the human nervous system; they
reflect the evolution of sentient life from single-celled amoebae to humankind
with our complex bipedal locomotion. Embodying and clarifying these
movement patterns, with a therapist's guidance and support, can help both
child and adult to achieve greater strength, coordination and gracefulness
in their movement, and posture can be improved. Positive changes are also

witnessed at other levels of functioning as neurological pathways are reorganized. Mills and Cohen describe *developmental movement therapy* with children whose emotional, social and mental skills improved as a result (Mills and Cohen 1979).

The movement patterns embody important developmental tasks with which the infant is engaged in the process of developing a sense of self, a healthy psychological core (Hartley 2004: 95–137). For example, in-utero movement, which is organized around the umbilical centre, enables the foetus to begin to develop a sense of coherence, of being a whole with separate parts that are nevertheless connected. *Self-coherence* is one of the *invariants* needed for the development of a *sense of core self* (Stern 1985: 82–9). In-utero, and during and after birth, touch to the skin is also crucial to the development of self-coherence, the sense of being a unified and boundaried whole.

Birth involves a monumental effort on the part of the infant and is a powerful act of agency, another of the invariants crucial to the development of a sense of core self (Stern 1985: 76–82). Then as the newborn begins to feed, they discriminate what is and is not desired, expressing their first 'yes' and 'no' as they turn towards or away from the breast in the *rooting reflex*.

Through *yielding* weight into earth or mother the infant bonds, then gradually finds the pathway to separate through *pushing* up out of this supporting ground. The infant is laying the foundation for developing independence and interdependence, the sense of being a separate yet related self. Soon they are *reaching out* in desire, curiosity, play or fear, and drawing in to grasp, embrace and incorporate into themselves. They are now fully engaged in the world of relationship. The experience of these movements will be coloured by the infant's sensations, emotions and the responses of others; these tones will become embedded into the movement experience, giving each person their own idiosyncratic movement signature. As a child or adult going back to embody these early movements, memories and feelings related to the original experience may be evoked, and insights can emerge from consciously reinhabiting the moving body and the memories held within it.

The process of movement development involves a powerful impulse outwards. From the confines of the womb there is a gradual emergence, unfolding, opening to ever wider and higher horizons, as first gravity and then space are mastered. There are many spiralling turns in and out, but the overall thrust is up and out. I am talking here about a healthy and unhindered development, and a birth that is natural, well-supported and free of unresolved trauma. When things go wrong we see the strong and passionate impulse of the infant and child to radiate and extend outwards become inhibited, restricted and fraught with fear or rage. This will manifest in blockages of energy within the body tissues and in restricted patterns of movement, perception and behaviour, as the natural cycle of sensory-perceptual-motor response is interrupted or inhibited in some way. As the child grows and other experiences become layered upon these powerful early imprints, they will be influenced by and may reinforce early patterns of disturbance that have not been resolved.

Birthing the self

When a traumatic birth is not resolved the child (and often the mother too) is left in a state of shock which creates imbalance in the autonomic nervous system. The great challenge of birth stimulates sympathetic activity in the infant, which then needs to be modulated by quiet rest, nursing and comforting contact to support parasympathetic activity, as well as bonding. When this does not occur the natural cycle of activity and rest – the movement outwards followed by the return inwards to centre – is disrupted, and various physiological and psychological problems can evolve.

Sam showed such an imbalance: he tended towards hyperactivity or emotional collapse, and could not relax into recuperative states of creative rest or quiet interaction. He showed high muscle and organ tone in the centre of his body, with limp, flaccid extremities which did not support his meeting and full engagement with the world. The strong outward thrust of birthing energy had been blocked and turned inwards, locked into his body tissues. Sam was 5 when he first came to therapy and his development was being seriously hindered by unresolved birth trauma and the bonding failure which ensued. Because therapy with a child has to occur through bodily expression, and because a young child is still close to and involved with their birth experience, Sam's process vividly elucidates some of the ideas outlined above.

Sam's mother, Lianne, described him as tense and hyperactive with low concentration and movement problems. He had not been ready to start school that year and was attending a nursery school with children much younger than himself. He was uncooperative and would sometimes attack other children or hide under a table. His mother was concerned he would not be able to attend school and would be diagnosed as having special needs; she feared he might be autistic, or would grow up to be a 'delinquent' adolescent. Her immediate goal was to get him accepted into school the following year. Their relationship was also difficult. Lianne found Sam's states of high energy and high-pitched screaming intolerable, and tension would escalate between them until they got into a 'vicious cycle' which she could not find a way out of. This could be an expression of feeling trapped in the birth canal with 'no way out'; Sam may have been trying to show his mother what it had been like for him, how intolerable his experience was.

When Sam arrived for our first meeting he burst into the large room where we were to work, racing around for some time, wildly kicking the big green ball. I saw the limp hands and tense shoulders, the flailing arms and the lack of clear organization in his body. Sam's spine was rounded over, as if he had not fully emerged from the enclosed space of the womb; his forehead jutted forward and his head was slightly turned and tilted to the right. He tended to run in curves rather than straight forward, following the angle of his head. Again I was reminded of birth, as if his head were caught in the moment of spiralling through the birth canal, frozen in time, and the extension of his spine and the realigning of head with body had not been completed. I saw an interrupted birth process, and on asking Lianne about his birth she was clearly relieved that I would consider this relevant, affirmed and supported in her own feelings and concerns. This helped to build trust between Lianne and myself, so crucial if Sam's therapy was to be successful.

Lianne's father had died seven months into the pregnancy and a difficult relationship with her mother had added to Lianne's emotional stress during this time. At birth Sam presented with his forehead instead of the crown of his head, which led to a long and difficult labour. Eventually forceps were used; because of his position there was a risk that his eye could have been damaged.

The birth was traumatic for both mother and child and Lianne described being unable to bond with Sam afterwards, suffering a long period of depression during which she stayed at home most of the time. Sam missed out on a lot of physical activity, play and social interaction that would have helped him develop physically and psychologically. Lianne felt guilty about what had happened and wanted deeply to help him; her commitment to this task did undoubtedly support Sam's therapy, and she was very much part of the process. The healing of their relationship was an integral part of our work. In therapy with adults we work with the remembered and internalized parents of childhood. It was both fascinating and complex to work with Sam and his mother together, as we sought to repair the early trauma and bonding failure they had both suffered.

One aim was to restore balance within Sam's autonomic nervous system, alternating periods of high activity which supported Sam to find channels to release the held energy in a creative and organized way, with periods of quiet rest and inwardly-focused attention. In the beginning there was little respite from activity and Sam would quickly reach a threshold of tolerance beyond which overexcitement would lead to aggressive behaviour or distress. A first moment of contact was made when he finally lay over the big green ball and allowed me to gently touch his back and rock him, with a focus on supporting him to release weight and the tension in his organs; for a brief moment there was a qualitative change in energy and attention as he became still and quiet. He moved in a more measured way after this.

Over time Sam allowed more such moments of contact. On one occasion he was able to receive a very gentle contact to his forehead, the part that had led him into the desperate birth struggle. He settled into a quiet parasympathetic state, as if listening inwardly and recognizing that something different was happening. After this he readily accepted and often sought contact and bodywork experiences, offering a foot to be held, or his head to be touched, or leaning into me for fuller body contact. Through touch and gently guided movements I could work to repattern the distribution of energy throughout his body and support the integration of his posture, movement patterns, and muscle and organ tone.

Aligning his head, spine and limbs and feeding gentle compression through the bones and joints helped Sam to begin to find the core of support which the skeleton provides. As his spine aligned more centrally, Sam was beginning to develop his sense of core self, expressed in a growing confidence and boldness. The work through the bones also helped him to yield his weight into gravity and to push – first against my hands, then against the floor as he learned to integrate the early crawling patterns which he had not fully embodied. Learning to push through his hands and feet was essential for Sam to learn to make boundaries, to establish his sense of core self, and to be able to separate from his mother. Engaging with these movements Sam was also revisiting his first separation from his mother, his birth experience, but in a playful way which allowed him to develop his power.

Through integration of his spine, pushing through his feet and gentle work with his head, Sam was being 'taught' the movements of birthing. At this point in the therapy he began speaking about being in mummy's tummy, and often regressed into baby talk and play with Lianne. During one session he was leaning against me, his head in my hands and his feet placed against Lianne's feet. He suddenly found the power to push her right away from him. He then turned around and did the same thing with his feet pushing against me – clearing space, pushing us away, he was making space for himself, preparing for birth.

The birth moment finally came gently and Sam discovered it all by himself. He began nuzzling his head into a soft ball which he liked to play with and rest on. He came onto his hands and knees and began purposefully rolling and pushing the ball across the floor with his head, flexing and extending his neck and spine to do this – the movement which initiates birthing. He travelled in a wide arc, deeply engrossed in the movement, then emerged and crawled onto Lianne's belly where he lay for some time, resting. Lianne did not know what he was doing but felt it was important and told me afterwards that she was moved to tears, just wanting to stroke and kiss him as he lay there. Sam had completed his birth process, even crawling up to his mother's breast as a newborn will do if laid on her belly after birth, and this time she had been able to welcome him with love.

Soon after this Sam took some tests which would determine whether he would be selected for a place at school. He did very well and was offered the place. The doctor praised him and Lianne felt proud of her son; Sam's progress had been generously affirmed.

Embodying relationship

The action of pushing allows the body to extend fully, and Sam had been finding the pathway to unfold out of his curved, foetal posture. Fully embodied pushing naturally leads into wholehearted reaching out and into relationship. A game of pushing with his feet against my hands to roll over the green ball and reach with his outstretched hands towards Lianne, who sat in front of him, became a favourite for Sam; he was embodying the necessary task of separating from his mother in order to come into relationship with her as a separate individual. Alternating with the pushing games there evolved lots of affectionate embraces and cuddles, their bodies learning to mould together, to bond. Cuddling had formerly involved Sam being very clingy or hurting Lianne, and Lianne drawing away; now they were finding a way to be together in intimacy. Sam was learning through his body to negotiate the complex relationship with his mother, and she was now able to respond. Stern claims that an infant must first develop a sense of core self in order to relate to and experience merging with another: 'the infant's first order of business, in creating an interpersonal world, is to form the sense of a core self and core others ... the capacity to have merger- or fusion-like experiences ... is secondary to and dependent upon an already existing sense of self and other' (1985: 70). With a clearer sense of himself, Sam was now able to enter into intimate moments with his mother without the fear of being swallowed up.

The pushing games Sam now loved to play were usually high-energy activities, and in time Sam came to know when he was tired and in need of rest. He was learning to self-regulate his levels of activity and rest as his nervous system came into better balance. He learnt to throw, catch and kick a ball, which he had been unable to do before. Ball games demand full externally focused attention and quickened reflexes. They challenge eye-hand-foot coordination and require alertness of the body extremities, all of which Sam needed. This helped him release held energy and the tension created by an overactive sympathetic nervous system, and support fuller engagement with his world.

After the birthing process Sam needed to create his own play, and invented games which helped him to deal with difficult feelings, acting-out inner dramas and finding his own creative solutions. He evolved a game of 'piggy and wolf' where I was the bad wolf-mother and had to try to catch him, the baby-piggy; Sam was able to work out this transference in a safe and enjoyable way through the game. He created four 'safe houses' in the room where he could not be caught, and would spend a long time in one of his houses before tricking me to look away and running very fast to another place of safety. With slight variations, we played this game for many months as he learnt to deal, at another level, with his need to separate and protect himself from the devouring wolf-mother – first physically through the pushing games, and now symbolic-ally through story. Eventually he learnt to symbolize the safety; now he could run freely about the room but if he was forming a letter T with his fingers, he was safe and could not be caught.

On one occasion Sam became very upset and left the room. I followed and sat with him until he could articulate his feelings. He was angry because mummy had rescued a ball from under the cupboard when he had wanted to get it himself. Every child must go through this development, but it may have had special significance for Sam because of his forced delivery at birth. With support he was able to tell Lianne of his anger; he was learning to differentiate and express his chaotic feelings, and this incident led to them finding ways to negotiate boundaries together.

Sam developed a passion for drawing and this became an integral part of our work. In the drawings, too, he was expressing and resolving difficult feel-ings and dynamics within the family. His first drawings were of black mon-sters, robots and devils. One day he surprised us by producing a flower. I was touched to see this and, perhaps recognizing that it was meaningful for me, he offered it to me at the end of the session. I later had an opportunity to compare it to a Little Red Riding Hood doll that transforms into Grandmother and the Wolf, which he had been fascinated by. I told him it reminded me of his drawings, the black monsters transforming into the beautiful red and yellow flower. He gave me a long and focused look which communicated to me that he felt seen. He was emerging from his dark inner world into a world of colour and light. After this, colourful and inventive stories began to evolve through Sam's drawings, telling the story of his inner emotional life.

Sam was now 7 and doing well at his new school. He had made many friends, and was growing into more independence. A new level of separation was occurring as Sam looked towards a wider world of school and friends and activities that took him away from his mother; he was also ready to end ther-apy. His drawings showed he had internalized a good and nurturing mother and learnt to mediate through his creative play the difficult and frightening feelings that had once overwhelmed him.

Persona and shadow embodied

Working with early wounding and perinatal trauma in therapy with adults will of course look different from therapy with a child, but there are many similar-ities in the core issues and the process of therapy. In both adult and child the exuberant expansion of energy outwards has been inhibited, and bodily tensions and weaknesses reflect underlying psychological contractions or dis-sociation. Each has struggled in his or her own way to connect to and express from an authentic and vital sense of self, and been thwarted in this to some degree. There is an infant self seeking to grow, expand and engage fully with life, but fear and unresolved trauma inhibit this.

As for the child, bodywork and movement can help the adult client integrate a more fully embodied sense of core self, which is a foundation for development in the domains of relatedness and symbolization through image and language. In working with early disruptions to the sense of self in adult psychotherapy, I might combine work on infant movement patterns with bodywork that seeks to free energy blocked in the tissues, and integrate areas of the body that feel disconnected or dissociated. By bringing conscious awareness into specific tissues, information can be accessed as to how energy is flowing or blocked within them, and the quality of responsiveness and integration between tissue layers and body areas may be sensed. Memory and feeling held in the tissues might be accessed and can be explored and integrated in various ways.

The Body-Mind Centering approach explores the physiological functions and the *mind*, or quality of awareness, perception and feeling, which each tissue and organ system expresses. Body tissues, and their corresponding physiological and psychological functions, can be thought of as *shadow systems* when they are not embodied, when there is no conscious awareness and expression in that tissue. For example, one person may not fully embody his bones. The bones form the architecture, the bedrock of the body, offering qualities of support, clarity, containment and groundedness. This person may feel a lack of these qualities, or have an uncomfortable relationship to them, perhaps preferring to be 'up in the air' than on the ground. Another person may not embody his organs but be well grounded in his bones; he might be experienced by others as a clear and grounded but unemotional person. These are just two possibilities out of a multitude of 'choices' we all make about which parts of ourselves we inhabit and express and which are unacknowledged and unexpressed aspects of the shadow. The split between persona and shadow is as much a somatic as a psychological phenomenon.

Boundaries and containment

Creating enough trust and safety within the therapeutic relationship to address the core woundedness is the first task of therapy. Bodywork can support other therapeutic approaches in this. When a client with a wounded or undeveloped sense of core self has suffered violation of physical and psychological boundaries this might be approached through mindful touch focused on restoring a healthy sense of body boundaries and containment. Care must be taken with the timing of this; for some clients the body is experienced as an unknown and frightening place and any physical contact may be experienced as invasive. With some it may be advisable, at least in the beginning, to help the client develop their ability to feel their body and ground themselves in bodily sensation without the use of touch; this can also help create boundaries and safety (Rothschild 2000).

If the client and I agree, physical contact may be one method we use. When I touch a client I first make contact with the skin, focusing my awareness there; the client's experience of their psychological boundaries is often embodied in the way they experience the skin and subcutaneous tissues. For example, the client might have no awareness of the skin; this tissue might not be present to them at all. Or it might be imaged as something vague and cloudy, or a dry and brittle barrier, or a too-permeable membrane with holes in it. Going deeper, the client might experience the layer of subcutaneous fat as an insulating and protective cushioning, or as something alien and frightening, or again it might not feel present at all. Sometimes there is the feeling that there is no outer membrane to the body, and my hands are drawn immediately into the deep inner spaces of the visceral organs which embody our 'gut feelings'. The issues that arise might be explored using touch, dialogue, imagework, drawing and movement.

Other body systems can help create a sense of boundary, containment and safety. For many the bones, embedded with mineral deposits of the earth, offer support and security; this seemed to be the case for Sam. For another who feels fragmented and dissociated as a result of early trauma, the connective tissue may give a feeling of connectedness, of being a unified and integrated whole. The lymphatic system, an essential part of the immune system which provides protection and defence, can be experienced as a clear support for maintaining personal boundaries when embodied. And we use our muscles to provide feelings of containment and defence. When the skin and other layers are not supporting the embodied experience of boundaries, excessive muscular tension may compensate for this; finding the support of other body tissues can help to release excessive muscular contractions. In Sam's work, embodying the bones and releasing tension in the organs helped him to release chronic muscular holding and distribute energy more evenly throughout his musculature.

The child in the adult

As I touch the skin to offer a sense of containment I may also focus my attention towards the cellular membranes of the body, offering a deepening sense of holding and containment as I focus on the first movement of life, *cellular breathing*. This may allow the client to find a deep level of rest, and by bringing awareness into the cellular membranes they may begin to heal their damaged boundaries at the cellular level. *Cellular holding* reflects the uterine world, and the hope is that the client may experience the 'therapeutic womb' as a containing and nurturing enough environment to enable them to revisit and resolve early woundings (Hartley 2004: 95–119).

As we follow the unfolding developmental process, work with the connective tissue might lead into movement which integrates all the body parts, reflecting the *navel radiation* pattern which develops in-utero around the umbilical centre. When addressing imbalance in muscle tone throughout the body, such as chronic holding patterns or weak, flaccid muscles, a movement pattern which stimulates the development of *physiological flexion and extension* might be introduced. This involves a specific whole-body flexion pattern alternating with whole-body extension, and can support in an organic way the movement from the closed foetal posture into an expanded state. Physiological flexion and extension develop in-utero during the last three months, and provide the underlying muscle and organ tone which will allow integrated movement and posture to evolve. A client who has been born prematurely will have missed out on some of this development and may show either chronic holding patterns which seek to compensate for the lack of underlying tone, or low tone throughout the body. Psychological development will unfold upon this incomplete foundation.

As described in Sam's story, movements which support the ability to push can also help the creation of personal boundaries and empower the adult client to, literally as well as metaphorically, 'stand on their own feet'. It is important that the client is helped not only to regress and resolve early issues, but that they are supported to continue the developmental journey up and out towards individuation and healthy functioning in the world. Themes of reaching out for contact and relationship, or towards goals, may also be addressed using movement as a support for exploration and integration of the complex themes that can be involved. Embodying early movement patterns can facilitate access to unconscious memories and feelings related to these issues, uncovering needs and longings, fear and shame as well as the joy of reaching out for what we desire.

Integrating the personality

With some clients, when enough safety and trust in themselves, their body and the therapeutic container has developed, it may be appropriate to explore the myriad of feelings and attitudes embodied in the organs, glands, nervous system and fluids of the body. This is a rich area of exploration where unconscious memories and feelings can be accessed and integrated. As a secure enough sense of self is forming, the client may be ready to enter this world and engage with integrating the many aspects of their personality. Body awareness, touch and movement might be used to support this exploration.

Authentic Movement is one approach I may use with clients who have a secure enough ego structure to allow for exploration of the deeper layers of the psyche; it is generally not appropriate for those with a fragile ego, or borderline or psychotic condition, who may be overwhelmed by material from the unconscious. Chodorow (1999: 238) writes:

> When movement is used in psychotherapeutic intervention, it activates both conscious and unconscious processes. By its very nature, movement as a therapeutic tool will explore, strengthen and integrate multiple aspects of the human psyche. However, in order to determine specific interventions, the dance therapist needs a sense of direction. This includes knowing whether the immediate goal is to move toward the unconscious or toward a more conscious, concrete reality.

When a client is ready to open more fully to the unconscious, they are invited to close their eyes and attend to their inner world, waiting to be moved by sensations, images, feelings and movement impulses arising within them. As the process unfolds, memories, feelings, images, archetypal energies and healing moments may be evoked and find expression through movement. The movement that arises is an expression of the movements of the psyche, and in attending to the details of physical movement we engage with messages from the self.

The presence of the therapist/witness offers a container, a safe space, in which the mover can surrender their ego consciousness for an agreed time and enter their inner world. The witness seeks to see the mover with clarity, compassion and non-judgemental acceptance; they pay attention to the sensations, feelings, memories and images evoked in them by the presence of the one moving. When, after the movement, mover and witness share their experiences, the witness endeavours to recognize and own their projections, interpretations and judgements, coming to understand how these may obscure clear seeing of the other. Thus the inner witness of each develops within the context of relationship. The discipline of witnessing is a metaskill for being in relationship with a client no matter what approach is used, and it facilitates awareness of countertransference.

Emily, a young university student, was drawn to Authentic Movement as a way to make deeper contact with herself and explore her inner conflicts. She had come into therapy suffering from depression, anxiety attacks and a compulsion to pull out her hair. In her teens she suffered from an eating disorder which, after a period of psychoanalysis, had been overcome but was later replaced by the hair-pulling. The complex issue of self-harming behaviour has deep roots in parental complexes (Gardner 2001), and as we explored Emily's symptom of hair-pulling it seemed that she was attempting to pull out the roots of something unacceptable within herself.

Throughout the therapy, which included exploring current relationships and parental conflicts, Emily frequently asked to move. Through the movement she came to recognize two aspects of her personality. One was clear, rational and organized, the side of her which studied hard and could excel academically. The other she named 'degenerate'; it was laid back and unmotivated, and she feared becoming lost in the inertia of this side of herself. The two sub-personalities were embodied in movements which were clear, focused and upright on the one hand, and which slumped and drew her down into the floor on the other. In the beginning of our work Emily's rounded posture, when sitting talking with me, unconsciously expressed this feared and rejected side of herself. She would twist her body around herself, drop her head into her chest, often scratch her skin or pick at her clothes, and gave a general sense of lack of support. She projected the quality of 'degeneracy' onto her father and boyfriend; it was associated in her mind with sexuality and being out of control.

Through many movement explorations, work with sub-personalities and dialogue, Emily engaged with the relationship between these parts of herself and the conflicts she experienced in relationship to them and the men who represented them. As the movement qualities became more integrated she was also integrating these sides of her personality, coming to recognize and value the rejected 'degenerate' side as a softer, more relaxed, 'feminine' and sensual aspect of herself. With this acceptance she was able to find more support for her intellectually ambitious and focused 'masculine' side, and the stress that her studies had been putting her under dissolved. By the time her final exams came she felt calm, accepting and able to take care of herself with breaks from study to rest or be with friends. By now she was enjoying this formerly rejected side, and it showed in a transformation of her appearance. She had emerged from a tense and anxious body twisted up around itself, dressed in sweatpants and ragged sweaters, into a beautiful and self-possessed young woman taking care of her appearance and dress, who sat relaxed and upright, looking at me directly. She now only occasionally pulled her hair, but said it no longer felt like a problem. As Gardner writes: 'The attack . . . needs to be replaced by a genuine sense of self-esteem and self-worth' (2001: 101).

By integrating, through movement and dialogue, two polarized sides of her personality Emily was finding her self. With a growing sense of selfhood and self-confidence she was now able to separate from her parents and an unsatisfying relationship. As she came to the end of her studies, and her therapy, she felt ready and excited to face the new challenges ahead.

10 Continuum Movement

Emilie Conrad

Introduction

Although Continuum officially emerged in 1967, the work basically represents a lifetime of freeing myself from the confines of culture.

As a very young person, my intuition sensed that all life was imbued with a unifying spirit and somewhere within my body this spirit could be experienced. The impression I received from the world around me was, 'God was elsewhere'.

For years, I had a recurring image of the movement of fish dissolving into the undulating waves of the ocean, becoming one inseparable reality. I felt that somewhere in a secret long ago, we were all swimming with the very same boundless wave movements of ocean fish, and if only I could discover how to get there, the 'real' world would be revealed to me.

In 1953, I received a scholarship at the Katherine Dunham School in New York, where I steeped myself in the magical world of Haitian dance. A few years later, I arrived in Haiti, and through a series of fortunate events I became involved in a newly-formed folklore company as choreographer and lead dancer. It was there that I had an epiphany that would change the course of my life.

What I witnessed in the prayer rituals was the undulating movements I had been searching for all my life. Though I had seen these same movements at the Dunham School, it wasn't until I was actually dancing in a Haitian hut and feeling myself drawn deeper into the primal call of the drums that my known self dissolved into the memory of those ancient rhythms. To this day, deep in my eyes, there still dances a timeless undulating resonance.

What I saw was how the undulating wave movements of the Haitian prayer became the connecting link to our spiritual bio-world. At last I saw the movement of ocean fish personified in human movement. I knew in that moment that these fluid undulating movements transcended time, place or culture and provided the crucial connection, linking organism to environment as an unbroken whole.

I returned from Haiti in 1960, and spent the next seven years exploring the universality of those undulating wave motions that so inspired me. These explorations eventually led to what is now known as continuum.

It's important to know that each of us carries billions of years of an ongoing global process, a sequenced continuum of life on earth, which is taking place within the galaxy and humankind alike. We are basically fluid beings that have arrived on land. All living processes owe their lineage to the movement of water. Our implicate pre-existent memory beginning with the first cell lies in the mysterious deep, quietly undulating, circulating, nourishing this aquatic being on its mission to planet earth. God is not elsewhere, but is moving through our cells and in every part of us with its undulating message. The fluid presence in our bodies is our fundamental environment; we are the moving water brought to land.

I would like to suggest that the far-reaching consequences of having a body are not just to serve as a conveyance, not just to propagate, but that we are composed of a mysterious substance that has no defined boundary. Without this substance we could not exist as humans. We may, at some time in the near future, learn to replace our pulsating wet body parts with metallic ones – in which case, we will become something quite different.

It was the vision of a universal human that beckoned me. I had no map to follow except my strong urge to experience our essential bio-lineage and my certainty that our existences were fed far beyond our cultural moorings. It is my belief that we carry in our cells, in our tissues, in the very throb of our existence, an underlying flow that urges, inspires, flares our nostrils and beats our heart. This encompassing atmosphere of love has its own destiny – perhaps using humans as its messengers, this love has arrived on earth.

Movement

> *Movement* 1. Moving or being moved. 2. moving parts of a mechanism (i.e. clock or watch). 3a Body of persons with a common object. 3b Campaign undertaken by them. 4. Activities or whereabouts of a person or group. 5. Mus. principal subdivision of a longer musical work. 6. Bowel evacuation. 7. Progress.
> (Oxford Dictionary, American Edition, 1995)

Science tells us we are a world of movement. Objects that we think of as static are moving, but not in discernible ways. Rocks and mountains are 'moving' with various rhythms and frequencies.

The conventional notion of movement is that it is something that turns on and off. It is usually thought of as a specific activity: walking, running or scratching our heads. When we stop these activities, we are 'still', 'not moving'.

I make a distinction between what we call *functional movement*, which implies a 'body', and *biological movement* in which the body is not a designated object and does not maintain a specificity of form. In this, we can say that movement is what we are, rather than something we do.

As living systems, can we engage in the formative tendency of life more directly? As intelligent beings, can we live in a culture but not be bound by it? Does our organism have a destiny separate and apart from the concerns of personality? What we commonly refer to as a body is basically movement that has became stabilized. When we see a newborn, essentially we are looking at the movement of water made flesh. We are seeing a fluid system meeting the vibrational field of the earth, where an elegant exchange begins to take place. As this exquisite system adjusts to its new atmosphere, a gradual stabilizing occurs. Liquid grasps, eyes focus, experiments are made. The baby rolls, thrusts, jerks, flails . . . trying out the best possible sequences to ensure survival on earth.

The very nature of stabilizing impels the fluid system to coalesce, giving the support that is needed to become functional. Fluidity consolidates as new requirements are met. Our oceanic memory pales as the demands of life on land become more immediate. All is forgotten, except for the primordial characteristics of our intrinsic environment.

We learn to crawl, to stand, to move forward through the savannahs, the mountains, the cities, outer space. This stabilized creature called human, what is it? Can we ever know?

The fluid presence in our bodies is our fundamental environment; we are the moving water brought to land.

In-utero the amniotic and the embryo engage in a sphere in which there is no separation. Our early existence is inclusive: the embryo recapitulates our planetary process, we contain all forms, all possibilities. A claw, a fin, a hand are all blueprints in this biomorphic plan. Chemical codes will determine whether we will have a snout or a nose. The web between our fingers, the membranous *dura mater* and oesophagus, the suspiciously protozoan curve of our brains and viscera that lie pulsating in water, are vestiges of ancient worlds here before we were, resonating in us through their varied undulating messages.

As human beings, we are an accrual of many life forms that have been shaped by our oceanic origins, still pulsating as the intrinsic world of our organs, our connective tissue, our nerve fibre. We are the result of millions of years of an open-ended experiment. Our forms have been designed and redesigned, unendingly adaptive and innovative.

All form is temporal. Its demise, or its need to reconfigure is inherent. In movement there are no objects. There is only fertile probability awaiting an urging. By defining an object or creating a boundary, such as a 'body', we establish a limit. In order to survive efficiently, we must stabilize and in a sense 'stop the world'. We must define ourselves as a designated self in order to survive. I must know that when I'm hungry I can feed my mouth and not yours. My ability to survive appears to need to identify this bounded state that I call myself. We can live successfully within our environment, and do all that is necessary to ensure that tomorrow will come. But that is not all we are. We are also the flowing expression of a divine and complex intelligence that has formed us for a purpose we may never know.

Stabilization is vital for efficiency, but it becomes rigid when uninformed by new probabilities. Maintaining an identity of the body as our only designated form we, as biological systems, actually narrow our vectors of expansion. With increased stabilization there is a compromise in adaptability. Infants have a capacity to heal because they are 'flux' – mutable and relatively open systems. Healing becomes a more arduous process as we fall victim to our assumptions about our bodily reality. We can encompass more than one description. We can learn from our 'flux', which gives us pure information and nourishment. It can improve our world by not limiting us to the boundaries of our own thought.

In 1974, I made a decision to experiment with spinal cord injuries. My question was, 'If we are movement, then what is paralysis?' Perhaps our medical model needs to be updated. Perhaps paralysis is in the model and not in the spine. If we acknowledge ourselves as dynamic, energetic systems that are primarily movement, we could say that in paralysis there is a compromise in function, but not in movement. What I have been discovering is that movement can innovate new function.

Movement, or the lack of it, relates directly to how we are breathing. In the case of trauma, breath is usually suspended, which will also suspend movement. Shock will contribute to paralysis by its emotional immobilization. Spinal shock sometimes wears off, but emotional shock can go on for years.

When working with people demonstrating such extreme physical compromise, I begin by introducing a variety of breaths. Breath will start to activate our fluid systems and bring about novel intrinsic interactions where the throb of life becomes apparent. Complex intrinsic movement, stimulated by using breath in a profusion of ways, brings warmth and flow to what once appeared to be frozen and unresponsive.

No official protocol has ever been developed for the elaboration of spinal movement in cases of paralysis. By using an embryogenetic (biomorphic) model I encourage movement in the cerebro-spinal core. As intrinsic movements become more abundant, a neurologically rich matrix is created for the budding of new neural pathways. I believe that our ability to innovate lies within our biological core.

As life currents become increasingly visible and articulate, and as rigidity melts into the mutable play of form, there is a gradual lowering of the level of injury and ambulatory movement eventually becomes possible.

My concern has always been with the ingenious ways we become self-limiting; and how all our various cultures define the parameters of what is knowable. Western culture, in particular, has brought about the industrialization of the body, with a devastating and alienating effect. For us, mechanical, repetitive movement is accepted as desirable, and this mechanization lies at the core of how we live and describe our world. Does this have any connection to a flowing vital process called a human being, whose form is based on the movement of water?

In these many years of teaching Continuum, whether I am dealing with a specific healing process or with the limits we put upon ourselves, my concern has always been to bring us to a greater participation with the underlying motif of life on earth: organism as environment.

As each of us becomes more fluid and resonant, defensiveness disappearing like worn out flesh, there emerges a larger unity in which communication at the level of cells and fluids becomes vastly enhanced. We are processes, terrestrial and beyond. Our relationship with our planet is maintained by the resonance of our fluid systems with all fluid systems, human and other.

Creative 'flux' is essential for the enhancement of our functioning. In 'flux', we cannot identify 'parts'. This 'flux' is our existential unity and creates a resonant chord with our planet. It provides us with an ability to function as biological systems rather than cultural entities. All distinctions dissolve into flowing variations, into a matrix of divine expression. There appears to be an intelligence and strength to this flux that goes beyond our thinking. Our ability to innovate lies, as far as I can tell, in this softening of form, where all becomes liquid.

We are open systems, able to respond to the immediacy of change. Our notion of 'body' undergoes a metamorphosis. We no longer identify with ourselves as bounded forms exclusively, but we can enter the waters of our own existence without reservation or plan. We are the process of life constantly unfolding itself. The universe we are living in is in a constant exchange of information and nourishment. I see this as a fundamental activity of the human on this planet and perhaps beyond our earth as well. Blood, rivers, oceans, cerebrospinal fluid, all fluids are in a state of resonance, a unity without boundary.

Our biomorphic ancestry makes itself known to us directly and informs us personally. God is not elsewhere, but in the very movement of our own formative tendency, continually manifesting itself through the play of mutable forms . . . continuum . . .

Thomas

Thomas sustained an injury to his skull and spine in a motorcycle accident a year previously. Although paralysed for a few months, he has recovered to some degree. He is ambulatory, but continues to maintain many areas of pain and immobility. There is a rigidity, particularly to his jaw, face and spine. I can see, although he is able to walk, there is not much communication in his system. His movements have a disrupted, robotic quality. Some of him has returned to life, but part of him is still in limbo.

He was a gymnast and has clearly maintained a well-muscled structure although it is quite limited in its expression. I am particularly aware of how he is holding his head, and the immense immobility of his jaw. He describes the constant pain in his head and back, and at the moment he is living a very cautious existence. A part of him seems to know that he is not exactly 'all there'.

As I watch him speak and tell me of his concerns I am aware that there continues to be a great deal of shock. As someone who has specialized in movement, my approach to shock is to address the mobility of breath and whether sensation is registering. What I often find is that breath is constrained, often trapped in the upper chest or throat. Sensation, if it registers at all, is minimal, a generalized fogging. In some situations, particularly with abuse, sensation can become hyper-responsive, in which the person registers an extreme heightened reaction to all sensation no matter how mild. To me, this response is shock with an alternative strategy.

In my experience, trauma, whether through an accident or some other means, becomes patterned into the system; much like a scar added to a fingerprint, the trauma continues. Our understanding of the continuance of post-traumatic stress syndrome has received great attention. A person surviving a concentration camp will certainly experience trauma. Someone falling off a bicycle will also be traumatized. All experiences in which one faces one's own death are similarly imprinted.

Extreme stress can also be seen as related to shock and trauma. Perhaps to a lesser degree, but stress paralyses and numbs, most likely due to the cortisol that floods our system. Considering paralysis to be a 10, stress can be seen as high as a 5 on our immobilizing desensitizing scale.

Depending on the degree of shock or stress will be the degree of suspension of breath, movement and sensation. Maintenance of shock signifies that vitality is also suspended. When vitality is elsewhere, our ability to interact has been compromised by the limitation of movement and sensation. Our primal tendency for self-organization has become compromised.

It is mystifying how some people will recover from an accident, while others do not. Much of what determines the healing potential of a situation is the degree and the length of stress or shock. Limitation of movement and sensation will inhibit the organism's capacity for self-renewal.

Primary to any healing process is to establish communication within the system. If there is no communication, or if it is faint or partial, the self-organizing processes of our bodies will become short-circuited. We still carry an inherited response to danger. Suspending breath mediates movement and sensation. In the animal kingdom one cannot be detected if there is no movement.

Breath determines intrinsic mobility and adaptability. Breath becomes key in summoning our life force. Breath equals movement, movement equals communication, which creates new interactions, inviting self-renewal and innovation. All of this takes place within the fluid system of our bodies. These movements are intrinsic, internalized, establishing an ancient rapport, a miniaturization of the cosmic soup, a creative flux in which fluid interactions have reached such complexity that new life is summoned.

What is required is to engage the person at their fullest. A person in shock cannot do this. The primitive responses of their bodies are held in suspension. Waiting . . . waiting to be released.

I begin by asking Thomas to create sounds.

Sound is audible breath, and for most people sound is an easier way to access breathing than concentrating directly on breath. Sound gives more obvious feedback than breath alone, which is much more subtle and requires a more nuanced attention. Sounds create different shapes; some are lateral and some are tubular. With each sound, different parts of the mouth, tongue and throat are stimulated in a variety of ways.

After exploring several minutes of sounding, I ask Thomas to go into open attention. Open attention is the harvesting of sensations and internal interactions as a result of a direct activity. At first, he is aware of very little sensation, in fact he is feeling a heightening of the pain in his jaw. This is not unusual. In the engaging of new interactions the increase of blood supply and activity will often intensify all sensation including pain. He is aware only of his pain.

I am aware that his shock may have suspended his ability to feel. The increase of sensation will soften the hard suspension of shock. The reptilian circuits through sensation will begin to buzz again.

Most people are rudimentary in their ability to feel. Sensation is not considered important, particularly in our western techno-society, which has moved far away from the river of life and the revelation of the human body. Sensation for most people will circle around pain, sexual arousal, things that feel good and things that don't feel good. Sensation becomes slotted into known categories and we take no further interest.

An array of sensation will represent an increased capacity for response. If I have only one response to a situation, my choices become very limited. If my responsive capacity becomes more developed, the intelligence of my system has the opportunity to broaden, and I am able to register more options within a given situation.

Pain is useful information, and can be a complex response to situations that may or may not be physical. For example, if someone is in a painful life situation, has a difficult boss, or is presented with a work situation where they feel helpless to express anguish, often the emotional response will go underground and surface as pain. Helplessness can become symptomatic, appearing in the arms or hands where we defend ourselves – this is usually referred to as 'somatizing'. A painful situation is being transferred to the body. Pain is important feedback. Our system is trying to tell us something. We have hidden our feeling and now the pain is being expressed in the back, neck, anywhere – sometimes everywhere.

Nature protects us from extreme pain by shutting off our sensation with a global numbing. We survive but we cannot feel. The problem is, when awareness locks into pain, we are unable to respond to anything else. We have localized our attention to such a degree that we are creating a stasis of awareness. Our pain will remain a repetitive response to sensory information and evolve into a defence strategy. When we have narrowed our perception, no matter how justified, we create a form of paralysis. We may still be ambulatory, but our awareness becomes truncated and unable to move. We are the living dead. Not able to be responsive at the most basic level of our system, we become cut off from the information around us and the primitive part of our nervous system becomes increasingly muted.

Habitual responses, whether painful or delightful, are basically manoeuvres of our defence system to maintain a status quo. The habitual response can be ecstatic or difficult, it doesn't matter. What matters is that my awareness is trapped in stable sameness and I am unable to shift it. My fear has now immobilized my awareness and I have created a feedback loop that keeps me safe from new information or communication. My system now is in a highly compensatory state.

When working with someone I always ask for their lens of awareness to enlarge, even slightly, to accept the pain as there, and to see what else is there. What else is happening no matter how faint? The atrophied awareness sometimes only registers what is within its immediate radius, almost as if it has shrunk itself to a situation. We want awareness to be mobile, to be able to generalize. To be able to receive information that is both local and non-local we want our awareness to be versatile. We want our sensation palette to be full and rich. Much like a painter with brilliant colours, we are informed by the pulsations of tones. Our capacity to know is not just cerebral. Our sense perceptions can become tentacular, spreading far and wide, allowing a new circumstance to take place within us.

As best I can, I explain this to Thomas. I tune in to him and to where he 'lives'. I adjust my language and my references to what would make sense to him. I want to interest him in his own process. To help him to see how his habitual response locks his attention and narrows the possibilities for healing.

I can see that I have engaged his interest. A gleam is in his eye, he appears more animated. He is eager to see if his lens of awareness can go beyond his habit. We try again. The sounds that lateralize combine with sounds that are tubular, creating a kind of music. These sounds engage different parts of his throat and tongue.

We go into open attention. I watch him smile as he sits in front of me with closed eyes, apparently registering something more than his usual response. He is in open attention for several minutes, harvesting the movements and sensations that the sounds have stimulated. After some time his eyes open, there is a general softening of his system, more colour to his skin, a quiet energy to his body. He is present.

He seems to materialize in front of me. He takes on more substance, as if he is being filled out from within. An awakening has occurred, the tone of his voice, the deepening of his colouring, the expansion of his field are evident.

He describes with wonder that he has been able to unlock his attention, and like someone snorkelling deep onto the ocean floor, he notices a new world existing within him. Sensations that would ordinarily be so muted as to be below the threshold of his awareness have been amplified by the soundings. The restrictiveness that he usually feels is melting, and he describes something that he tentatively calls pleasure.

I listen carefully, not just to his words. I am listening to the increased tones of his voice, and I am watching his body come alive in subtle ways. His entire expression has become more flowing, his movements more open. He is communicating with me far beyond language, I am with him, and he can feel this. Our rapport grows as our ability to communicate at the silent level increases.

I make some comments, and once again we return to the orchestration of textural sounds. After a bit he stops and goes into open attention. I can see that there is an increased softening. After a while he opens his eyes. He seems wetter to me, he has an 'afterglow', as if he had just finished making love. His experience was much deeper the second time. He felt that, as the first round opened him up and slowed him down, his awareness was able to move more and things became more interesting.

He felt his second round had become even more delightful, and surprisingly he was able to feel his system flow. Connections were being made internally that were bringing new life. He could feel an ancient intelligence being summoned. There was more to him as he spoke. Each round helped to materialize him further. It was as if he had been a ghost and now he was vivid. After talking for a few minutes we did another round of the same sequence.

I call this process of repeating a sequence 'layering'. This brings about a complexity of interactions in which sensation and movement are inter-penetrating in new ways. I often refer to this as 'creative flux'. As complexity increases and interactions become more diverse, there is a fecundity present in which new life processes are possible. The first round is a point of entry, the second brings an increase of exchanges, the third round is where 'creative flux' moves into an elaborate heightening of the basic fluid interactions of our bodies. Complex wave motions are evident as Thomas' structure becomes more mobile. Fecundity rises as form lessens, and once again we return to ourselves as movement.

When Thomas finishes layering, we enter into a verbal exchange and I feel his whole system has become kindled with an incandescence that I take as 'coming to life'. Much has occurred that goes beyond what we can make sense of. We are witness to a larger event that has not as yet been named.

As we sit together our exchange becomes richer. We are in a resonant field. In resonance or rapport we are communicating beyond verbal interaction. In a sense our words become the background, and the feeling tones or a field of meaning comes forward. Communication becomes a new activity. This is not unlike when we have made love in a truthful and satisfying way. We have merged in an exquisite contact that includes the physicality of the moment and yet goes far beyond it.

Defensiveness or excessive self-description decreases resonance and limits our intelligence. We cannot grow healthy within a bounded self that is deadened to its own primary existence. A defended or rigid body is not only hampered in communicating within its own system, but is removed from a depth of contact with others. Resonance is a deeply sensual way of existing. It allows wholeness to occur in which there is a mutuality of being that, again, is similar to making love. Resonance brings forth new qualities of contact, communication and certainly relationship.

We go back to the soundings. This time I show Thomas movements that involve his jaw and throat. These movements are what I call 'biomorphic', meaning that they are universal movements that are at the basis of all life forms. I believe the human structure to be a species blend, a synthesis of primordial forms. The biped or human, as we know it, can recall its ancient past where form is mutable. Species boundary is softened. Recapitulating our oceanic origins, we become a kaleidoscope of forms that were here before we were. We are in the sea of fecundity from which all life has emerged.

As I watch Thomas I see intrinsic protozoan-like elongations changing the contours of his throat and face. His throat has now softened in form to such a degree that I feel I am watching an oceanic creature at the bottom of the sea. His movements have a liquidity that becomes obvious when we have invoked the ancient intelligence of the human system, that is represented in form but goes beyond it. 'The thousand faces of Shiva', come to mind as I watch the movement spread to his torso. Thomas is becoming more mutable. I see an elegant dance of life taking place within him. A flickering of primordial domains appears, moving in and out through his skin, like watching the history of species development.

I believe that this protozoan liquid world is our 'dreamtime'. We cannot become Aborigines, it is too late for that. But we, in our techno-society, can discover, through our capacity to explore new terrain, the remarkable human.

Conclusion

We are astounding beings held hostage by our cultural values. Our organism is a spiritual biological legacy that invites us to enter the liquidity of a merged self with the encoding of a humanness that has not as yet arrived. I feel that the work that I have brought forward through all of these years points to our birthright. The human is an explicate of our planetary process. We are inexorably and umbilically connected to the origins of life. We are not bound by time space or condition. As yet, I believe that we have not even begun to tap the immensity of our heritage.

11 The body in Process Work

Jean-Claude Audergon

Introduction

Process Work, or Process-Oriented Psychology, is a wide-spectrum approach to working with people's experience and perception of life's flow. At its origin is Arnold Mindell, originally a physicist and Jungian analyst. In a recent interview, he described how in his early years as an analyst he became interested in 'getting out of his chair' – getting up from the chronic sitting position, and moving more deeply into body experience (Mudie 2004).

Getting out of the chair

I saw Arnold Mindell for the first time in the mid-1970s at his lecture on Carlos Castaneda's writings about the teachings of the Man of Knowledge, Don Juan, and their relevance for dream and bodywork (Mindell 1993: viii). I'd been seeking ideas and ways to explore the relationship between dreams, body symptoms and illness for a while. I had worked for seven years with a Jungian analyst in Zurich on my dreams. When I finished that work, I read a lot of psychology, attended some bodywork seminars and found myself dissatisfied by it, because I missed the Jungian scope. When my girlfriend of the time told me I might be interested in listening to a Jungian analyst talk about the body, I jumped at the chance to attend the next lecture. Crowded in a large lecture room with 200 people, I remember listening to Arnold Mindell recounting a story of how a marathon runner had come to him complaining of getting completely stiff in his hips within ten minutes of running. A doctor had sent him to Mindell because nothing else had worked and if seeing Mindell might not be helpful, it certainly would not be harmful. I remember being delighted when hearing Mindell recount how he had invited the client to put on his running shoes and go running with him along the lake. I remember being thrilled at the idea that a Jungian analyst would move from his chair and run with his client. I listened to the details of the story – how they ran for a couple of minutes, how the stiffness of the client's hips came up, how Mindell then asked him to make movements that made the stiffness a tiny bit worse (a process called 'amplification'), and how the runner then exclaimed that he could not, because if he did that he would walk a 'certain way'. Mindell's client had just stated his 'edge' or belief system that limited him and simultaneously structured his identity.

Here also was my first encounter with the fact that symptoms have a social context. The runner could not walk a certain way because he considered that kind of walk 'womanly'. Asked what he understood by 'womanly', he said, 'feelings, emotions and crying', unaware of the poverty of the male image he was trying to live up to, unaware that he was willing to marginalize his own feelings, emotions and impulses to cry and be warm-hearted – and unaware that this attitude supports sexism and homophobia and perpetuates the privileges of patriarchy. Mindell might have been aware of all of this, but he chose at the time to ask him to walk like a woman, talk and behave like one and he (Mindell) would now voice the criticism exactly as the runner had just done. At this point the runner started to understand his dilemma. This was the mid-1970s and men with feelings were 'news' – men who were willing to do 'women's work' and share responsibility at home were still an oddity, and conflicts concerning old values were arising in people's awareness. Mindell would make the collective aspect of such issues a more central part of his focus ten years later in his World Work approach to social issues and conflict resolution (Mindell 1995: 66). That day, it seemed, he talked about feelings and being a man with his client. It helped the client.

I was hooked and phoned Mindell for an appointment the next morning. Over the next 27 years I became one of several co-founders and trainers of the Research Society for Process Oriented Psychology, Zurich, and later the Process Work Centre of Portland, Oregon. I'm also a co-founder of RSPOPUK, the Research Society for Process Oriented Psychology, the umbrella organization for the Process Work training programme in the UK. I'm also on the faculty of several other Process Work training programmes across Europe and internationally.

In the three decades since, Arnold Mindell has deepened and widened Process Work's theory and application extensively, working with dreams, perceptual awareness in proprioception (body sensation), movement, auditory, visual, symptoms and illness and their relevance in relationships and group life, coma, extreme states associated with mental health disorders, creativity, inner work, relationships, groupwork, organizational development and community conflict resolution (or World Work) with social and political issues.

The dreaming body

Process Work consistently focuses on the body to gain contact with the wisdom of nature and the creative process that is emerging through body signals and symptoms. No matter the application of Process Work, it always includes awareness of the body's signals. Process Work also includes working directly with body symptoms and illness as one of its applications.

The body is a teacher to live life fully. It teaches you to differentiate your perception and your ability to welcome the creative part of yourself that often first manifests as a disturbance, a symptom, an illness, a weird body feeling (Mindell 1998). Rather than trying to get rid of a symptom or seeing it as a sign of something gone wrong, Process Work's orientation and methods consider symptoms to carry essential information. When this information is unfolded, it makes you feel you have dipped into the creative process. You discover specific patterns meaningful to you, your situation in life, or a project or relationship that you are entangled in.

One reason to focus on the body is that it carries information that is not structured by our intentions and will. Rather, dreaming patterns structure body signals and symptoms. When Mindell began exploring body symptoms, he used methods of amplification to discover the body's message. Time and again, he discovered that the experience in the body mirrored the person's night-time dreams. He coined the term 'dreambody' to refer to the patterns that express themselves both in our body and in our dream images.

Mindell tells an early story about a man with a tumour. He asked the man to feel the tumour more. He did so and said, 'I feel as though I could explode.' Then he said he had dreamed of fireworks exploding on Independence Day. The 'explosion' in the tumour was in essence his medicine, or the direction of his personal development. The man then went on to metaphorically 'explode' with feelings that had been bottled up for years.

Process Work is an awareness method. Its methods do not impose a change of behaviour or attitude from the outside, but rather the methods facilitate noticing what is occurring and unfold it according to the feedback from all parts. A basic idea is that the client's body signals how to work with them. Awareness itself is transformative. Feedback is considered the ethical regulator of process work, because it is the whole process that has the wisdom for the individual's process. The feedback comes from the client's intended and unintended communication and, similarly, the facilitator's. While as facilitator, I will focus on the client's unintended signals as well as on the content of their intentions, I will also notice the feedback of the interaction between us. If, for example, a client comes with a headache to work on, and leaves happy without a headache, and I mysteriously have a headache afterwards, then the overall feedback is to be looked at together with the client.

The roots of process work

- *Jung's analytic psychology*. The original interest of Mindell had been the teleological approach of Carl Gustav Jung, the creator of the analytical psychology movement in Zurich. Rather than asking where dreams *came from* in the client's personal history, Jung asked where dreams were *leading*. The dream carried patterns guiding the person's individuation or becoming their whole self. Mindell, a Jungian at the time, realized that if dreams carried meaningful patterns for the person's evolution, so must symptoms. He narrates in his first book, *Dreambody: the Body's Role in Revealing the Self*, how he was advised in his dream to focus on the same alchemical God Mercury that Jung had used to understand the meaningfulness of dreams. This would help him to understand the mercurial nature of symptoms and the body, the potential of symptoms to transform and change. In later years, Mindell would name the Process Work school a daughter of Jung's analytical approach to the unconscious.
- *Physics*. With its theoretical framework, its phenomenological and empirical tools of observation, its demand for accuracy of observation, its demand for the reproduction of the experiment leading to results and hence its 'teachability', Mindell's physics background influenced his ceaseless reframing of his findings, his persistent curiosity, questioning and research into the mystery and wonders of the human condition (Mindell 2000: 13). We train from the perspective that a hypothesis is to be named, applied, tested and rejected if the feedback and the observation do not validate it. In fact, a principal method of Process Work is to follow the feedback of the client's intended and the client's unintended signals.
- *Taoism*. The 'Tao that can't be said' reflects the idea of ever-flowing processes and the interconnectedness of events. The 'Tao that can't be said' from a process perspective is considered a sentient preverbal feeling experience that transcends duality. Following the Tao and in Process Work, we attempt to accurately follow and unfold the mysteries of nature, even when they are apparently disturbing or negative (Mindell 1989: 90).
- *Shamanic tradition*. Process Work training reflects shamanic traditions. Process Work methods involve facilitating and consciously entering into altered states and bringing back information useful to an individual or a community. It is basic to the training of the process worker to enter their *own* altered states and learn to explore them as the future of their creative life. It is about training to enter the unknown and discover the process on its own terms, from within the so-called

altered state, rather than to remain outside of it and interpret the experience. People tend to name an experience as disturbing or fascinating and never enter the experience itself. In Process Work, we focus on entering an experience and unfolding it rather than interpreting it.

- *Alchemy*. Alchemy was the process of cooking the *prima materia* to transform it into gold. Jung studied alchemy. He describes the process of cooking and transformation of the psyche. Mindell expanded upon the Jungian techniques of 'amplification', such as active imagination and dream interpretation, by adding methods for working directly with nonverbal, body-level experience (Mindell 1989: 118).

Growing from these roots

Building upon these sources, Mindell developed a theoretical and practical framework for encouraging clients to consciously inhabit a previously unconscious experience and to 'unfold' the process. This unfolding process is a deconstruction of the client's named experiences (their first interpretation of experience), that relies not only on verbal material and imagery but also on movement, deep somatic experience, interpersonal relationship and social context. Process Work theory emerges from Mindell believing in unravelling and living the message and task of the dreamworld, as Jung has modelled to many and as have countless 'healers' or 'shamans' before them.

With his Jungian and physics orientation, Mindell first explored working with the body's dreaming, and explored processes of illness and of dying people, including work with comatose states. He differentiated short-term processes reflected in night-time dreams, and body symptoms and long-term processes reflected in childhood dreams and collective or archetypal material found in deeper levels of body experience. He also explored working with people with extreme states using psychiatric diagnosis. Mindell observed how the dreaming body appeared in communication signals that influenced relationships, and went on to study and formulate a theory of 'systems with awareness' that he called the 'global dreambody' (Mindell 1998: 104–5). The inclusion of awareness and hence conscious change differentiates this concept from the other systems theories. Mindell applied this concept in his studies and work with large groups dealing with social and political issues and explored these and other ideas of Process Work in relation to the creative process. He and his students and colleagues continue to explore the application of Process Work in organizational development, conflict resolution, theatre and the arts.

Mindell and his colleagues consistently re-evaluate the theory and its application. When I once asked him about how it was that he was always able to continue developing the theory, he told me that it was a natural process, like going out in the bay with a boat to enjoy the day – but, if the boat was leaking, he'd go back to the dock and either fix it or take a new one, before going back to enjoy the bay again.

In essence, the Process Work facilitator needs and seeks to constantly grow from their own holes of perception. This attitude has a lineage in the shaman's practice to take himself apart to find out what plagues the client, or in Jung's dedication to consistently reinventing his theory to fit his client's needs and psyche rather than condemn the client for being 'resistant'. While it is natural to say that the individual client or group is resistant, or the symptom or conflict is intractable, it is more interesting to recognize that the facilitator's awareness or skills need expansion. That expansion will happen when the facilitator focuses on their growing edge. This occurs not only in supervision or therapy, but in moment-to-moment inner work while facilitating.

Chasing an antelope

I have profited in the last 30 years from regularly working with my somatic experiences, my symptoms and dreams, several chronic symptoms and some illnesses. I still always find myself searching anew for my path.

Unfolding my symptoms has always made me aware of the limits of my belief systems that have been part of my youth and culture. I acquired these systems, as all of us do, through familial and cultural socialization. I also developed belief systems to support me to give me more privileges, power or rank within the social context I was growing up in. I did not notice when these patterns had become redundant and my growth demanded of me to separate myself from them and start exploring the flow of unfamiliar processes. When young, I was not taught to meet the unexpected, step into the unknown or grow by interacting with and learning from difficulties, or from my dreams, intuition, impulses and moods. On the contrary, I was taught, as countless of us are, to focus solely on achieving socialization – at school, at home, within my culture.

I had lots of exposure to unpredictable events, but no philosophy to profit from them consciously. I was unconsciously encouraged to identify with the background I came from, which was lowest in the echelon, even among the working class. Don't overstretch, recognize your limits, and recognize what you can't do and implicitly, where you do not belong. We know today no one belongs, few of us fit the mould that parents and cultural norms prepare for us. Few of us fit the mould we construct for ourselves.

What Mindell researched and formulated in the dreambody concept is that what does not fit our mould or concept of our identity, and what we therefore marginalize, appears nonetheless in signals in our channels of perception and expression: visual, auditory, proprioception and movement (Mindell 1989:11). In his present work, Mindell also emphasizes how these experiences first manifest in pre-signals which can be picked up in fleeting signals, tendencies or 'flirts' (Mindell 2000: 215).

Marginalizing does not imply bad faith from us. It means that we do not have patterns to do differently. Many indigenous cultures have or have had a different relationship to the dreaming level. Take the Aboriginal culture of Australia. Their cultural inheritance includes a belief that the outer world we live in comes from the world of dreams, and that we are constantly shaped by the world of dreams. Dreaming is the foundation of life, and this corresponds to the importance of following the subtle impulses of the body and signals of the environment. This notion is a far cry from the modern western causal and mechanistic explanations of life, and the belief among many that dreams are irrational or irrelevant. In the western world, we tend to be suspicious of experiences which are 'only subjective' and try to hold ourselves accountable to 'consensus reality': those things we feel are 'objective', that we can agree upon.

I recently saw a film on an African indigenous groups' way of living and hunting. The documentary depicted the hunting day of a warrior, who was in pursuit of an antelope, how he ran after her for six hours, how the antelope rested in some shrubs, and then left. The warrior arrived at the shrubs, studied the ground carefully and found absolutely no further tracks. He proceeded to immerse himself in 'being the antelope', acting like her, moving like we had seen her some hours before on the hidden camera. Trusting his perceptions as the antelope, he left the shrubs and started running, in the same direction we had seen the antelope run. Sometime later, he found her tracks again and came upon the exhausted antelope. He had identified with the spirit of the antelope, rather than fight it, became it and so was one with what he was seeking. Consequently, he deeply thanked both her and her spirit for the food she and her spirit were granting his family and him for the months to come.

In a nutshell, this illustrates the theory of Process Work. Rather than fighting the body and its symptom(s), the idea is to enter its spirit, become it, be it, act like it, live it, because you are 'it' beyond your usual identity, and assume responsibility for the advantages 'it' gives you.

Body symptoms and signals indicate the method of working with them. A variety of methods for working with body experiences fall under the category of 'amplification', which we have mentioned. It is an extension of Jung's method of working with dreams. While Jung asked for an association to the dream image, a process worker will ask the person to feel the symptom *more*. One's personal subjective experience of any symptom is unique and therefore relevant to understanding its meaning for the individual. No interpretation can replace the subjective experience.

Identity and edges

Take the story of a young woman who asks me about the pain in her shoulder. She is a graduate student in the field of economics, and also prides herself in her studies and knowledge of psychology. She is from South America, trilingual, living and studying in Europe.

I ask her to feel the pain and to adjust her posture or make a movement to make it a tiny bit worse, so that she can feel it better and perceive her experience more specifically. She lifts her shoulder a bit, grins and tells me, 'Oh yes, I know about that, I tend to be too pushy, too aggressive.' And she drops her shoulder.

Although many people think that symptoms are meaningless, others rapidly assign 'meaning' to the symptom, as a sign that something is wrong and needs correction. For example, 'My symptom is telling me I have too much stress, and I need to slow down.' This sort of 'meaning' reflects an underlying orientation that symptoms are disturbances that need to be removed. The symptom is not yet fully grappled with and understood on its own terms.

I noticed that the woman with her shoulder pains had reacted quickly with her belief system, that she should be less pushy and more relaxed. But we had not yet explored the experience of her shoulder, and what 'it' wanted and what it was like. I asked her to lift her shoulder again, to feel the symptom, while I touched her shoulder with my hand. I asked her to find out what her shoulder felt like doing. She agreed. I put my hand lightly on her lifted shoulder, and I sensed a slight push upwards against my fingers. I pressed back, and her reaction was way stronger – she pushed back with her shoulder. Soon, she was pushing with her shoulder against my outstretched arm and laughing. I asked her how she had enjoyed the interaction. Apparently she had enjoyed her strength a whole lot, yet she said she was 'too feisty, too aggressive', and that people were constantly telling her she should be more relaxed and open, and always advised her to cool down.

So I asked her to step into the role of these people, these critics or gate-keepers reflecting the internalized belief system. She now pushed down on my shoulder, and said, 'You are too feisty, too emotional, cool down!' I kept pushing relentlessly against her pressure and request to be calm. She laughed and relaxed in her posture, rejoicing in how energizing it felt to her to see me expressing and enjoying the energy that was in her symptom.

I anchored the work by then putting my hand against her shoulder and she started immediately to push against my pressure, this time refusing to heed my requests to cool down. She said she now realized how she'd been giving up her own excitement and drive at her university, believing people when they said she should be calmer. She realized she wanted to live her passion, her tendency to have strong points of view and to tussle with people.

We also spoke about the cultural aspects of her process. As a South American living in Europe, she often felt unwelcome, not only in her personal style but in her cultural style. She decided she would voice her perceptions and engage at her leisure with the uncomfortable discussions that were bound to arise.

Edges and awareness

This young woman felt disturbed by a shoulder pain. She identified as needing to be more open and relaxed. Without being conscious of it, she was in agreement with an internalized critic towards her own exuberance, that was thus marginalized. The exuberance remained in her shoulder. As with many physical symptoms, her shoulder pain reflected two parts or attitudes in conflict with each other. One part called for her to cool down. The other part didn't want to cool down, but wanted to push through with exuberance and excitement. The symptom occurs at the 'edge': a term used in process work to describe the belief system that defines the limit to our identity or who we think we should be. The 'critic' defined the edge or belief system: that it is better to be cool and calm, and that one ought not be too pushy. In this work, she becomes aware of her experience in proprioception and movement, the urge to push and the verbal dictate that she should be calmer. She becomes aware of how these processes are in conflict inside her. Rather than feeling stuck between the two, she starts to enjoy her feistier, exuberant nature. This in turn relaxes her! Both sides of the process are now more accessible.

Edges, collective processes and change

The woman suffered from feeling slighted by her friends and teachers, who said she was too rebellious, pushy or temperamental. But all this is not very conscious. It occurs just outside her conscious perception. She is attempting to fit into the culture where she lives and studies, and unwittingly sides against her own exuberance, which resurfaces in her symptom.

Edges, or belief systems, stem from personal, family, cultural, social and religious norms and values. These define how we identify, and what we marginalize. The woman with the shoulder pain voiced an internalized value of the dominant culture of Europe which criticized and marginalized her exuberance. As she also identified her exuberance as belonging to her culture of origin, the edge was enforcing a kind of internalized oppression and prejudice against her as a member of a minority culture. The symptom thus carries extremely valuable information. Just trying to remove symptoms has far-reaching implications for our personal and social development.

Edges and rank

Emphasis on the importance of social awareness of privilege and rank is an important milestone in the evolution of Process Work theory. The dynamics of social rank are also relevant to body experience and symptoms. Unconscious use of power and privilege is oppressive and creates symptoms and illness. Power and privilege, and the associated rank are also easily misused to enforce prejudice. They tend to appear as double signals.

I recall a client who complained of headaches and stomachaches and pressure that had been ongoing for a few weeks. She told me she was going to change her job and that she was happy about it. I said I was happy to hear that, but noticed pauses and a slowness in her voice that were not congruent with the message of happiness. She paused and then told me the following story. She'd been working for many years at her current job, in a social organization. She was loved and respected by many people in the organization, due to her innovative ideas, commitment and hard work. She had recently come up for a review, in order to renew her contract. While having a tea break in the cafeteria, two senior managers whom she vaguely knew came up to her, asking questions about her work, but implicitly challenging her training and qualifications. After a while, she realized that she was feeling intimidated, and asked them to state their purpose in questioning her in this way. They stopped and left her table. She then told her boss about this incident, and asked him if it had to do with her review, and if there was any question in the organization as to her skills and qualifications. The boss refused to answer, saying he would give her the evaluation in a week. The boss then went on holiday, without leaving word about the evaluation and contract renewal. There had been rumours that changes were under way in the organization and people would be made redundant, but she had never been told or considered that this could involve her job. She now realized that the rumours probably involved her, and so she was looking for work elsewhere.

I described my perception to her regarding the misuse of rank and the tactics of intimidation employed by the senior managers and her boss, whether intended or not. In relation to the hierarchy in the organization, they had rank over her and had misused it (Mindell 1995: 49). She felt witnessed and validated in her perception. I then helped her to become aware of how she had not let herself get intimidated, how she had reacted with presence of mind in the cafeteria, and when approaching her boss to find out what was going on. I pointed out that she had a 'psychological' rank, in her ability to stay emotionally centred within a conflict, and able to communicate directly. This psychological rank was sorely missing in her boss and managers. I suggested that it might be useful to her to recognize this rank and act with this rank in relation to her boss and managers.

She asked to pause for a moment and then said that she realized I was right, that she tended to ignore her own presence and abilities to handle difficult situations, and in this way left the action and accountability for the situation she was in with others, which furthered her feeling of intimidation. She decided on the spot that rather than just leaving, she would first go back and clear up the whole situation and request clarification of the managers' actions. She also said with surprise and delight that all the symptoms she'd had in the last weeks since the incident had disappeared during the session.

She shifted identity by first recognizing the signals that she suffered from, rather than enduring them. In this way, she more clearly recognized the misuse of power by her boss and managers. She then also became aware of her own rank in this situation – her ability to demand that the managers and her boss be accountable for their actions.

Edges and double signals

The edge structures our communication in double signal. The double signal consists of an intended signal and an unintended signal. The intended signal originates from our primary process (i.e. how we identify and what we intend to communicate). The unintended signal arises from our secondary process, the 'dreaming' process we do not identify with. In between is the edge, the belief system that organizes how we identify and what we marginalize. Another way to look at this is that a double or unintended signal that 'you' don't send is sent by a dream figure.

With the dreambody concept Mindell suggests that the dream pattern is not only reflected in a symptom, but is also mirrored in the double signal. The 'dreaming' is occurring at all times. At night, it appears in our dreams. It also appears in our body experience and symptoms, our unintended communication and in our relationship patterns and entanglements. We can access the 'dreaming' at any moment by unravelling a double signal. To illustrate this: a client of mine tells me that he is feeling afraid of talking to his wife and father about their demands on him. He wants to learn to be more assertive. While he tells me this story, he unconsciously touches his lips. I ask him to notice the feeling he gets while lightly stroking his lips and then to inhibit himself (another method of amplification), to stop the stroking and to notice what he misses. He does this and tells me that he misses the feeling of tenderness that stroking his lips gives him. As we explore this a bit, he tells me his dream. In it, he pushes down earth with his fingers around the bulbs of the tulips he has planted. In the dream, he realizes the tulips need more earth around their bases and stems so that they can stand up straight. For him to stand up straight (to discover the assertiveness he was looking for) did not mean that he needed to be tougher, but rather that he needed more earth (i.e. more support to his tenderness). He easily saw the connection between his dream, double signal and relationship.

Principles of process work

Almost nothing principle

The most subtle signals carry the seeds of transformative life-changing experiences. These subtle signals self-amplify until they reach our awareness. This means we have the opportunity to work with many symptoms and body experiences long before they become overtly disturbing. This in turn means that you focus on the minimal signals and cues you have been trained to ignore, bring them to foreground and, by inhabiting them, bring to the middle what is usually marginalized.

Deep democracy principle

Deep democracy refers to the inner wisdom and direction that arises when we support the interaction of all parts of our experience and all dimensions – the concerns of everyday life, the dreaming that structures our symptoms, night-time dreams and unintended signals, and the subtlest levels of experience.

Eldership and facilitation

Elders – not necessarily age-related – are no longer attached to one particular point of view dominating the other. Rather, an attitude of eldership supports the interaction of all parts. Jung described the individuation process as a shift in the locus of awareness from the ego as the centre of personality to the self as the centre of personality.

Similarly, in Process Work, we focus on developing fluidity to welcome and facilitate an interaction among all parts and the resulting transformation, rather than impose one part over another. Thus its premise lies in *awareness* and *facilitation*. This is very relevant to working with the body. People generally side with one part over the other or attempt to impose one part over the other. For example, relaxing is valued over tension. This marginalizes tension and its potential for the person who might need tension to finish a project, for example.

One classic example from Mindell's early work is the story of one of his occasional seminar participants who, attending a seminar on bodywork offered by a visiting teacher, was made aware by the seminar leader that his protuberant jaw muscles needed relaxing. The seminar leader demonstrated his technique with the assent of the participant, releasing the tension in these muscles. Mindell saw this young man shortly after. His mouth was slack, and he felt heavily depressed. Mindell asked the client to consult the I Ching with him about how to go further. He got Hexagram 16 – biting through. The young man's process that appeared in his jaw was to bite through – to 'bite through the problems in his life' with all his focus and intensity, and not to relax (Mindell 1989: 25–6).

Metaskills

Metaskills refer to the attitude with which the tools and skills of Process Work are used. Attitude affects process work, just as the attitude when you cook affects your food, or the attitude when you pick up a pen affects your calligraphy. There are attitudes that are recommended as useful when applying skills of process work, such as beginner's mind, interest in the unknown and the ability to be compassionate to all parts. Another approach is to become aware of the attitude you *do* have, to name it and facilitate it as part of the whole interaction with the client (Mindell 1995).

The tendency in most of us when working with people is to unconsciously identify with a certain attitude, such as friendliness, criticism, mothering or optimism. When you unconsciously do that, you and your client get polarized. You might be optimistic rather than facilitating your client's awareness between their optimism and their depression or pessimism.

Perception of our metaskills makes such skills work. Another way of saying this is: *not* noticing your attitude as you apply a skill makes you fall into the process with your client.

Personal myth and pilot wave

Process Work's teleological orientation (i.e. focusing on the evolution, meaning and direction of processes), perceives life's creative process in the body, its signals, symptoms and illnesses as an expression of the individual's myth. Jung defined the individual myth as a long-term orientation in life. Its pattern is mirrored in the childhood dream. While researching the connection between dream and body, we studied the interaction between childhood dreams as long-term patterns and chronic symptoms as somatic long-term patterns. Process Work in recent years has reformulated the personal myth idea in dynamic terms and borrowed the concept of the 'pilot wave' from quantum physicist David Boehm. The 'pilot wave', the 'flux behind all events' is the sum of all dream-figures across your lifetime (Arnold Mindell 2004: 69–70, 84). It gives you the sense that your life has direction.

Three dimensions: CR, dreaming and sentience

We've seen how body experience, symptoms and unintended signals arise from the dreaming process and shape our long-term individuation. Body symptoms and double signals reflect the conflict and the complementarities of parts to parts. Working with the relationship of parts leads to transform-ation, a creativity that arises out of their interaction and often an experience that transcends the duality. Amy Mindell used to refer to this as reaching an irreducible core experience. At this point, there is a momentary resolution, a sense of discovery and meaningfulness that transcends siding with one part or the other.

In recent years, Arnold Mindell has focused on working with pre-signals and tendencies originating from what he calls the 'sentient level of expe-rience'. This is the level before a signal becomes repetitive and precedes the polarization of parts and roles. While we used to unfold signals and the interaction of all parts of the process to its irreducible core, we now also focus on accessing these core experiences through fine-tuned awareness of subtle pre-signals before they become signals and symptoms.

Alternatively, with special methods that begin with attention to a somatic experience, symptom or signal, it is possible to discover and connect to the underlying impulse at the origin of the signal or somatic experience.

Mindell describes three dimensions:

1 *Consensus reality* refers to ordinary reality. Experiences are consented upon or 'objective', repeatable and measurable. They can be captured on a video or measured, and most people will agree they exist.
2 *Dreamland or dreaming level* refers to the level of double signals, dreams, subjective experiences of the body, deeper feelings, mythic polarizations, dream images and visions.
3 *Sentience or essence level* is the area of subtle tendencies before some-thing manifests as a dream image or an identifiable feeling, or a specific or repeatable signal.

A specific category of pre-signals are fleeting signals, sensations, visual or auditory flirts, moods and hunches. These fleeting signals manifest at the margins of our perception in the various channels. They arise from the sen-tience level and seek our attention. These flirt-like experiences are of such brief duration that we normally do not hold onto them long enough for them to come into our consciousness (Amy Mindell 2004: 60–5).

Mindell describes the sentient level as a creative field from which our dreaming and consensus realities arise. The creative process is central to Pro-cess Work theory and practice. Bringing awareness to the existence of this field is creative in itself. Mindell formulates methods to move fluidly between these levels of experience. By returning to his earlier interest in physics, his interest in psychology and formulating the relationship between the two disciplines, he has deepened his first concept of the dreambody and his attempt at unifying the gap between mind and body.

Conclusion: awareness, healing and creativity

The idea of Process Work is to go where our perception is called by the dreaming and somatic experience. For example, when working with comatose people or terminally ill people, we follow and support their subjective experiences/dreaming within their altered states (Mindell 1994). The idea of healing as 'making the symptom or illness go away' is worthwhile, but not necessarily possible or relevant to the wholeness of the person. Working with people with terminal illness makes the process worker perceive that people may begin to identify with their eternal self, with a quality that is beyond time and space, feeling in that space more alive than ever, even while their body may be dying.

This attitude of welcoming and unfolding the subjective experience of the symptom is an important contribution of Process Work. It is of course natural and important to have empathy for that part of a person who is suffering and just wants the symptom to go away and get better. What is less often seen is the importance of also supporting the symptom to be experienced and unfolded – to enter it and discover its potential creativity. It is a kind of paradox that an attitude that sides against the symptom, in hopes of health, tends to try to remove it rather than discover its creative information. This 'healing attitude' thus keeps the person locked within a limiting identity, and away from the spirit that seeks personal growth and contribution to community. Because the information in the symptom still tries to express itself, this attitude can also inadvertently exacerbate the symptom.

An alternative usage of the term 'healing' refers to wholeness. Arnold Mindell writes: 'I predict that focusing on and appreciating subjective body experience as a fundamental reality will have remarkable and positive effects upon health issues' (Mindell 2004: 270).

12 Embodied-Relational Therapy

Nick Totton

Introduction

Embodied-Relational Therapy (ERT) integrates body-oriented work, psycho-analytic thinking, process approaches, and spiritual and political perspectives. About 15 years old, it was developed by myself and Em Edmondson, for and through the psychotherapy training courses which we led under the name of 'Selfheal'. Currently I lead one-year post-qualification courses in ERT, together with follow-up advanced courses, and a group of graduates are learning to teach the work. In what follows, as well as discussing ERT from a technical and theoretical point of view, I shall be trying to convey some of the flavour of the work.

ERT starts out from the perception that, as human beings, we are integrated body-mind-spirit, and that on the whole, we find this condition hard to manage. Our nature seeks to *express itself freely*, while at the same time *protecting itself*, sometimes in conditions of great difficulty. This double task of expression and protection makes us often subject to contradictory pulls, and offering double messages about what we feel, want and need. Through a relationship which is challenging but supportive and non-invasive, it is possible to disentangle our doubleness and allow our process to unfold – which is what has been trying to happen all along.

The fundamental assumption of ERT is that *we all do the best we possibly can*; the best that we know so far. Each individual has come up with a brilliant and brave solution to the conditions in which we have found ourselves: the optimum available style of relating, the optimum balance between body and spirit. (Often, when a person has been brought up in distorted circumstances, the best they can do is certainly not good enough, either for themselves or for those around them.)

Equally, each person is seeking, consciously or unconsciously, to *change* their behavioural style to meet current possibilities and conditions, which may be very different from those in which we grew up. Whatever appears in a person's life as a problem, a symptom, a conflict, can also be understood as an incomplete attempt to change and grow. ERT tries to use the therapeutic relationship as a space in which these issues can unfold, unwind and reach their natural fullness. The fundamental tool of therapy is *awareness*, which tends to unpack and transform any stuck situation.

Hence, ERT places emphasis on spontaneity, and what resists it. It believes that simply relaxing and allowing life to happen will be profoundly healing. Relaxation could be said to be the entire goal of therapy! However, we have all learnt that relaxation and spontaneity can be very dangerous, leading to failure, humiliation and punishment ('Sit still! Keep quiet! Be good!'). Undoing this learnt avoidance means developing trust – of process, of embodiment, of relationship. Spontaneity and relaxation are *spiritual* qualities: in developing them, we develop a trustful and respectful attitude towards the great universe of which we are part. In stalking the spontaneous, we cultivate an internal quietness and humility. At the same time, many of the ways in which we are oppressed and struggle against our oppression are *political* phenomena, which require political framing and courageous confrontation.

Like other body psychotherapies, ERT is a whole psychotherapy which explores human embodiment equally with other channels of expression – for example, words (see the Introduction to this volume). In this chapter, I will concentrate on the different ways in which humans try to deal with the problematic situation of being a body, and the implications for our life. However, focusing on our embodiment reveals that it cannot be separated from relationship.

Because we are embodied beings, our whole lives revolve around our need for relationship. To be a body is to need other bodies. We come into the world with our lives literally depending on our ability to form relationships with the adults around us, and with an innate drive to do so. (Infants as young as 42 *minutes* will try to imitate adult expressions: Meltzoff and Moore 1995.) Our most profound desire is for the Other, for the embodied pleasure, satisfaction and transcendence which connection with the Other can (in reality or in fantasy) provide. At the same time, we represent the Other for other people, and the web of mutual need and desire can become very twisted indeed. We grow up needing relationship, and fearing it – fearing the uncontrollable, which we locate most painfully in our bodies and in our relationships. ERT explores the possibility of relaxing into embodied relating.

Embodiment

Our experience as human beings is that, apparently, we are spirit, and we are matter. Often this is understood as spirit *in* matter – soul in body. That little word 'in' is very difficult and confusing. Are we in our bodies like snails in shells? Like prisoners in cells? Like babies in bathwater? Or salt in seawater? Like thoughts in heads? Like minds in brains? Like people in trouble? Or like people in couples? Like oaks in acorns, then? Like seeds in soil?

If spirit is in matter, then matter is, equally, in spirit.

ERT finds it more helpful to think of 'spirit' and 'matter' as directions or polarities of energy: tendencies *between which* every being exists and moves. More like verbs than like nouns, in fact: all energy 'matters' and 'spirits' constantly, in varying proportions. We are spirit becoming matter, matter becoming spirit, constantly passing ourselves both ways on the spiral stair.

To explore these experiences we will have to use metaphor. Nothing about spirit will translate completely into 'concrete' language. However, metaphors don't have to be vague and woolly; after all, 'gravitational attraction' and 'electrical current' are both metaphors, referring to scarcely understood processes but allowing very practical procedures. ('Concrete' itself is a metaphor when applied to language. 'Metaphor' means 'to carry across': in a sense, matter is spirit carried across.) The metaphor we start out with, then, is of a series of concentric layers, nestling one inside another like the layers of an onion; except that they go on to infinity – and exist in many more dimensions than our everyday three. At the heart of the onion is our physical being, and the material world in and through which that being manifests. Each layer out from the centre is made up of 'stuff' which is a bit less like 'matter' and a bit more like 'spirit'.

A key quality of matter is its definiteness: fixed and limited in both space and time. Matter is simply, flatly, *there*, one bit of it in one place at one time; its nature is to be obstinate, resistant to being changed and moved around. There's no arguing with it. And from these basic material qualities follow a range of experiences like frustration, disappointment, grief, death, predictability, effort, satisfaction, creation and pleasure.

Spirit, on the other hand, tends towards being everywhere and everywhen at once, and partaking of every identity at once. And again, from this basic quality follow experiences like ecstasy, illumination, play, imagination, ease, boredom, indecision, pointlessness and vapidity.

From the viewpoint of matter, spirit is free, expanded, indefinite, open – and ungrounded, vague, illusory. From the point of view of spirit, matter is bounded, concentrated, precise, closed – and limited, pedantic, imprisoning. Spirit is linked to awareness; matter to existence. We could say that 'pure awareness' cannot really exist – and 'pure existence' cannot be aware.

The layers of our multidimensional onion are spread along the spectrum between these two impossible poles, but real directions, of 'pure spirit' and 'pure matter'. An embodied human being exists simultaneously in every layer of the onion.

We become embodied, it seems, in order to temper our being, as a sword is tempered by plunging it red-hot into water. The plunge into matter *defines* us:

challenges us to exist in a particular way, to be one person rather than another, to manifest the lightness of spirit under conditions whose difficulty and limitation is also their richness and profundity. The recalcitrance of material incarnation, its awe-ful difficulty, its precision of consequences, offers an extraordinary teaching potential.

Our struggles and choices in life can usefully be understood within the polarity of matter/spirit which we have been considering. Whenever we begin a new involvement or commitment, we are 'embodying' ourselves, identifying with a position of limitation and definition. Whenever we step back, 'see through' or 'beyond' a specific position, we are 'disembodying' ourselves, identifying as spirit and awareness. When we wake up in the morning we embody; when we go to sleep we enspirit – which is a different kind of waking up. Both matter and spirit, ground and sky, are awake to particular aspects of reality which the other tends to ignore.

For many people the issue of embodiment, of choosing to be here, is crucial: it functions as an underlying metaphor to every situation they live through, a choice they have to keep remaking. Often a part of them refuses to commit, to incarnate, to forget its own spiritual nature (fall asleep into matter). But they won't usually be aware of the process in these terms: they're more likely to see themselves (and be seen) as wimpish, useless, ill, daydreamers or crazy people. If someone can become aware of their own disembodied aspect and start to own it without shame, then they can begin to use it as a resource, a doorway, a messenger – something to make life brighter and less restricted. Equally, many people are so committed to body that they ignore or reject spirit – treat ideals and aspirations as foolish and 'unrealistic'. Interestingly, this attitude is called 'hard-headed'. Very often it goes along with depression.

This is very general. For each person there is an individual knot of issues concerning embodiment/disembodiment, with their experience of birth a key element of the knot – but only an element; many other circumstances and situations will affect and be affected by our whole attitude towards materiality. As I sit with a client, these issues are always in the back of my mind, and frequently move into the foreground and cast light on the problems and satisfactions being described.

Relationship

Embodiment directly implies relationship. Our characteristic style of embodiment, our willingness or otherwise to *be* embodied, expresses itself through our way of relating to the world and to people – our needs, our desires, our projections, our defences – sometimes creative, sometimes problematic.

A central factor in therapy is the relationship between client and therapist.

Nothing can be done without adequate contact between the two participants. And the sort of relationship that comes into being, the way it opens up and closes down possibilities as it flows through different aspects and intensities, tells us about the client's patterns, history and belief systems. People together are in a field relationship, a state of mutual co-arising where each continuously affects and conditions the experience of the other. As therapists we seek to bring awareness to this field.

Using relationship therapeutically means practising detachment – we still have strong feelings about people, but witness them, study them, rather than identify with them or act as if they are transparent. Habitually, humans treat the way we relate to another person as if that's what the other person *is*: I feel angry so you must be irritating, I love you so you must be wonderful. Training as a therapist, or being in therapy, means re-owning these projections. But as well as studying the projection and transference in an interaction, we must also recognize and honour the actuality of what's going on. In particular, we need to acknowledge that the client's feelings about us may be – to some extent always are – *a response to how we behave*, not just to their fantasies about us.

Here is a body-centred example of how one can work in and out of the relationship trance. When I started working with 'James' (a fictionalized and composite character), I was fascinated by the tension in his jaw, and convinced that releasing it would be a tremendously helpful thing that I could offer him. I pressed strongly on the insertion point of the muscles at the hinge of his jaw, and encouraged him to breathe and make a sound. He found this unbearable, and very quickly asked me to stop; his resulting distrust lasted for more than one session.

Despite this, however, in a state of temporary amnesia I found myself trying exactly the same thing again a few months later – and then yet again! – each time producing a similar and highly understandable reaction of anger and distrust. Once I managed to mobilize my awareness around this, to apologize fully, and to think together with James about what was going on, we focused on his childhood experience of being repeatedly teased and physically bullied by his older brothers, and his inability to speak out about this, either to them or to his parents. Both the pain of being abused, and the holding back from speaking, were held in his locked jaw. My own contribution, what hooked me in, was a compulsive desire to fix things and be helpful – traits which James also manifested.

Contact

Contact is vital to the healing space: people are *in touch*, and energy flows between them. Our most primal experience of this is in the womb, surrounded and supported by fluid, with nourishment and information flowing directly into us through the umbilical cord. After birth, we need to remake that connection, through skin, eyes, ears, mouth, heart, energy field; and throughout life every relationship is partly a reminder of this original contact. We need contact in order to live, and our primary model of contact, however abstract it may become, is a bodily one.

We also all have experiences of difficult contact, difficult connection, difficult energy, difficult feeding, which can make us very reluctant to open up to someone else. We may have to spend a lot of time in therapy – hours, weeks, years – working around contact: it is useless and dangerous to do any other work if living contact is not there. So establishing contact can easily become the whole of therapy with a particular person; and recognizing contact and its absence, and different styles of resistance to contact, are key therapeutic skills.

Contact is importantly different from some other kinds of relating.

Merging

Womb experience is perhaps more like this: with no clear boundaries between us and the universe, we are part of the whole, floating in a sea of bliss. Everyone needs to dissolve like this sometimes – through sex, love, meditation, worship, time in nature, sleep. But losing boundaries needs to be voluntary, rather than being overwhelmed, flooded, seduced. And we need to *have* boundaries in the first place: some people are still trying to separate themselves off fully, to learn where they stop and the world starts.

Penetration

One way of reaching someone is to come inside their being. Some qualities of penetration – assertiveness, passion, demand – can be valuable aspects of contact. Some people sometimes can only be reached through insisting. As therapists, though, we have to learn to approach someone's boundary, and stop. Many people have had terrifying experiences of feeling invaded, abused, shattered, poisoned, which may derive from sexual, physical or mental abuse, from horrific births and other traumatic experiences, or from more chronic long-term relationships and atmospheres. The difference from involuntary merging is that instead of having weak or absent boundaries, the person has brittle, rigid, over-defined boundaries: they are cut off from contact through their fear of invasion.

Separateness

While some people are trying to separate themselves off, others are stuck in a separateness which they cannot overcome – a lonely, isolated life. Just as losing our boundaries needs to be voluntary, *having* boundaries also needs to be voluntary.

These three qualities of merging, penetration and separateness are all distinct from contact, yet related to it; at different times we need a flavour of each in order to improve our contact with someone. With each person we meet therapeutically, we have to sense their issues concerning contact, and find a way of building trust, forming relationship, allowing energy to flow safely between us. For some people, the fear is mainly of invasion or flooding; for others it's about lack of connection. Some believe they have to hide their insides because others will reject them; some feel they have to manipulate others or smash their defences in order to preserve themselves. Another sort of person plays constantly with contact and separation, advance and retreat.

Contact as a way of life

Contact happens not only *between* people; it happens *within* a person, and between them and their environment. Grounding is a form of contact, and so is what ERT calls 'skying', contact with the cosmos and with spirit. We need contact with ourselves, with other people and with our environment; all three depend on our capacity to tolerate spontaneity, to give up some control, to let the boundaries of our identity become relaxed and porous while still remaining comfortable about what is 'me' and what isn't. All this depends on our embodiment, which determines our capacity to contact our own feelings, sensations, impulses, thoughts and fantasies. These in turn give us most of our information about what is going on in the relationship field. Being in touch with ourselves, the world and other people models for our clients the possibility of living in a more relaxed and flexible way.

The key is to offer contact consistently, without overriding the other person's 'keep off' signals. Sometimes these are impossible to miss; but some people find it very hard to say 'No', and have no belief that others will stay out. We need to be alert to and respectful of any feeling of hesitancy or resistance. Sometimes in therapy circles 'resistance' is spoken of as if it is a bad way to behave, something to overcome. But if we think of it in the sense of resistance to oppression, or resistance to infection, we may be able to support people's need to protect their integrity.

At the same time, though, it is necessary to offer contact in a convincing and authentic way – which means above all working on our own resistance to and avoidance of contact, giving ourselves just as much respect and support as we do our clients, but finding our way through to a place where we can genuinely want to be with the other person. Times when we don't may tell us about what is going on for them, as well as for us: our impatience or repugnance may mirror their negative expectation.

Character, embodiment and relationship

ERT's understanding of character has developed out of the work of Wilhelm Reich, who was himself exploring some implications of Freud's theories. Character expresses the unity of embodiment and relationship: it is each person's fundamental mode of being in the world, apparent equally in their attitudes and beliefs, their ways of relating in and out of the therapy room, and their bodily structure and appearance (for a fuller account see Totton and Jacobs 2001).

For ERT, character is essentially *creative*: a central way to express our existence. Each character position defines a *theme* arising from key developmental encounters during early life: existence; nurturing; validation; self-regulation; assertion; meta-communication; or some blend or combination of these. These themes all play themselves out in every life: each reflects a developmental stage we all go through, and need to go through to attain adult competence and creativity. We all need to be able to think and imagine ('boundary stage'), to take in nourishment and stand on our own feet ('oral stage'), to use play and fantasy to manage our internal and external objects ('control stage'), to regulate our own bodily processes and engage with the material world ('holding stage'), to push ourselves forward and conquer reality ('thrusting stage') and to play, flirt and meta-communicate ('crisis stage'). Each of these psychological thresholds has bodily corollaries.

But individual circumstances – together, perhaps, with elements which we 'bring with us', and ongoing family stories – determine which of these universal themes will be of central significance. Everyone has a character, because to be here we have to be *someone*: character is inseparable from embodiment, the particular 'colour' or blend of colours which each person contributes to the rainbow. This understanding of character as creative has led ERT to rename character positions from their traditional, rather pathologizing and limiting labels: instead of the 'schizoid' we speak of the boundary character, instead of the 'phallic' and 'hysteric', the thrusting and crisis characters, and so on.

Although everyone does the best they can in the circumstances, this best can be disastrously inadequate. The same goes for character: although essentially creative, how creatively it functions in practice is determined by the degree, type and timing of any trauma we encounter in our initial attempts to *express* each developmental need, and the strategies we therefore adopt to *protect* each need, even at the cost of disguising or concealing it; together, of course, with whatever work of self-understanding and self-acceptance we may later undertake. Character is a means of functioning, and a means of survival: it constitutes 'resistance' not only as avoidance, but also as appropriate struggle against oppression and invasion.

Reich says that for everyone 'the *first* impulse . . . must be the desire to establish contact with the outer world' ([1945] 1972: 271). If this is frustrated by prohibition, coldness, avoidance or hostility in those adults with whom we seek a close relationship, a personality structure develops which both conceals and presents, expresses and protects our desire. Its specific form will match the key points when traumatic frustration was experienced; for example, oral frustration – deprivation of nurturing and support during the oral 'window' in early childhood – gives rise to a character which both expresses the need for nurturing and defends against it.

Character embodies our history, our individual experience of passing through key developmental stages as infants and young children. At each developmental 'window', we are available for specific learning and depending what happens to us, we acquire more or less creative or restrictive maps of reality. We all have all these maps, and use each of them in certain circumstances, but we tend to specialize in one or two, which we try to use as the key for every door we encounter in life. These are our embodied character. In therapy, with its offer of deep contact, childhood issues are intensely reactivated, and the attitudes which a person uses in life to defend against damage and disappointment are used to defend against becoming aware of these buried issues.

What I have been saying about contact styles is one example, indicating a person's imprinting in relation to the 'boundary' position, the window which seems to open and close in the first days or weeks of life. A more familiar name for this is 'schizoid'; Reich called it 'ocular', indicating its embodied relationship with eyes, ears and head (also with the skin) – zones which are very active in a newborn infant. The developmental journey through early life is also a *journey through the body*, from the head downwards to the pelvis. It follows a specific, curving trajectory down the front of the body, back through the diaphragm to the sacrum, and up through the pelvis to the genitals, as each zone in turn is activated.

The concept of character anchors particular styles of being in the relational events of developmental life. Our experiences of trauma are felt initially in particular bodily zones and only have a structural effect if they happen while that zone is at the centre of our developmental agenda – during its activation phase. Traumas at other periods will colour our character style, but will not define its core elements. There is considerable evidence from neuroscience to support this view (Carroll, this volume; Perry *et al.* 1995; Schore 2001a, 2001b), hinting at a potential unification of attachment theory and post-Reichian character theory.

Here we are concerned with sub-critical or non-catastrophic trauma, relatively tolerable experiences, generally ongoing rather than single events – often interactions with carers – which shape not only our psychic structure, but our *physical* structure: character can be recognized before the person even speaks. Overall body shape, distribution of muscle and fat, breathing, skin colour and texture, posture, movement style, even metabolic style – character is literally *embodied* in all these ways, so that for example a spindly 'oral' body may powerfully convey lack of support, or a stocky 'holding' (traditionally, 'masochistic') body may appear literally 'squashed'.

Character is a *quality of embodiment* – linked with Stern's 'vitality affects' (1985): an expression of the individual's experience of bodily impulse and its satisfaction or denial. As an example, from a bodily point of view, the key quality of the boundary character is *incompleteness*, so that the body seems not fully incarnate: unintegrated, immature or semi-material. Types include the 'professor' or 'nerd', awkward, large-headed, stiff-limbed, myopic; the pudgy baby; the ethereal elf. Different versions are represented by Spock from *Star Trek*; by Sinead O'Connor; by Woody Allen; or by Stan Laurel.

The complete list of basic character types used in ERT, together with the key issues and body areas involved, is as follows, in sequence of development:

- *Boundary character* (eyes, ears, head; skin. Existence: the right to be).
- *Oral character* (jaw and mouth, arms, legs. Need: the right to be fed and supported).
- *Control character* (chest, arms. Validation: the right to be recognized).
- *Holding character* (buttocks, thighs, shoulders. Regulation: the right to do it my way, in my own time).
- *Thrusting character* (pelvis, lower back, thighs, shoulders. Assertion: the right to be recognized, to make one's own way).
- *Crisis character* (pelvis, thighs, chest, eyes. Meta-communication: the right to choose, to play, to be ambiguous).

Ultimately, the limiting aspects of character result not from internal conflict, but from external, socially-driven frustration of desire. Social organizations based on authority and exploitation require character structures which can tolerate the pressures this creates. The family mediates authority's need for a pliable and obedient individual character – through sexual inhibition, and more generally through the inhibition of all forms of pleasure, empowerment and self-expression. Hence ERT's work with character has an intrinsic political dimension.

ERT in action

ERT sees therapy (all therapy, not just our own approach) in four phases or stages, which operate equally during one particular session or part of a session, or over the course of a therapeutic relationship: that is, they are fractal, and can be identified at any level of the therapeutic process. We call these phases making contact; gathering information; amplifying; and integrating. I have already discussed the role of contact in therapy; there is no space to look at all four phases, so I will say a little about amplification.

Under this heading we can place most of the explicit skills, techniques and methods of psychotherapy. Amplifying means taking something that we have noticed going on, and helping it to happen more. In so doing, we are encouraging the client to get more in touch with their own process; especially the bits that they either don't know about, or experience as alien, coming from outside themselves. Once a part of the process has been amplified, it can hopefully be owned, experienced and completed.

To amplify something that is going on, we can ask the client to do it *more* (e.g. 'Say that again, louder'; 'I notice your fingers are tapping – what happens if you focus on that action?'); or ask them to do it *less*, so as to amplify the *impulse* to do it ('What happens if you keep your fingers still?'; 'Let's see what it feels like if you try not to say sorry'). Sometimes we also need to quieten and slow down the rest of what is happening, so that this one feature can stand out more. So we might help the client relax and go inside, then ask them to focus on a body part, a sensation, an image etc. We can amplify any aspect: all roads lead to Rome, everything will take us deeper into the person's process. But it's important to deal with signals that say 'No' before we go any further. For instance, if we ask the client to do something and they comply, but as though they don't really want to, then we need to amplify that unwillingness.

Even leaving aside all channels except embodiment, there are many, many options for amplifying – we could work with posture; gestures and movements; tones of voice; breathing; body sensations; the bodily expression of emotions; symptoms; and many other phenomena. We aim for a playful, imaginative, flexible approach that lets us follow and facilitate the flow of the client's energy from one issue to another, from one channel of expression to another (e.g. a body sensation becomes an emotion, an image arises, leading to a thought . . .) It's easy for the therapist to actually impede the client's process by being rigid and clumsy – for example insisting that the client stay in the embodiment channel when their energy has moved elsewhere. Especially important is amplifying the relationship between client and therapist, which carries a tremendous amount of information about the client's issues and history. This means amplifying our *own* feelings as well as theirs: our reactions to them are part of their process.

A small example: 'Joan' (another fictional/composite character) arrived with a sense of pressure and breathlessness in her chest, and asked me if I could 'help her get rid of it'. My spontaneous response was listless and reluctant, as if I couldn't be bothered. I had an impulse to override this and 'be a good therapist'; but instead, I shared some of my response with her, and asked whether it might illuminate what she was experiencing. Immediately she said, 'Yes, I feel under constant pressure to be cooperative and deliver the goods.' Now my energy changed, I became interested and wanting to explore the process. I asked Joan to put physical pressure on me and try to make *me* deliver. She put her weight on my shoulders and, with increasing enthusiasm, ordered me to get my act together and help her!

After a while we swapped roles: I put my open hand on her sternum and 'leant into' her until she felt the external pressure matched what she was feeling internally, repeating lines she had used like, 'You've got to come through!' She growled in protest, the growl became a roar, and she connected with anger against these demands being put on her. At the same time, through my touch I experienced a stuck, toxic quality in her chest which, as she expressed anger, transformed into a vibrant and vital energy; we were able to develop a new shared vocabulary from discussing these perceptions. The demand to perform, and the resistance to it, had been passed around between Joan, her environment and myself, ending in a creative 'delivery' of the emotional 'goods' rather than just 'getting rid of' (aborting) the experience. A few weeks later a birthing process occurred – a different kind of 'delivery' and 'coming through under pressure'. Joan no longer felt that her baby self was being 'got rid of' in the act of being born.

The therapist's impulses and reactions are one part of the therapeutic field which the client may experience as external and alien. A wider example is 'symptoms': all the things our body/mind/spirit field creates, but our conscious self *suffers* – anything from a cold to cancer, a bad back to toothache; but also more subtle experiences – we can feel 'overcome' by jealousy or 'poisoned' by depression; we can feel at the mercy of many forces, including our habits and addictions, other people's behaviour, institutions, the weather – all can be invited to tell us what they are trying to bring to our attention. It's worth noticing all the events that a client describes as having happened, or being done, *to* them. Amplifying these aspects of the process is often very valuable: they represent the unknown, the bits the person doesn't identify with – the unconscious.

Breathwork

I shall illustrate ERT's approach to amplifying embodiment with one specific way of working which is close to my own heart, since it grew out of the Reichian breathwork technique that was central to my own original training. I need to emphasize, though, that this is not the central technique of ERT, which in fact does not have a central technique – it aims to improvise a creative response to each client in each session. However, we obviously have some tried and true methods, and breathwork is one of them.

ERT redefines Reichian work as centred on breathing and relationship, asking: can I breathe and relate to someone at the same time? Whenever we have difficult feelings in relation to someone, we instinctively restrict our breathing to suppress those feelings. Alternatively, to keep breathing we cut off relating, for example by turning away or closing our eyes. Trying to stay open both internally and externally opens up core therapeutic issues, immediately highlighting transference – and also countertransference: this is intense work for therapist as well as client.

Working with a client in this way, I encourage them to lie down or lean back and relax. I sit near them, offer them eye contact, and ask them to bring their attention to their breath: not to do anything about it or to it – although this may well happen automatically, in which case it should be accepted – but simply to be aware of it, be warmly interested in what it does, as I am myself.

When one tries to let the breath happen freely while attending to it consciously, consciousness and spontaneity begin to interfere with each other: resistance emerges, embodied in the breath. Breathing is right on the interface between voluntary and autonomic functioning: any attempt to 'control ourselves' shows up here. Through breath control we create and maintain 'the spastic I' – the ego based in body *tension* rather than body *awareness*. The 'spastic I' learns to regard awareness as a matter of self-consistency, a continuous self-commentary which saves appearances. Like free association, attention to breathing reveals the impossibility of maintaining both consistency and spontaneity; or rather, it reveals that we cannot *deliberately* be consistent or spontaneous – because we can never be anything else.

Attention to the breath acts as a gateway into a tremendous range of experiences, which seem to self-select according to the client's needs at the time. It can lead to a session focused on relationship and resistance; discharge of pent-up emotions; exploration of embodied sensation and impulse; trance-like journeys into the unknown; experiences of ecstacy and (temporary) enlightenment. Touch will very frequently feature here – as contact, as comfort, as emotional expression – but as the process develops, I may also use touch to help free the client's energy flow, to allow the breath to move more deeply through the body, using 'intricate tactile sensitivity' (Johnson 2000) to a range of subtle sensations from the client's body, and employing language to represent these sensations in rich imagery which in turn informs my touch. When a client has allowed their breath to take them into deep realms of non-verbal bodily expression, I will be accompanying them through my touch, and using it to amplify and support their bodily impulses and flow of energy.

The central focus of ERT breathwork, then, is on re-establishing a fuller, more spontaneous breath – not by efforting, but by gradually letting go of our need to protect ourselves from feeling by not breathing. Exploring resistance to spontaneous breath – to 'being breathed' – therapist and client encounter all the relationship issues which emerge through sustained encouragement to let things happen spontaneously and without censorship.

Conclusion

This perhaps brings us back to our starting point, the relationship between matter and spirit – between the impulses towards embodiment and disembodiment, ground and sky, protection and expression that, for ERT, so much define the human space. The matter/spirit pair is closely related to that of state and process (Totton and Jacobs 2001: 111–14). ERT tries to hold an even-handed tension between these two ways of seeing therapy, or people – recognizing that they are both opposite and complementary. Organisms, including humans, are goal-seeking adaptive systems, which have to balance stability with change. Just as a cell needs a surrounding membrane to delineate the place where it is, human beings need 'edges' (Mindell 1985) – psychological boundaries which resist change – in order to define themselves; in order to exist at all. These edges are our grip on embodiment. However, edges which are too tightly fixed render life impossible.

Either process or stasis, if taken to extreme, will flip over into the other. While edges are the limit point of processes, the point at which flux becomes stability, symptoms mark the equivalent limit point of fixed psychological states like character. Symptoms are how stasis moves into process, and edges are how process moves into stasis. So if someone becomes too rigid and resistant to change, they tend to develop a symptom, an irritation which destabilizes their boundary; conversely, if movement and change go too far and too fast, the person will develop an edge, which stabilizes into a boundary. In this and many other ways, human beings are self-regulating and self-healing. As I said at the beginning of the chapter, our job as therapists is to support what is already trying to happen.

Acknowledgements

Thanks to Hélène Fletcher, Sandy Goldbeck-Wood, Melanie Johnson and Allison Priestman for reading and commenting on a draft of this chapter.

References

Adler, J. (2002) *Offering from the Conscious Body*. Rochester, VT: Inner Traditions.

Alhanati, S. (2002) Silent grammar, in S. Alhanati (ed.) *Primitive Mental States: Psychological and Psychoanalytical Perspectives on Early Trauma and Personality Development*. London: Karnac.

Anzieu, D. (1990) *A Skin for Thought: Interviews with Gilbert Tarrab*. London: Karnac.

Aposhyan, S. (2003) *Body-Mind Psychotherapy: Principles, Techniques, and Practical Applications*. New York: W.W. Norton.

Aron, L. (1998) The clinical body and the reflexive mind, in L. Aron and F.S. Anderson (eds) *Relational Perspectives on the Body*. London: The Analytic Press.

Aron, L. and Anderson, F.S. (1998) *Relational Perspectives on the Body*. Hillsdale, NJ: Analytic Press.

Asheri, S. (2004) Desire in the therapy room, *AChP Newsletter*, 26: 21–32.

Atwood, G.E. and Stolorow, R.D. (1988) *Structures of Subjectivity: Explorations in Psychoanalytic Phenomenology*. London: Analytic Press.

Balint, M. (1984) *The Basic Fault: Therapeutic Aspects of Regression*. London: Routledge.

Bar-Levav, R. (1998) A rationale for physical touching in psychotherapy, in E.W.L. Smith, P.R. Clance and S. Imes (eds) *Touch in Psychotherapy*. London: The Guilford Press.

Barlow, J. and Coverdale, D. (2004) *Embodied Relational Dynamics: Course Prospectus*. www.somaticpsychotherapy.com.au/courses/ERD_Course_Outline.pdf.

Bartenieff, I. (1980) *Body Movement: Coping with the Environment*. New York: Gordon & Breach.

Bartuska, C. (2001) Neurobiologie und biodynamik, *Zeitschrift für Körperpsychotherapie*, 8(29): 17–28.

Bartuska, C. (2002) Das 'bauchhirn', *Zeitschrift für Körperpsychotherapie*, 9(32): 5–20.

Beck, A. (1986) Theoretical perspectives on clinical anxiety, in A. Hussain Tuma and J.D. Maser (eds) *Anxiety and the Anxiety Disorders*. Hillsdale, NJ: Lawrence Erlbaum.

Beck, A. and Emery, G. (1985) *Anxiety Disorders and Phobias; A Cognitive Perspective*. New York: Basic Books.

Beebe, B. and Lachman, F. (2002) *Infant Research and Adult Treatment: Co-constructing Interactions*. Hillsdale, NJ: Analytic Press.

Begley, S. (1998) Living hand to mouth, *Newsweek*, 18: 81.

Bernsen, A., Tabachnick, B.G. and Pope, K.S. (1994) National survey of social worker's sexual attraction to their clients: results, implications, and comparison to psychologists, *Ethics & Behaviour*, 4: 369–88.

Bick, E. (1968) The experience of the skin in early object relations, in A. Briggs (ed.) *Surviving Space: Papers on Infant Observation*. London: Karnac.

Bick, E. (1986) Further considerations on the functions of the skin in early object-relations, in A. Briggs (ed.) *Surviving Space: Papers on Infant Observation*. London: Karnac.

Bion, W. (1962a) *Learning From Experience*. London: Karnac.

Bion, W. (1962b) The psychoanalytic study of thinking II: a theory of thinking, *International Journal of Psychoanalysis*, 43: 306–10.

Blackledge, C. (2004) *The Story of V*. London: Phoenix.

Bloom (forthcoming) *The Embodied Self: Movement and Psychoanalysis*. London: Karnac.

Boadella, D. (1987) *Lifestreams: An Introduction to Biosynthesis*. London: Routledge & Kegan Paul.

Boadella, D. (1997) Awakening sensibility, recovering motility: psycho-physical synthesis at the foundation of body psychotherapy: the 100-year legacy of Pierre Janet (1859–1947), *International Journal of Psychotherapy*, 2(2): 45–56.

Bosanquet, C. (1970) Getting in touch, *Journal of Analytical Psychology*, 15(1): 42–58.

Boyesen, G. (1987) *Über den Körper die Seele heilen: Biodynamische Psychologie und Psychotherapie. Eine Einführung*. München: Kösel.

Boyesen, G. and Bergholz, P. (2003) *Dein Bauch ist klüger als du*. Hamburg: Miko-Edition.

Boyesen, G. *et al.* (1980) *The Collected Papers of Biodynamic Psychology*, Vols 1 and 2. London: Biodynamic Psychology Publications.

Boyesen, G., Leudesdorff, C. and Santner, C. (1995) *Von der Lust am Heilen: Ouintessenz meines Lebens*. München: Kösel.

Breckenridge, K. (2000) Physical touch in psychoanalysis: a closet phenomenon? *Psychoanalytic Inquiry*, 20(1): 1–20.

Briggs, A. (ed.) (2002) *Surviving Space: Papers on Infant Observation*. London: Karnac.

Bucci, W. (1997) *Psychoanalysis and Cognitive Science: A Multiple Code Theory*. New York: Guilford Press.

Buck, R. (1993) Spontaneous communication and the foundation of the interpersonal self, in U. Neisser (ed.) *The Perceived Self: Ecological and Interpersonal Sources of Perceived Self-knowledge*. New York: Cambridge University Press.

Cameron, R. (2002) Subtle energy awareness: bridging the psyche and the soma, *Person-Centred Practice* 10(2): 66–74.

Carroll, R. (2000) The autonomic nervous system: barometer of intensity and internal conflict. www.thinkbody.co.uk.

Carroll, R. (2002a) Interdisciplinary thinking: an introduction to some neuroscientists, *The Psychotherapist*, 18: 17–19.

Carroll, R. (2002b) Biodynamic massage in psychotherapy: re-integrating, re-owning and re-associating through the body, in T. Staunton (ed.) *Body Psychotherapy*. London: Taylor & Francis.

Carroll, R. (2003) On the border between chaos and order: neuroscience and psychotherapy, in J. Corrigal and H. Wilkinson (eds) *Revolutionary Connections: Neuroscience and Psychotherapy*. London: Karnac.

Carroll, R. (2004) *Emotion and Embodiment: A New Relationship Between Neuroscience and Psychotherapy*. www.thinkbody.co.uk.

Carroll, R. (2005) Rhythm, re-orientation and reversal: deep re-organization of the self in psychotherapy, in J. Ryan (ed.) *How Does Psychotherapy Work?* London: Karnac.

Carswell, M.A. and Magraw, K. (2001) Embodiment as a metaphor in therapy, *Organdi Quarterly*, 2. www.geocities.com/organdi_revue/February2001/Embodiment.html.

Casement, P. (1986) Some pressures on the analyst for physical contact during the reliving of an early trauma, in G. Kohn (ed.) *The British School of Psychoanalysis: The Independent Tradition*. London: Free Association Books.

Challis, J.R. and Smith, S.K. (2001) Fetal endocrine signs and preterm labour, *Biology of the Neonate* 79: 163–7.

Chodorow, J. (1991) *Dance Therapy and Depth Psychology: The Moving Imagination*. London: Routledge.

Chodorow, J. (1999) Dance therapy and the transcendent function, in P. Pallaro (ed.) *Authentic Movement*. London: Jessica Kingsley.

Clarkson, P. (1995) *The Therapeutic Relationship*. London: Whurr.

Clarkson, P. (2002) *The Enemy of My Enemy is My Friend (Heraclitus' Wisdom; Plato's Errors)*. www.physis.co.uk.

Cohen, B.B. (1993) *Sensing, Feeling and Action*. Northampton, MA: Contact Editions.

Conger, J.P. (1988) *Jung & Reich: The Body as Shadow*. Berkeley, CA: North Atlantic Books.

Conger, J.P. (1994) *The Body in Recovery: Somatic Psychotherapy and the Self*. Berkeley, CA: Frog.

Cooper, P. (2000) *The Healing Power of Light*. London: Piatkus.

Cornell, W.F. (2003) Entering the gestural field: the body in relation, *Energy and Character*, 32: 45–56.

Csordas, T.J. (ed.) (1994) *Embodiment and Experience: The Existential Ground of Culture and Self*. Cambridge: Cambridge University Press.

da Silva, G. (1990) Borborygmi as markers of psychic work during the analytic session, *International Journal of Psychoanalysis*, 71: 641–58.

Damasio, A. (1994) *Descartes' Error: Emotion, Reason and the Human Brain*. London: Papermac.

Damasio, A. (2000) *The Feeling of what Happens: Body and Emotion in the Making of Consciousness*. London: Harcourt Brace.

De Zulueta, F. (1993) *From Pain to Violence: The Traumatic Roots of Destructiveness*. London: Whurr.

Diamond, N. (2005) When thought is not enough, in J. Ryan (ed.) *How Does Psychotherapy Work?* London: Karnac.

Diamond, N. and Marrone, M. (2003) *Attachment and Intersubjectivity.* London: Whurr.

Dodge, K.A. and Frame, C.L. (1982) Social cognitive biases and deficiencies in aggressive boys, *Child Development,* 53: 620–35.

Eiden, B. (2002) Application of post-Reichian body psychotherapy: a Chiron perspective, in T. Staunton (ed.) *Body Psychotherapy.* London: Brunner-Routledge.

Eigen, M. (1998) *The Psychoanalytic Mystic.* London: Free Association Books.

Epstein, M. (2001) *Going On Being: Buddhism and the Way of Change – a Positive Psychology for the West.* New York: Continuum.

Fairbairn, W. (1958) On the nature and aims of psychoanalytic treatment, *International Journal of Psychoanalysis,* 39: 374–85.

Fairbairn, W. (1974) *Psychoanalytic Studies of the Personality.* New York: Routledge, Chapman & Hall.

Ferenczi, S. (1988) *The Clinical Diary.* London: Harvard University Press.

Flew, A. (1971) *Body, Mind and Death: A Reader.* New York: Macmillan.

Frank, A.W. (1990) Bringing bodies back in: a decade review, *Theory, Culture and Society,* 7(1): 131–62.

Frank, R. (2001) *Body of Awareness: A Somatic and Developmental Approach to Psychotherapy.* Cambridge, MA: Gestalt Press/Analytic Press.

Freud, S. (1894) *The Neuro-Psychoses of Defence,* in J. Strachey (ed.) *The Standard Edition of the Complete Works of Sigmund Freud* [hereafter SE], Vol. 3. London: Hogarth Press.

Freud, S. (1895) Case histories, in Freud, S. and Breuer, J. (1893–5), *Studies on Hysteria,* SE 2.

Freud, S. (1900) *The Interpretation of Dreams,* SE 4 and 5.

Freud, S. (1904) Freud's analytic procedure, SE 7.

Freud, S. (1915a) *The Unconscious,* SE 14.

Freud, S. (1915b) Instincts and their vicissitudes, SE 14.

Freud, S. and Jung, C.G. (1974) *The Freud/Jung Letters,* ed. W. McGuire. London: Hogarth and Routledge & Kegan Paul.

Gallup, G.G. and Maser, J.D. (1977) Human catalepsy and catatonia, in J.D. Maser and E.P.S. Martin (eds.) *Pyschopathology: Experimental Models.* San Francisco: W.H. Freeman.

Gardner, F. (2001) *Self-Harm.* New York: Brunner-Routledge.

Geib, P. (1998) The experience of nonerotic physical contact in traditional psychotherapy, in E.W.L. Smith, P.R. Clance and S. Imes (eds) *Touch in Psychotherapy.* London: The Guilford Press.

Gelhorn, E. (1967) *Autonomic-Somatic Integrations; Physiological Basis and Clinic Implications.* Minneapolis, MN: University of Minnesota Press.

Gendlin, E. (1981) *Focusing.* New York: Bantam.

Gendlin, E.T. (1991) On emotion in therapy, in J.D. Safran and L.S. Greenberg (eds) *Emotions and the Process of Therapeutic Change*. New York: Academic Press.

Genet, J. (1987) *Thief's Journal*. New York: Grove Press.

Gerhardt, S. (2004) *Why Love Matters: How Affection Shapes a Baby's Brain*. Hove: Brunner-Routledge.

Gershon, M. (1999) *The Second Brain*. New York: HarperPerennial.

Goggin, J. and Goggin, E.B. (2001) Politics, ideology, and the psychoanalytic movement before, during, and after the Third Reich, *Psychoanalytic Review*, 88: 155–93.

Gomez, L. (1997) *Introduction to Object Relations*. London: Free Association Books.

Greenberg, J. and Mitchell, S. (1983) *Object Relations in Psychoanalytic Theory*. Cambridge, MA: Harvard University Press.

Greene, A. (1984) Giving the body its due, *Quadrant*, 17(2): 9–24.

Greene, A. (2001) Conscious mind – conscious body, *Journal of Analytical Psychology*, 46(4): 565–90.

Grennel, M.M., Glass, C.R. and Katz, K.S. (1987) Hyperactive children and peer interaction: knowledge and performance of social skills, *Journal of Abnormal Child Psychology*, 15: 1–13.

Gross, O. (1907) *Das Freudsche Ideogenitätsmoment und seine Bedeutung im manisch-depressiven Irresein Kraepelins*. Leipzig: Vogel.

Hammer, E. (1990) *Reaching the Affect: Style in the Psychodynamic Psychotherapies*. Northvale, NJ: Jason Aronson.

Hancock, P., Hughes, B., Jagger, E., Paterson, K., Russell, R., Tulle-Winton, E. and Tyler, M. (2000) *The Body, Culture and Society*. Buckingham: Open University Press.

Hartley, L. (1995) *Wisdom of the Body Moving: An Introduction to Body-Mind Centering*. Berkeley, CA: North Atlantic Books.

Hartley, L. (2004) *Somatic Psychology: Body, Mind and Meaning*. London: Whurr.

Hawkins, P. and Shohet, R. (2000) *Supervision in the Helping Professions*. Maidenhead: Open University Press.

Heiman, P. (1950) On countertransference, *International Journal of Psychoanalysis*, 31: 60–76.

Hellinger, B., Weber, G. and Beaumont, H. (1998) *Love's Hidden Symmetry*. Heidelberg: Carl Auer.

Henley, N.W. (1973a) The politics of touch, in P. Brown (ed.) *Radical Psychology*. New York: Harper & Row.

Henley, N.W. (1973b) Status and sex: some touching observations, *Bulletin of the Psychonomic Society*, 2(2): 91–3.

Heuer, B. (1998) Sein oder Nichtsein. Überlegungen zu Körperlichkeit und Seinserfahrung in der Analyse, *Analytische Psychologie*, 29: 83–98.

Heuer, G. (2002) Psychoanalysis at the crossroads, *International Journal of Psychoanalysis*, 83: 1181–4.

Heuer, G. (2004) *The Influence of the Life and Ideas of Otto Gross on the Life and Ideas of C.G. Jung.* Ph.D. Thesis, University of Essex.

Hillman, J. (1978) *The Myth of Analysis: Three Essays in Archetypal Psychology.* New York: Harper Colophon.

Hillman, J. (2004) *The Azure Vault: The Coelum Experience.* XVI Congress Papers of the International Association for Analytical Psychology: *Edges of Experience, Memory and Emergence.* Barcelona (CD-ROM).

Holland, R. (2004) *Wilhelm Reich's 'Mission Impossible': A Psychoanalytic Exploration and Critique of Wilhelm Reich's Life (1897–1957) and Some of His Basic Theoretical Assumptions.* MA Thesis, Tavistock/UEL.

Holroyd, J.C. and Brodsky, A. (1977) Psychologist's attitudes and practices regarding erotic and non erotic physical contact with clients, *American Psychologist,* 32: 843–9.

Hunter, M. and Struve, J. (1998) *The Ethical Use of Touch in Psychotherapy.* London: Sage.

Ian Paul, M. (1997) *Before We Were Young.* New York: Esf Publishers.

Issaroff, J. (1989) Personal communication regarding Winnicott's conceptualizations of aggression in utero.

Jacobs, M. (1986) *The Presenting Past.* Milton Keynes: Open University.

Jacobs, T. (1973) Posture, gesture, and movement in the analyst: clues to interpretation and countertransference, *Journal of the American Psychoanalytic Association,* 21: 77–92.

Jacobs, T. (1994) Nonverbal communications: some reflections on their role in the psychoanalytic process and psychoanalytic education, *Journal of the American Psychoanalytic Association,* 42: 741–62.

Jagger, E. (2000) Consumer bodies, in P. Hancock *et al. The Body, Culture and Society.* Buckingham: Open University Press.

Johnson, D.H. (2000) Intricate tactile sensitivity, *Progress in Brain Research,* 122: 479–90.

Johnson, S. (1994) *Character Styles.* New York: W.W. Norton.

Jones, E. (1955) *The Life and Work of Sigmund Freud.* New York: Basic Books.

Journard, S.M. (1966) An exploratory study of body accessibility, *British Journal of Social and Clinical Psychology,* 5: 221–31.

Juhan, D. (1987) *Job's Body: A Handbook for Bodywork.* Barrytown, NY: Station Hill Press.

Jung, C.G. (1945) *The Psychology of the Transference.* Collected Works Vol. 16. London: Routledge & Kegan Paul, 1981.

Kaplan-Solms, K. and Solms, M. (2001) *Clinical Studies in Neuro-psychoanalysis: Introduction to a Depth Neuropsychology,* 2nd edn. London: Karnac.

Keleman, S. (1975) *The Human Ground.* Berkeley, CA: Center Press.

Keleman, S. (1975) *Your Body Speaks Its Mind.* Berkeley, CA: Center Press.

Kemp Welch, A. (2001) Rituals of chaos: the movement work of Suprapto Suryodarmo, *Contemporary Theatre Review,* 11(2): 55–68.

Kepner, J. (1987) *Body Process, A Gestalt Approach to Working with the Body in Psychotherapy*. New York: Gestalt Institute of Cleveland Press.

Kertay, L. and Reviere, S.L. (1993) Touch in context, in E.W.L. Smith, P.R. Clance and S. Imes (eds) *Touch in Psychotherapy*. New York: Guilford Press.

Kestenberg, J. (1965) The role of movement patterns in development II: flow of tension and effort, *Psychoanalytic Quarterly*, 36: 356–409.

Kestenberg-Amighi, S., Loman, P., Lewis, M. and Sossin, K.M. (1999) *The Meaning of Movement*. New York: Brunner-Routledge.

Kim, J. (1995) The mind-body problem, in T. Honderich (ed.) *The Oxford Companion to Philosophy*. Oxford: Oxford University Press.

Krystal, H. (1997) Desomatization and the consequences of infantile psychic trauma, *Psychoanalytic Inquiry*, 17: 126–50.

Laban, R. (1950) *The Mastery of Movement*. London: MacDonald & Evans.

Langs, R. (1981) *Interactions: The Realm of Transference and Countertransference*. Northvale, NJ: Jason Aronson.

Leites, A. (1976) *Countertransference*. New York: Institute for the New Age.

Levine, P.A. (1986) Stress, in G.H.M. Coles, E. Donchin and S. Porges (eds) *Psychophysiology*. New York: Guilford Press.

Levine, P.A. (1997) *Waking the Tiger: Healing Trauma*. Berkeley, CA: North Atlantic Books.

Lindon, J.A. (1994) Gratification and provision in psychoanalysis: should we get rid of the 'rule of abstinence', *Psychoanalytic Dialogues*, 4: 549–82.

Little, M. (1985) Winnicott working in areas where psychotic anxieties predominate: a personal record, *Free Associations*, 3: 9–41.

Litton, R. (2004) 'Sex in the city': understanding how your insurance policy deals with claims of sexual misconduct. Unpublished paper.

Lothane, Z. (2001) The deal with the devil to 'save' psychoanalysis in Nazi Germany, *Psychoanalytic Review*, 88: 195–224.

Lowen, A. (1958) *The Language of the Body*. New York: Collier.

Lowen, A. (1976) *Bioenergetics*. Harmondsworth: Penguin Books.

Lowen, A. (1977) *The Way to Vibrant Health*. New York: Harper & Row.

Macnaughton, I. (2004) *Body, Breath, & Consciousness: A Somatics Anthology*. Berkeley, CA: North Atlantic Books.

Malatic, V. (1987) *Body, Space, Expression*. Berlin: Walter de Gruyter & Co.

Martin, E. (1992) The end of the body? *American Ethnologist*, 19: 121–40.

Masson, J. (1985) *The Complete Letters of Sigmund Freud to Wilhelm Fliess*. London: Belknap.

Masterson, J. (1985) *The Real Self: A Developmental, Self and Object Relations Approach*. New York: Brunner/Mazel.

Maturana, H. and Varela, F. (1980) *Autopoiesis and Cognition*. Dordrecht: D. Reidel.

McDougall, J. (1989) *Theatres of the Body*. New York: W.W. Norton.

McGinnis, M. (2002) How the gesture summons the word, *Columbia Magazine*. www.columbia.edu/cu/alumni/Magazine/Spring2002/Krauss.html.

McNeely, D.A. (1987) *Touching: Body Therapy and Depth Psychology*. Toronto: Inner City.

McTaggart, L. (2003) *The Field*. London: Element.

Meltzoff, A.N. and Moore, M.K. (1985) Newborn infants imitate adult facial gestures, *Child Development*, 54: 702–9.

Meltzoff, A.N. and Moore, M.K. (1989) Imitation in newborn infants: exploring the range of gestures imitated and the underlying mechanisms, *Developmental Psychology*, 25: 954.

Merleau-Ponty, M. (1962) *The Phenomenology of Perception*. London: Routledge & Kegan Paul.

Mills, M. and Cohen, B.B. (1979) *Developmental Movement Therapy*. Amherst, MA: School for Body-Mind Centering.

Mindell, A. (1989) *River's Way: The Process Science of the Dreambody*. London: Arkana.

Mindell, A. (1993) *The Shaman's Body: A New Shamanism for Transforming Health, Relationships and the Community*. San Francisco: Harper.

Mindell, A. (1994) *Coma, Key to Awakening, Working with the Dreambody near Death*. New York: Penguin Arkana.

Mindell, A. (1995) *Sitting in the Fire*. Portland, OR: Lao Tse Press.

Mindell, A. (1998) *Dreambody: The Body's Role in Revealing the Self*, 2nd edn. Portland, OR: Lao Tse Press.

Mindell, A. (2000) *Quantum Mind, The Edge between Physics and Psychology*. Portland, OR: Lao Tse Press.

Mindell, A. (2001) *Meta-skills: The Spiritual Art of Therapy*. Tempe, AZ: New Falcon.

Mindell, Amy (2004) A brief review of recent evolution of process work theory, *Journal of Process Oriented Psychology*, 11(1): 63–5.

Mindell, Arnold (2004) *Quantum Mind and Healing, How to Listen and Respond to Your Body's Symptoms*. Charlottesville, VA: Hampton Roads.

Mintz, E. (1969) Touch and the psychoanalytic tradition, *Psychoanalytic Review*, 56: 365–76.

Mitchell, S. (2002) *Can Love Last? The Fate of Romance over Time*. New York: W.W. Norton.

Mitchell, S.A. and Aron, L. (1999) *Relational Psychoanalysis: The Emergence of a Tradition*. Hillsdale, NJ: Analytic Press.

Montague, A. (1986) *Touching: The Human Significance of the Skin*. New York: Harper & Row.

Morris, D. (1969) *Primate Ethology*. London, Weidenfield & Nicholson.

Mudie, L. (2004) Edges of experience: Jung, process work and collective change. www.aamindell.net/edges_of_experience.htm.

Nitzschke, B. (1999) Psychoanalysis during National Socialism: present-day consequences of a historical controversy in the 'case of Wilhelm Reich', *Psychoanalytic Review*, 86: 349–66.

Novalis (1798) *Pollen and Fragments* (excerpts). www.birchlane.net/june03.htm.

Odent, M. (2002) *Primal Health: Understanding the Critical Period Between Conception and the First Birthday*. Forest Row: Clairview.

Ogden, T.H. (1989) *The Primitive Edge of Experience*. Northvale, NJ: Jason Aronson.

Ogden, T.H. (2001) *Conversations at the Frontier of Dreaming*. Northvale, NJ: Jason Aronson.

Orbach, S. (2004a) There is no such thing as a body, in K. White (ed.) *Touch, Attachment and the Body*. London: Karnac Books.

Orbach, S. (2004b) Presentation to United Kingdom Council for Psychotherapy Annual Conference, University of Cambridge.

Pallaro, P. (ed.) (1999) *Authentic Movement*. London: Jessica Kingsley.

Pally, R. (2000) *The Mind-Brain Relationship*. London: Karnac.

Panksepp, J. (1998) *Affective Neuroscience: The Foundations of Human and Animal Emotions*. Oxford: Oxford University Press.

Pennefather, J.N., Patak, E., Pinto, F.M. and Candenas, L. (2004) Mammalian tachykinins and uterine smooth muscle: the challenge escalates, *European Journal of Pharmacology*, 500: 15–26.

Perls, F., Hefferline, R. and Goodman, P. (1951) *Gestalt Therapy: Excitement and Growth in the Human Personality*. New York: Julian Press.

Perls, L. (1993) *Living at the Boundary*. New York: Gestalt Journal Press.

Perry, B.D. and Pollard, R. (1998) Homeostasis, stress, trauma and adaptation: a neurodevelopmental view of childhood trauma, *Child and Adolescent Psychiatric Clinics of North America*, 7(1): 33–49.

Perry, B.D., Pollard, R., Blakley, T.L., Baker, W.L. and Vigilante, D. (1995) Childhood trauma, the neurobiology of adaptation, and 'use-dependent' development of the brain: how 'states' become 'traits', *Infant Mental Health Journal*, 16(4): 271–91.

Pert, C. (1986) The wisdom of the receptors: neuropeptides, the emotions and the body-mind, *Advances: The Journal of Body-Mind Health*, 3(3): 8–16.

Piaget, J. (1954) *The Construction of Reality in the Child*. New York: Basic Books.

Pierrakos, J.C. (1990) *Core Energetics*. Mendocino, CA: Life Rhythm.

Piontelli, A. (1992) *From Fetus to Child*. London: Routledge.

Pope, K.S., Keith-Spiegel, P. and Tabachnick, B.G. (1986) Sexual attraction to patients: the human therapist and (sometimes) inhuman training system, *American Psychologist*, 41: 147–58.

Pope, K.S. and Vasquez, Melba J.T. (2001) *Ethics in Psychotherapy and Counselling*. San Francisco: Jossy-Bass.

Porges, S.W. and Bazhenova, O.V. (n.d.) Evolution and the autonomic nervous system: a neurobiological model of socio-emotional and communication disorders. www.idcl.com//porges.html.

Prescott, J. (1975) Body pleasure and the origins of violence, *Bulletin of Atomic Scientists*, November: 10–20.

Prescott, J.W. (1996) The origins of human love and violence, *Pre- and Perinatal Psychology Journal*, 10(3): 143–18.

Quinodoz, D. (2003) *Words That Touch*. London: Karnac.

Rees, D. and Rose, S. (2004) *The New Brain Sciences: Perils and Prospects*. Cambridge: Cambridge University Press.

Reich, W. ([1945] 1972) *Character Analysis*. New York: Touchstone.

Reich, W. ([1942] 1973) *The Function of the Orgasm*. London: Souvenir Press.

Reich, W. (1980) *Genitality*. Toronto: McGraw-Hill Ryerson.

Rogers, C. (1970) *Carl Rogers on Encounter Groups*. New York: Harper & Row.

Rosenfeld, D. (1984) Hypochondrias, somatic delusion and body scheme in psychoanalytic practice, *International Journal of Psychoanalysis*, 65: 377–88.

Rothschild, B. (2000) *The Body Remembers: The Psychophysiology of Trauma and Trauma Treatment*. London: W.W. Norton.

Ryle, A. (1994) Projective identification: a particular form of reciprocal role procedure, *British Journal of Medical Psychology*, 67: 107–14.

Salzen, A.E. (1967) Social attachment and a sense of security, *Social Sciences Information*, 12: 555–627.

Samsonov, E.v. (1995) Über Giordano Bruno. Einleitung, in E.v. Samsonov (ed.) *Giordano Bruno*. Munich: Diederichs.

Samuels, A. (1993) *The Political Psyche*. London: Routledge.

Samuels, A., Shorter, B. and Plaut, F. (1986) *A Critical Dictionary of Jungian Analysis*. London: Routledge & Kegan Paul.

Sayers, J. (1996) On kissing, touching and shaking hands, *Changes*, 14(2): 117–20.

Scaer, R. (2001) *The Body Bears the Burden: Trauma, Dissociation and Disease*. New York: Haworth.

Schoppe, G. (1600) Brief an Rittershausen über die Verbrennung Giordano Brunos, in E.v. Samsonov (ed.) *Giordano Bruno*. Munich: Diederichs.

Schore, A.N. (1994) *Affect Regulation and the Origin of the Self*. Hove: Lawrence Erlbaum.

Schore, A.N. (2000) Attachment, the developing brain, and psychotherapy. Notes to a lecture given at the Bowlby Conference 'Minds in the Making', London, 4 March.

Schore, A.N. (2001a) Effects of a secure attachment relationship on right brain development, affect regulation, and infant mental health, *Infant Mental Health Journal*, 22(1–2): 7–66.

Schore, A.N. (2001b) Effects of early relational trauma on right brain development, affect regulation, and infant mental health, *Infant Mental Health Journal*, 22(1–2): 201–69.

Schore, A.N. (2002) Clinical implications of a psychoneurological model of projective identification, in S. Alhanati (ed.) *Primitive Mental States: Psychological and Psychoanalytical Perspectives on Early Trauma and Personality Development*. London: Karnac.

Schore, A.N. (2003a) *Affect Regulation and the Repair of the Self*. New York: W.W. Norton.

Schore, A.N. (2003b) *Affect Dysregulation and Disorders of the Self*. Hove: Lawrence Erlbaum.

Schore, A.N. (2003c) The seventh annual John Bowlby Memorial lecture: 'Minds in the Making: attachment, the self-organizing brain and developmentally-oriented psychoanalytic psychotherapy', in J. Corrigal and H. Wilkinson (eds) *Revolutionary Connections: Neuroscience and Psychotherapy*. London: Karnac.

Schuetzenberger, A.A. (1998) *The Ancestor Syndrome*. London: Routledge.

Schwartz-Salant, N. (1982) *Narcissism and Character Transformation*. Toronto: Inner City Books.

Schwartz-Salant, N. (1998) *The Mystery of Human Relationship: Alchemy and the Transformation of the Self*. New York: Routledge.

Searles, H.F. (1999) *Countertransference and Related Subjects: Selected Papers*. Guildford, CT: International Universities Press.

Sella, Y. (2002) Integrating the use of touch with psychodynamic psychotherapy, in G. Shefler, Y. Achmon and G. Weil (eds) *Ethical Dilemmas in Mental Health and the Counseling Professions*. Jerusalem: Magnes – Hebrew University Press (in Hebrew).

Sella, Y. (2003) Soul without skin, bones with no flesh: bodily aspects of the self in the treatment of women patients with restrictive anorexic eating patterns, *International Journal of Psychotherapy*, 8: 37–51.

Sharpe, E.F. (1940) Psycho-physical problems revealed in language: an examination of metaphor, *International Journal of Psycho-Analysis*, 21: 201–13.

Shaw, R. (2003) *The Embodied Psychotherapist: The Therapist's Body Story*. London: Brunner-Routledge.

Smith, D. (1989) Biodynamics and object-relations. Part one: Reich and Fairbairn, in D. Boadella (ed.) *Maps of Character*. London: Abbotsbury Publications.

Smith, E.W.L. (1985) *The Body in Psychotherapy*. Jefferson, NC: McFarland.

Snelling, D. (2001) *Philosophy, Psychoanalysis and the Origins of Meaning: Prereflective Intentionality in the Psychoanalytic view of the Mind*. Burlington: Ashgate.

Solms, M. and Turnbull, O. (2002) *The Brain and the Inner World: An Introduction to the Neuroscience of Subjective Experience*. London: Karnac.

Solomon, M.F. and Siegel, D.J. (2003) *Healing Trauma: Attachment, Mind, Body and Brain*. New York: W.W. Norton.

Soth, M. (1999) Relating to and with the objectified body, *Self & Society*, 27(1): 32–8.

Soth, M. (2000) The integrated body/mind's view on 'body/mind integration', *AChP Newsletter*.

Soth, M. (2003a) What is working with the body? A response to Maggie Turp's paper from a body psychotherapy perspective, *European Journal for Counselling, Psychotherapy & Health*, 5(2): 121–33.

Soth, M. (2003b) Psychotherapy: paradoxes, pitfalls & potential, *Self & Society*, 30(6): 34–44.

Soth, M. (2004) What therapeutic hope for a subjective self in an objectified body? Keynote address, UKCP conference 2004. www.soth.fsnet.co.uk.

Staunton, T. (ed.) (2002) *Body Psychotherapy*. London: Brunner-Routledge.

Stern, D.N. (1985) *The Interpersonal World of the Infant: A View from Psychoanalysis and Developmental Psychology*. New York: Basic Books.

Thelen, E. and Smith, L. (1993) *A Dynamic Systems Approach to the Development of Cognition and Action*. Cambridge, MA: MIT Press.

Tolle, E. (1999) *The Power of Now: A Guide to Spiritual Enlightenment*. Novato, CA: New World Library.

Tolle, E. (2003) *Stillness Speaks*. London: Hodder & Stoughton.

Totton, N. (1998) *The Water in the Glass: Body and Mind in Psychoanalysis*. London: Rebus.

Totton, N. (2002) Foreign bodies: recovering the history of body psychotherapy, in T. Staunton (ed.) *Body Psychotherapy*, pp.7–26. London: Brunner-Routledge.

Totton, N. (2003) *Body Psychotherapy: An Introduction*. Maidenhead: Open University Press.

Totton, N. and Jacobs, M. (2001) *Character and Personality Types*. Buckingham: Open University Press.

Trevarthen, C. (2003) Neuroscience and intrinsic psychodynamics: current knowledge and potential for therapy, in J. Corrigal and H. Wilkinson (eds) *Revolutionary Connections: Neuroscience and Psychotherapy*. London: Karnac.

Trevarthen, C. and Aitken, K.J. (2001) Infant intersubjectivity: research, theory and clinical applications, *Journal of Child Psychology and Psychiatry*, 42(1): 3–48.

Tune, D. (2001) Is touch a valid therapeutic intervention? Early returns from a qualitative study of therapist's views, *Counselling and Psychotherapy Research*, 1(3): 167–71.

Turner, T. (1994) Bodies and anti-bodies, in T.J. Csordas (ed.) *Embodiment and Experience: The Existential Ground of Culture and Self*. Cambridge: Cambridge University Press.

Ukairo, C. (2004) *Naked Celebrity: The Body Language of Power*. London: Granada Television (TV documentary).

Ware, R.C. (1984) C.G. Jung und der körper: Vernachlässigte möglichkeiten in der therapie? in U. Sollmann (ed.) *Bioenergetische Analyse: weiterentwickelte Konzepte und Praxisanalysen*. Essen: Synthesis.

Weiss, G. (1998) *Body Images: Embodiment as Intercorporeality*. London: Routledge.

White, K. (ed.) *Touch: Attachment and Body*. London: Karnac.

Whitman, W. (1891) *I Sing the Body Electric*. www.bartleby.com/142/19.html.

Wiener, J. (1994) Looking out and looking in: some reflections on 'body talk' in the consulting room, *Journal of Analytical Psychology*, 39: 331–50.

Wilber, K. (2000) *Integral Psychology*. Boston, MA: Shambala.

Williams, G. (1997) *Internal Landscapes and Foreign Bodies: Eating Disorders and Other Pathologies*. London: Duckworth.

Wilson, J.M. (1982) The value of touch in psychotherapy, *American Journal of Orthopsychiatry*, 52(1): 65–72.

Wilson, R.A. (1995) *Wilhelm Reich in Hell*. Tempe, AZ: New Falcon.

Winnicott, D.W. (1953) Transitional objects and transitional phenomena, in *Playing and Reality*. London: Tavistock, 1970.

Winnicott, D.W. (1958) Mind and its relation to the psyche-soma, in *Collected Papers: Through Paediatrics to Psychoanalysis*. London: Tavistock.

Winnicott, D.W. (1960) True and false self, in *The Maturational Process and the Facilitating Environment*. London: Karnac.

Winnicott, D.W. (1963) Fear of breakdown, in D.W. Winnicott, R. Shepherd and M. Davies (eds) *Psychoanalytic Explorations*. London: Karnac.

Winnicott, D.W. (1971) *Playing and Reality*. London: Tavistock.

Winnicott, D.W. (1987) Communication between mother and infant and infant and mother, compared and contrasted, in D.W. Winnicott, R. Shepherd and M. Davies (eds) *Babies and Their Mothers*. London: Free Association Books.

Wortis, J. (1963) *Fragments of an Analysis with Freud*. Indianapolis, IN: Charter.

Wyman-McGinty, W. (1998) The body in analysis: authentic movement and witnessing in analytic practice, *Journal of Analytical Psychology*, 43: 239–60.

Zimbardo, P.G. (1977) Understanding madness: a cognitive-social model of psychopathology. Invited address at the annual meeting of the Canadian Psychological Association, Vancouver.

Index

Related books from Open University Press

Purchase from www.openup.co.uk or order through your local bookseller

THE POLITICS OF PSYCHOTHERAPY
NEW PERSPECTIVES

Nick Totton (ed)
Psychotherapist and trainer in private practice, UK

A unique collection by leading authors, *The Politics of Psychotherapy* explores the links between therapy and the political world, and their contribution to each other. Topics covered include:

- Psychotherapy in the political sphere, including the roots of conflict, social trauma, and ecopsychology, political dimensions of psychotherapy practice, discrimination, power, sexuality, and postcolonial issues
- Psychotherapy, the state and institutions, including the law and ethics, and psychotherapy in healthcare
- Working at the Interface, examples of therapy in political action from Croatia, the USA, the UK and Israel/Palestine.

How to 'place' political issues in therapy is highly controversial – for example, whether political themes should be interpreted psychologically in the consulting room, or respected as valid in their own right: Similar issues arise for the role of therapeutic insights in political reality. This book provides a map through these complex and demanding areas for therapists and counsellors in training, and also for experienced practitioners and other interested readers.

Contributors
Lane Arye, Arlene Audergon, Emanuel Berman, Sandra Bloom, Jocelyn Chaplin, Petruska Clarkson, Chess Denman, Dawn Freshwater, Kate Gentile, Susan Gutwill, John Lees, Hilary Prentice, Mary-Jayne Rust, Judy Ryde; Andrew Samuels, Nick Totton.

Contents

192pp   0 335 21653 6 Paperback £19.99   0 335 21654 4 Hardback £60.00

BODY PSYCHOTHERAPY
AN INTRODUCTION

Nick Totton
Psychotherapist and trainer in private practice, UK

Body psychotherapy is a holistic therapy which approaches human beings as united bodyminds, and offers embodied relationship as its central therapeutic stance. Well-known forms include Reichian Therapy, Bioenergetics, Dance Movement Therapy, Primal Integration and Process Oriented Psychology.

This book examines the growing field of body psychotherapy. It:

- Surveys the many forms of body psychotherapy
- Describes what may happen in body psychotherapy and offers a theoretical account of how this is valuable drawing in current neuroscientific evidence
- Defines the central concepts of the field, and the unique skills needed by practitioners
- Is accessible and practical, yet grounded throughout in current research

Body Psychotherapy: An Introduction is of interest to practitioners and students of all forms of psychotherapy and counselling, and anyone who wants to understand how mind and body together form a human being.

Contents
Introduction – What happens in body psychotherapy? – Foundations of body psycho-therapy – Models, concepts and skills – Varieties of body psychotherapy – Clinical and ethical issues – The future of body psychotherapy – Resources – Bibliography – Index.

160pp   0 335 21038 4 Paperback £23.99   0 335 21039 2 Hardback £65.00

RESEARCHING PSYCHOTHERAPY AND COUNSELLING

Rudi Dallos and Arlene Vetere

University of Plymouth; University of Surrey, UK

This book focuses on the issues facing practicing clinicians attempting to engage in research. It outlines approaches which are collaborative in involving clients and other professionals in the research. It argues for approaches which can combine an exploration of the experience as well as the effectiveness of therapies, and importantly help clinicians and clients to identify not just whether therapy works but what the active ingredients of change are.

The book also addresses some of the dilemmas and challenges for clinicians in recruiting participants and combining research with clinical practice. These issues represent a set of threads running through the book:

- Collaborative research
- The ethics of research and emancipator approaches
- Researching the experience of therapy
- Research which is do-able for busy clinicians
- Practice-based evidence and evidence-based practice

Both authors have extensive experience of research teaching with clinicians. It is essential reading for trainee and practicing counsellors as well as allied mental health professionals.

Contents
Preface – Introduction: Research in psychotherapy and counselling – Getting started: Generating and refining research questions – Sampling and generalizability – Choosing a qualitative method – Questions of evaluation and outcome – Psychotherapy process research: Exploring what happens in psychotherapy – Single case and case study approaches – Observing and participating – Interview methodology – Approaches to validity – Final reflections – References – Index

320pp   0 335 21402 9 Paperback £18.99   0 335 21403 7 Hardback £55.00

HEALTH PSYCHOLOGY
SERIES EDITORS: SHEILA PAYNE & SANDRA HORN

THE PSYCHOLOGY OF APPEARANCE

Nichola Rumsey and Diana Harcourt
The University of the West of England, Bristol, UK

Appearance related concerns and distress are experienced by a significant proportion of people with visible disfigurements, and are also reaching 'epidemic proportions' in the general population. Coverage includes:

- A comprehensive summary and critical evaluation of research and understanding concerning the psychology of appearance
- A historical review of research to date
- A review of the methodological challenges for researchers in this area
- An overview of current understanding of appearance-related concerns and distress in the general population and amongst those with visible disfigurements

This book explores the psychosocial factors which are protective and those which exacerbate distress. Furthermore, it reviews current interventions, and offers a vision of a comprehensive approach to support and intervention in the future. It provides essential reading for undergraduate and postgraduate students of psychology, health professionals caring for the broad range of patient populations with disfiguring conditions, health psychologists, health care and social policy makers, and those interested in the evaluation of appearance.

Contents
Preface – Appearance matters: The history of appearance research – The challenges facing researchers in the area – Appearance and image issues for those without visible differences – Psychological difficulties associated with visible difference – Psychological predictors of vulnerability and resilience – Current provision of support and intervention for appearance related concerns – The potential for more effective support and intervention – Conclusions, dilemmas and challenges still ahead – References – Index

192pp   0 335 21276 X Paperback £19.99   0 335 21277 8 Hardback £60.00